CRITICAL ISSUES IN SOCIAL WORK LAW

CRITICAL ISSUES IN SOCIAL WORK LAW

EDITED BY ALISON BRAMMER AND
JANE BOYLAN

First published 2017 by
PALGRAVE

Palgrave in the UK is an imprint of Macmillan Publishers Limited,
registered in England, company number 785998, of 4 Crinan Street,
London, N1 9XW.

Palgrave® and Macmillan® are registered trademarks in the United States,
the United Kingdom, Europe and other countries.

ISBN 978–1–137–54150–5 paperback

This book is printed on paper suitable for recycling and made from fully
managed and sustained forest sources. Logging, pulping and manufacturing
processes are expected to conform to the environmental regulations of the
country of origin.

A catalogue record for this book is available from the British Library.

A catalog record for this book is available from the Library of Congress.

Printed and bound by CPI Group (UK) Ltd, Croydon, CR0 4YY

Dedicated to Paul Boylan (1961–2015)
'Justice always a winner in his company'

CONTENTS

NOTES ON THE CONTRIBUTORS

Jonathan Dickens is Professor of Social Work at the University of East Anglia, UK. His research interests focus on the role of the law and the courts in social work practice with children and families. Research undertaken includes studies on care proceedings, decision-making in edge of care cases and care planning for children in care. He is the author of *Social Work and Social Policy: An Introduction* (2nd edn, 2016, Routledge) and *Social Work, Law and Ethics* (2013, Routledge).

Beverley Burke is Senior Lecturer in Social Work at Liverpool John Moores University, UK. She has practised as a social worker with children and families and has published widely in the areas of anti-oppressive practice, values and ethics. Beverley is co-editor of the practice section of the international peer-reviewed academic journal *Ethics and Social Welfare*.

Jane Dalrymple has extensive experience in social work practice and education. Currently she works as a freelance trainer and consultant, an associate lecturer at the University of the West of England and is an assessor for the National Advocacy Qualification. Her previous publications include *Anti-Oppressive Practice: Social Care and the Law* co-authored with Beverley Burke and *Effective Advocacy in Social Work* co-authored with Jane Boylan.

Jonathan Herring is a Fellow in Law at Exeter College, Oxford University, and Professor of Law at the Law Faculty, Oxford University. He has written on family law, medical law, criminal law and legal issues surrounding care and old age. His books include: *Vulnerable Adults and the Law* (2016, OUP); *Caring and the Law* (2014, Hart); *Older People in Law and Society* (2009, OUP); *European Human Rights and Family Law* (with Shazia Choudhry, 2010, Hart); *Medical Law and Ethics* (2016, OUP); *Criminal Law*, (2016, OUP); *Family Law* (2015, Pearson); and *The Woman Who Tickled Too Much* (2009, Pearson).

Robert Johns is Senior Lecturer in Social Work at the CASS School of Education and Communities, University of East London, UK where he has been Head of Social Work. He has over 30 years' experience in social work with children and vulnerable adults, and has written extensively on social work law. He is author of *Using the Law in Social Work*, now in its sixth edition, *Social Work, Social Policy and Older People* and, most recently, *Capacity and Autonomy*.

Kim Holt is Professor of Social Justice and family Law and Head of the Department for Social Work and Communities at Northumbria University, UK, and a qualified barrister in the area of Family Law. Prior to being called to the bar in 2005, Kim practised as a social worker in the area of child protection for 20 years.

Her Honour Judge Sally Dowding was educated at the University of Manchester (LLB) and at Keele University (MA Child Care Law and Practice), UK. She was articled in Manchester and thereafter practised as a solicitor in Reading and in North Wales. She was a partner in a firm of solicitors in Bangor, and a long-serving member of the Law Society's Children Panel, representing children in public and private law proceedings across the six counties of North Wales. She was appointed a District Judge, based in Birmingham, in February 2007 and a Circuit Judge in July 2013. She now sits at Wolverhampton and Walsall where she deals primarily with public and private law children work, with a special interest in adoption. She is also a Nominated Judge of the Court of Protection.

Martin Wasik CBE is Emeritus Professor of Criminal Justice at the University of Keele, UK. He is also a Recorder of the Crown Court.

Penny Cooper, Barrister, is a Professor of Law and is the international expert on intermediary schemes for vulnerable witnesses and defendants. She chairs The Advocate's Gateway (theadvocatesgateway.org), an internationally renowned website which she co-founded in 2012 to provide best practice guidance on the evidence of children and vulnerable adults. Penny is also a witness familiarisation specialist and former governor of the Expert Witness Institute. She is an academic associate at 39 Essex Chambers, London.

Tom Obokata is Professor of International Law and Human Rights at Keele University, UK. His expertise lies in transnational organised crime generally, and human trafficking in particular. He has published extensively on these topics, and provides expert advice nationally, regionally and internationally.

Margaret Flynn is the Independent Chair of Lancashire's Safeguarding Adults Board and joint editor of the Journal of Adult Protection. She has chaired and written several types of reviews addressing the deaths and abuse of adults with learning disabilities and adults with mental health problems, including the Winterbourne View Hospital SCR. She is Senior Associate Consultant at CPEA and previously held research positions at the Universities of Manchester, London and Sheffiled.

Hilary Brown is Emeritus Professor of Social Care, Canterbury Christ Church University. Throughout her career she has specialised in safeguarding vulnerable adults and her research has focused on sexual abuse, financial abuse, the policy framework, the efficacy of training and the use of the 2005 Mental Capacity Act in complex cases. Until 2013 she chaired a Safeguarding Adults Board and she conducts safeguarding adults reviews. She is also a UKCP accredited psychotherapist.

INTRODUCTION: CRITICAL ISSUES IN CHALLENGING TIMES

Alison Brammer and Jane Boylan

The idea for this edited collection arose out of an established collaboration between social work and law academics at Keele University. Several of the chapters are developed versions of papers presented at a social work law research seminar series held at Keele which brought together academics, practitioners and policymakers. For a number of years the recognition of social work law as a discrete academic discipline has grown (Preston-Shoot et al., 1998), and this is reflected in the growing body of knowledge in this area. Established texts provide detailed explanation of the law relevant to social work practice and applied illustrations through case studies of that law in practice (Brammer, 2015; Braye and Preston-Shoot, 2016). More critical research literature, however, is lacking, or has to be gleaned from journals on topics of relevance – for example, relating to care proceedings, but not necessarily from a social work law perspective. In bringing together this collection, we recognise that one of the challenges facing practitioners is keeping up to date with changes in the law and debates concerning its impact and application. Increasingly, there are calls for greater legal literacy among the social work profession emanating critically from the courts, policy documents and serious case reviews. Therefore we have attempted to address legal issues which are of contemporary relevance to social work practice, such as major changes in the family court system, trafficking, youth justice, promoting the rights of vulnerable adult witnesses and finding ways of protecting vulnerable children and young people. The text explores intersections between law, policy and practice, examining some of the challenges for social workers engaged in contemporary practice. Given the complexity of the intersecting issues social workers face when working with individuals and families, it is not always possible to address concerns in a discrete fashion; there is always a degree of overlap and common themes emerge such as questions of accountability, autonomy, impact of limited resources and restructuring services. Each chapter is designed to equip readers with relevant knowledge for practice while also addressing contemporary challenges for social work in a critical manner.

At the outset it is important to add two notes of caution about the reach of the text. First, inevitably there are areas of practice that have not been specifically addressed in this volume. The book contains a selection of some key topics of great importance, but the absence of others in no way reflects their lesser importance. This statement alone reinforces our view that the breadth of social work practice and associated law is expanding. The topics selected illustrate the reality of ever-evolving law in the context of the Human Rights Act 1998, and the changing face of social work practice to incorporate recently recognised phenomena such as trafficking. Chapters have been written primarily from the perspective of current law in England, though there are some comparative references to practice throughout the UK, and there will be some parallels in applicable law. Devolution has allowed lawmakers throughout the UK to adjust and reflect national priorities for social care. A consequence for practitioners is the existence of increasingly divergent approaches to law across the UK. This is one of the challenges for social workers, particularly those working across borders. Where possible, we have encouraged contributors to make reference to law in the UK beyond England in a comparative sense. However, it is outside the scope of this book to provide comprehensive consideration of the law beyond England.

This introductory chapter outlines the framework and some of the key themes in the book. We begin with chapters addressing values, ethics and theoretical approaches, followed by chapters applying these approaches to specific aspects of practice, and concluding with a challenging consideration of accountability.

Jonathan Dickens's chapter positions social work as a 'profoundly intellectual, ethical profession, as well as a practical one'. Dickens unpicks notions of values and ethics and examines the interaction between the values and aims of the law, courts and social work through the lens of judgement and justice. A distinction is drawn between the political creation of legislation and its judicial application in court. Dickens argues for cooperative approaches to collaborative working in order to produce better outcomes, but, utilising section 20 of the Children Act 1989, highlights the at times conflicting culture of lawyers, the courts and social work. He acknowledges that 'judges and social workers tend to come from very different worlds', and there are risks of misunderstanding and stereotyping on both sides.

Anti-oppressive practice and the law is considered next. Beverley Burke and Jane Dalrymple examine how the law can be used to promote anti-oppressive practice. The reality of contemporary social work is that resources are limited and legalism is a feature of practice. It can be argued that the emergence of national standards alongside guidance and regulations prescribing practice promotes and encourages good practice since it stresses the importance of prevention and rehabilitation as well as providing legal safeguards when compulsory intervention is needed. However the controlling and restrictive elements of legislation can draw social workers into a process of surveillance that is experienced by users of services as repressive and restrictive. The contradictions that consequently characterise the complex relationship between practitioners, services users and the legislative framework is examined within this chapter. By encouraging practitioners to critically reflect on the dilemmas they may face when working within restrictive policy and legislative frameworks, while at the same time advocating for people's rights, a more creative and nuanced response to using the law can be promoted. In recognition of the complex relationship which exists between the law and anti-oppressive practice, the authors argue that using the law alongside professional codes and guidance can contribute to the development of practice that is beneficial, supportive and promotes anti-oppressive values. Case studies encourage consideration of the impact of structural inequalities and discriminatory legislation on the lives of people who use services, and suggest innovative ways of using the law positively in practice.

In Chapter 3, Jonathan Herring explores the concepts of 'Care, vulnerability and law', examining the norms that underpin the law. Herring argues that the law presumes that citizens are autonomous, independent and self-sufficient. The law is designed to promote and protect those values. This works against the interests of those who fall outside the model. In particular, it leads to a devaluing of the importance and impact of care work. It also leads to a sharp divide between those who are labelled as vulnerable and those who are not. This causes particular problems for those in caring relationships who suffer from the lack of respect for care and a misapplication of the notion of vulnerability.

Chapter 4, by Robert Johns, questions the existence of coercion in social care, drawing on research of relevant case law, highlighting areas where courts have determined whether someone can make a decision for themselves. Case examples that have relevance for social work are examined with the intention of trying to discern patterns that clarify the boundaries for intervention across the age range. Johns's analysis suggests that courts are increasingly prepared to acknowledge the tensions of safeguarding while protecting people's rights to autonomy, especially in the context of the European Convention on Human Rights. The chapter goes on to consider what influence this might have on social work practice.

In Chapter 5, Kim Holt examines what is without question one of the most complex areas of social work practice influenced by a changing legal and political context. There have been recent changes to legislation and case law that have resulted in uncertainty for practitioners, children and their families. The Court of Appeal in *Re B-S (Children)* [2013] EWCA Civ 1146 delivered a judgement that has led to some confusion and uncertainty in adoption cases specifically, but in public law cases more generally. The judgement of the President of the Family Division, Lord Munby, highlighted the need for a greater degree of analysis and a weighing up of all the options for the child, including adoption. Significantly, Lord Munby stated that adoption without parental consent is an extremely draconian step, and as an option should not therefore be based on resource constraints if the most appropriate option for the child is to remain living within their own family with support. In April 2014 the Children and Families Act 2014, the revised Public Law Outline (PLO) and new statutory guidance all promised swifter decisions for children and a streamlined system with a single family court. In the context of the family justice reforms, Holt includes a discussion of the implications of *Re B-S:* the courts appear to be more willing to grant leave to appeal an adoption order, especially where parents are not legally represented. Members of the judiciary may be concerned to uphold the Article 6 rights of parents, but this must be carefully balanced against the welfare of the child. Furthermore, there is evidence in unreported cases of social workers being heavily challenged on their oral evidence in court. Holt suggests this will inevitably lead to further uncertainty among professionals who are already working under considerable strain, and will undoubtedly introduce delay for children, when the rhetoric of the modernisation agenda of the family courts is the importance of the timetable for the child.

Family justice is explored further in Chapter 6. Her Honour Judge Sally Dowding considers the extent to which the law and its processes helps or hinders timely adoption, while promoting the well-being of children and respecting the human rights of all parties, a concern encapsulated in *Re B (Placement Order)* [2008] 2 FLR 1404 at 1408, per Wall LJ: 'There is a public perception ... that local authorities/adoption agencies are target-driven, and are seeking adoption orders simply to meet their quotas, without any reference either to the well-being of children or the ... Convention rights of the parents'. Dowding also examines relevant case law and policy initiatives, including the Department for Education 'Tackling Delay' papers of 2012, 2013 and 2014 in the context of the new landscape of the family justice review initiatives, and the continuing challenges facing social work of searching for suitable adopters for children who wait, and ensuring that birth families' rights to fair and human rights compliant hearings are not jeopardised by the imperative of faster adoption.

Youth justice is an issue which continues to attract media and political attention, and the legal framework is subject to regular amendment. Legal and social work responses to youth crime may appear to be in conflict at times, and this tension is highlighted in Chapter 7. Martin Wasik examines the impact of diversionary measures, including a critique of the use of Asset and the resultant reduction of numbers of young people in the youth justice system. Wasik notes that 'those youngsters now within the system often present with a more entrenched and complex range of social and psychological problems' and explores the challenge this presents to social work and other agencies working in a multidisciplinary framework. For those young people, a range of disposal orders exist, including custodial sentences, and contemporary concerns over the circumstances of young people in custody conclude this chapter.

A further important aspect of the criminal justice system is discussed in Chapter 8, namely the approach to vulnerable witnesses. Penny Cooper's contribution critically examines the concept of 'vulnerable witness'. It interrogates key areas including the fundamental question of who is a vulnerable witness, 'reasonable steps' and 'special measures' available to help vulnerable witnesses. Case studies illustrate the use of special measures in practice. The chapter also considers who is a competent witness – what is meant by capacity to consent to being a witness and to cross-examination. Cooper considers the important role of social work practitioners engaging with witnesses in civil and criminal law, in particular suggesting a series of practical recommendations for the social work approach to supporting a service user who may be considered a vulnerable or intimidated witness.

The global problem of human trafficking in contemporary society is considered in Chapter 9 by Tom Obokata, who explores the relevance of victims of trafficking to both children and adults social work practice. Importantly, this chapter critiques definitions of trafficking and its causes. The profile of victims is examined, and strategies for identification, prevention and education are proposed. Current law applicable to human trafficking and exploitation, including the Modern Slavery Act 2015, is examined from a human rights perspective. Obokata argues that social workers need to be sufficiently trained, 'so that they become fully aware of relevant indicators and the complex nature of human trafficking'.

The concluding chapter is co-authored by Margaret Flynn, the author of significant serious case reviews including the cases of Winterbourne View and Steven Hoskin, together with Hilary Brown. It traces the role of reviews in services for adults at risk as a measure for improving practice and achieving systemic change. The current landscape for reviews provided by the Care Act 2014 and supporting guidance is described, and key issues from recent reviews are highlighted in the context of a critical examination of the underlying purpose of reviews and whether they can truly create an agenda for change.

The overall aim in bringing the collection together is to provide a critique of the law as it applies to social work practice and to contribute to contemporary debates in social work law. The topics selected illustrate the reality of ever-evolving law and the changing face of social work practice to incorporate recently recognised phenomena such as trafficking, as well as continuing tensions in approaches in established areas of practice such as youth justice and child protection and the challenge of embedding and further promoting change within legal structures. Each chapter identifies the very real challenges currently faced by practitioners in applying the law in times of austerity. Inevitably, these debates will continue and expand. We hope this collection contributes in raising further questions and exploring the intersections between social work law, practice and ethics.

References

Brammer, A. (2015) *Social Work Law*, 4th edn, Harlow: Pearson.

Braye, S. and Preston-Shoot, M. (2016) *Practising Social Work Law*, 4th edn, London: Palgrave.

Preston-Shoot et al. (1998) Social work law: from interaction to integration. *Journal of Social Welfare and Family Law,* 20 (1) 65–80.

1

SOCIAL WORK VALUES, THE LAW AND THE COURTS

Jonathan Dickens

The relationships between the law, individual values and society's values have long been matters of intense debate for politicians, judges and philosophers. And social workers, although they may well be seen to lack the professional power or social status of those other groups, find themselves firmly in the middle of those debates – or, as it may be better to put it, at the sharp end. Think of the sort of questions that social workers have to address as part of their everyday job. How much support should be offered to parents to help them care for their children, or when should the children be placed in a different family? When should an individual be detained in a hospital or a care home, without their own agreement? How much money should be spent to help an individual remain living in their own home in the way that they choose, when budgets are limited and demand is high? The law provides one framework for thinking about these difficult matters – what is required and what is allowed, what isn't allowed, what legal processes have to be followed. But the legal provisions have to be seen in the context of wider societal values about family life, the role of the state and the powers of the court; and social workers will also have their own personal beliefs about these matters. Furthermore, social workers have to take account of their organisation's priorities, policies and resources; the service user's wishes, in the light of the person's mental capacity and understanding; and their own professional knowledge, skills and values. Holding these different poles together is what makes social work a profoundly intellectual and ethical profession, as well as a practical one (Dickens, 2016).

In this chapter I want to think more about the relationships between the law, the courts and social work, to explore their different roles and the ways that they interact with one another. At times their values and aims coincide and reinforce one another, and other times different functions and approaches come to the fore, bringing tension and conflict. I shall take two particular issues to illustrate the themes: judgement and justice. Both words have powerful resonance for lawyers and social workers, but the meanings and practical implications are complex and at times contradictory. Social workers are required to exercise professional judgement, but one of their core professional values is not to be judgemental; the courts deliver judgements all the time, and sometimes in ways that are highly critical of social workers. What are the underlying issues here, and the implications? And how does social work's approach to justice square with the formal, legal justice of the courts, and what does it mean for social work's relationship with the law?

The law and the courts have come to play dominant roles in social work in the UK, but it is not certain that this always helps the people who use social work services. Their increasing importance chimes with other trends and forces that have given social work in England a highly regulatory character (Social Work Task Force, 2009; Munro, 2011). That is to say, it is tightly regulated itself, but also regulatory in its interactions with service users – highly procedural, often focused on rationing services and assessing and managing risk. But the legalistic approach distorts social work in two senses: it is not always a realistic or fair view of what actually happens, and it pushes social work in certain directions that can be unhelpful to workers and, most importantly, to service users. But things do not have to be like that, and there are examples of more collaborative working between social work and the courts that can help to produce better outcomes for service users. Some forms of independent scrutiny and adjudication will always be necessary, but new approaches to review, challenge and learning are likely to be more productive for longer-term constructive change. But first, we need to define our terms.

Values and ethics in social work

For many social workers, their values are at the heart of their professional identity. They are what motivate them in their day-to-day work, and what make their profession distinctive (e.g. Bisman, 2004; Barnard et al., 2008). A social worker's values – say, to treat people fairly, to respect people's choices, to avoid being judgemental or blaming, to empower people to live their lives as independently as possible – will be grounded in their personal beliefs, their professional duties and the wider expectations of their society. Studying the reasons why someone might hold any particular value or set of values, how those values link together, how defensible they are and what their limitations may be takes us into the realm of ethics – reasoning about values.

There are many different schools of thought about the underlying principles behind social work values. Four principal schools of ethical thinking are Kantianism (duty-based approaches: one must do one's duty, categorically, regardless of the consequences); utilitarianism (one's duty is to do the thing that brings the greatest good for the greatest number); virtue ethics (it's a question of character, one must train oneself to become the sort of person who makes the right decisions for the right reasons); and care ethics (the important thing is to respond to other people in caring ways, not to be tied to inflexible rules). All of these have direct implications for social work, in thinking about *why* a worker should act in a certain way, what makes something 'the right thing to do'; and (as we shall see later) there may sometimes be tensions between them (Dickens, 2013).

There are other understandings of what social work is really about, or should be about. In particular, in the current context in England, where social work has become so tightly regulated and regulatory, two powerful counter-trends have emerged. Both seek to recover older, traditional strands of social work and give them a new lease of life. First, there are those who call for a rediscovery of social work's *radical* edge, its social critique and activism. There has been a resurgence of books with the word 'radical' in the title (e.g. Ferguson and Woodward, 2009; Lavalette, 2011; Ferguson and Lavalette, 2013; Turbett, 2014), the launch of a journal called *Critical and Radical Social Work* and the creation of the Social Work Action Network, 'SWAN'. Second, there has also been a revival of *relationship*-based approaches, those arguing that social work best achieves change not through procedural compliance or political action but through skilful (helpful and realistic) interpersonal helping relationships (e.g. Howe, 2008; Ruch et al., 2010; Munro, 2011; Wilson et al., 2011). It is clear that there are significant differences between the two approaches, and they could well give different answers to what is the right thing for a social worker to do in a certain situation; but Payne (2006) has argued that one of social work's distinguishing features is that it tries to reconcile these two strands, to bring about social change through work with individuals.

So, perhaps one should not overplay the distinction, and think of 'both/and' rather than 'either/or'. We shall return to this in the conclusion. Likewise, one should not overplay the distinction between values and ethics. It is not a rigid or consistent boundary, and the word ethics is sometimes used simply as another term for 'values', rather than as a more considered way of thinking about values. Examples of this are the various national 'codes of ethics' published by different social work associations around the world, insofar as they tend to set out lists of expectations rather than debate the reasons behind them. There is also an international statement of ethical principles for social work, adopted in 2004 by the International Federation of Social Workers and the International Association of Schools of Social Work (IFSW and IASSW, 2004). National codes are compared usefully in Banks (2012), and it is possible to read a selection on the IFSW website (see their 'National Codes of Ethics' webpage).

Social work values in a nutshell

The British Association of Social Workers, BASW, is the largest professional body for social workers in the UK, although membership is not compulsory and the large majority of social workers do not belong to it. In September 2014, total membership in the four countries of the UK was 17,000, the highest in the association's history (BASW, 2014a: 7). Despite the relatively low numbers, it has been established since the 1970s and has an influential voice in ongoing debates about the role and the future of social work.

BASW first published its code of ethics for social work in 1975. It was revised in 1986, to give greater weight to anti-oppressive values, and again in 2002, to enhance the human rights dimensions. A further revision was published in January 2012, to take account of more recent understandings of social work and the challenges that social workers face. The latest code is a succinct summary of social work values and a good route into thinking about them, but it should not be considered 'the' definitive statement. It has evolved over time and will no doubt be revised again in the future; and as noted above, other countries have their own codes, which may use different language and emphasise different aspects of professional activity.

The BASW code draws closely on the IFSW and IASSW international statement, highlighting three ways that ethical dilemmas can often arise for social workers (BASW, 2012: 6):

- Dealing with conflicting interests and competing rights

- Having a role to support and empower people, alongside statutory duties and other obligations that may be coercive and restrict people's freedoms

- Being constrained by limited resources and organisational policies

The code goes on to describe three key dimensions of social work ethics: human rights, social justice and professional integrity (the international statement uses the term 'professional conduct'). The BASW code gives five bullet points for each of these headings, and then elaborates on each of them with a further paragraph.

Under the heading *human rights*, the five points are:

- Upholding and promoting human dignity and well-being

- Respecting the right to self-determination

- Promoting the right to participation

- Treating each person as a whole

- Identifying and developing strengths

Social workers are unlikely to disagree with any of these general objectives. The challenge, of course, is putting general objectives into practice, in two senses: first, because for every general principle there is likely to be another that conflicts with it, and second because social workers have to implement them in the complex and uncertain realities of service users' lives and wishes, the worker's own individual and organisational circumstances and available resources (time, money, services, community and family support).

In terms of conflicting objectives, these are neatly illustrated in the paragraph that expands on the point about self-determination. It reads:

> Social workers should respect, promote and support people's dignity and right to make their own choices and decisions, irrespective of their values and life choices, provided this does not threaten the rights, safety and legitimate interests of others.
>
> (BASW, 2012: 8)

Two very different approaches to ethical reasoning are bolted together in this sentence, without any explanatory comment or recognition of the potential clashes. The first part of the sentence expresses a categorical view about the importance of an individual's rights to choose and decide about their lives, echoing the Kantian tradition; but the second part goes on to qualify this, balancing it against the rights and well-being of others, a more utilitarian approach. So the absolute importance of the service users' rights to choose, 'irrespective of their values and life choices', is restricted by other considerations that take account of wider, longer-term and social consequences.

Under the heading *social justice*, the five points are:

- Challenging discrimination
- Recognising diversity
- Distributing resources
- Challenging unjust policies and practices
- Working in solidarity

It is notable here that the requirement on social workers is not simply not to discriminate themselves, but to *challenge* discrimination. And under the bullet point on challenging unjust policies and practices, the paragraph reads:

> Social workers have a duty to bring to the attention of their employers, policy makers, politicians and the general public situations where resources are inadequate or where distribution of resources, policies and practice are oppressive, unfair, harmful or illegal.
>
> (BASW, 2012: 9)

This phrase seems to reflect the radical and campaigning vision of social work. In the current political and economic context, with tightly restricted resources, and policies that seem to be particularly harsh towards people who are poor, unable to work or from other countries, one might expect social workers to be raising issues about resource shortages and unfair policies all the time. But it is important to interrogate exactly what this phrase means, what its implications are for social work as a profession and for social workers as individuals. For a start, there are considerable differences between drawing matters to the attention of one's employers or to others outside one's agency, possibly including the general public; and there are differences between situations 'where resources are inadequate' and those where practice is 'illegal'. We return to these issues in more detail later in the chapter.

Under the heading *professional integrity*, the five points are:

- Upholding the values and reputation of the profession

- Being trustworthy

- Maintaining professional boundaries

- Making considered professional judgements

- Being professionally accountable

One of the implications of the professional integrity heading is that it extends to social workers' behaviour outside their work, and covers the sometimes blurred boundaries between personal and professional lives. An individual's conduct in their private life may possibly damage the values and reputation of the profession; and in some cases may even cause direct harm to vulnerable service users. It raises the question: how private is one's private life? The extreme cases will be clearly unacceptable, but many of the issues are likely to be more ambiguous, with uncertain lines between what is tolerable, what is best dealt with through advice and support and what requires disciplinary action (Doel et al., 2010).

One of the other points in this section concerns 'making considered professional judgements', and the challenge here is that another of social work's well-known core values is to be non-judgemental. The difference, of course, is that judgementalism is based on prejudice, not knowing (or not taking proper account of) the facts and circumstances. Social workers should certainly avoid this, but as part of their professional duties they are clearly called upon to exercise professional judgement. As the explanatory paragraph in the BASW code puts it:

> Social workers should make judgements based on balanced and considered reasoning, maintaining awareness of the impact of their own values, prejudices and conflicts of interest on their practice and on other people.
>
> (BASW, 2012: 10)

But as with all these things, it is often easier said than done; and it is intriguing that there is no mention here of national and organisational policies, team structures and supervision, other agencies or resources. It gives the impression that social workers exercise their judgement alone, but in modern social work practice that is not the case. Social work judgement is not simply an individual matter. And when social work comes into contact with the law and the courts, the tensions between non-judgementalism and proper judgement take on added complexities. These are explored further, later in the chapter.

Legislation and courts

Just as there is an important distinction between values and ethics, but also overlap and sometimes ambiguity between those terms, so there is an important distinction in the law, between legislation and the courts. Legislation refers to Acts of Parliament, and the related regulations ('secondary legislation'). The important thing to appreciate is that these are political creations, not judicial. They are passed by the government of the day, and are intended to help them achieve their political and policy objectives. In that sense, some Acts are more obviously political than others – that is, they are clearly a response to a wave of public opinion or a media-enhanced scandal, and are meant to show that the government is taking things seriously and is going to tackle these problems. Legislation about immigration controls could be seen under this category, or the repeated calls from some Conservative politicians to repeal the Human Rights Act 1998. Other legislation is designed to introduce policy reforms, such as restructuring the NHS, and even if the policy does not work well it is unlikely that anyone will be brought before the courts for failing to implement it properly. Sometimes legislation may be introduced to set a trap for other political parties. An example would arguably be the Child Poverty Act 2010, which was introduced by the Labour government in the run-up to the 2010 general election. No politician could be seen to be in favour of children being poor (especially just before an election), so the Act was passed. Subsequently many politicians in the coalition government expressed unhappiness about the way that child poverty was defined in the Act, with income-based targets, saying that it should not just be about money, but about parental and family circumstances such as worklessness, poor educational achievement and poor parenting (e.g. HM Government, 2011). Shortly after the Conservatives won the general election of May 2015, they announced that they would repeal the targets and change the definition.

So, Acts of Parliament are political, and in some cases the courts will not have any part to play in them. And although individuals may sometimes take their case to court to argue that they should be given a certain service, or allowed to do something, the UK courts cannot overturn decisions about public policy and public spending that are properly made by democratically elected politicians. Under the Human Rights Act 1998, they do have the power to declare legislation incompatible with the European Convention on Human Rights, but not to strike it down. A declaration would mean that the law is referred back to the government, and it would then be for Parliament to decide whether or not to amend it. Courts may declare that a particular decision or action by a public authority is unlawful through the process of judicial review, or, under the Human Rights Act 1998, they may declare that it contravenes the European Convention. Under both procedures, the court may award damages to the person who has been wronged, or refer the matter back to the relevant agency for reconsideration.

So the courts can contribute to the evolution of law and policy, through the way that judges interpret and apply the law. Indeed, even though their formal powers to change the law or government policy are limited, their judgements may well have considerable impact on the way that a policy is put into practice. An example of this occurred in 2013, in relation to the government's policy of promoting adoption as a permanence option for children who have been removed from their families because of abuse or neglect. The New Labour government, and then the coalition government, had both promoted this through legislation, target-setting and funding initiatives. But in three high-profile cases that year, *Re B (A Child)* [2013] UKSC 33; *Re G (A Child)* [2013] EWCA Civ 965 and *Re B-S (Children)* [2013] EWCA Civ 1146, the courts expressed strong views against what they saw as poor practice, from local authorities and the courts. The judgements led to a drop off in adoption plans and orders, and considerable disagreement between the government, social work agencies and the courts (National Adoption Leadership Board, 2014; and see Dickens and Masson, 2014). The impact of these particular cases is discussed in more detail in other chapters in this book, so will not be pursued now; the point here is to highlight the way that courts can affect the implementation of national policy even if they do not have the formal powers to overturn it. But the cases also raise an important issue about the language of blame in the courts. It leads us into discussing the theme of judgement in law and social work.

Judgement and judgementalism

In *Re B-S* the language used to criticise the local authority, and by extension other local authorities, was particularly strong. They were criticised for submitting material that was too often 'anodyne and inadequate', with the judge, Sir James Munby, insisting that 'this sloppy practice must stop' (paras 39–40). (Sir James Munby is the President of the Family Division, the leading family judge in England and Wales.) There have been other high-profile cases where similarly strong language has been used to criticise individual workers and/or particular local authorities. Two notable examples from child care cases in 2015 are *Northamptonshire County Council v AS and Others* [2015] EWHC 199 and *Re A (A Child)*

[2015] EWFC 11. In highlighting the critical language, it is not my intention to downplay the fact that practice in these cases fell short of the best standards; rather, it is to show the blaming culture of the courts and the antagonism towards local authorities. One of the consequences of the high levels of mistrust between the courts and local authorities has been the long delays in care proceedings that have been damaging to the interests of children and families (Family Justice Review, 2011: esp. paras 4.111–4.120).

In the Northamptonshire case, the judge found there had been delays by the local authority in starting care proceedings on a baby boy (referred to as 'DS'), undertaking the necessary assessments and filing the court statements and reports. The judge concluded that 'neither the social workers, nor the senior managers at Northampton Children's Services Department had DS's welfare best interests at the forefront of their minds. Worse still they did nothing to promote them. Their chaotic approach to this young baby's care and future life was dismal' (para 14). He spoke of the 'egregious failures' and 'appalling conduct' of the local authority (paras 4 and 32), their 'wholesale failure of DS and his family' (para 34) and a 'catalogue of errors, omissions, delays and serial breaches of court orders [that was] truly lamentable' (para 35). It is clear that there were shortcomings, although it is worth noting that the judge acknowledged that the outcome for DS was 'wholly satisfactory' (para 29). The local authority's evidence shows that there were serious staffing difficulties. It is highly questionable whether such language really helps to improve practice, and whether it helps local authorities to recruit and retain skilled social workers.

The Re A case involved Darlington Borough Council and was another matter heard by Sir James Munby. He described it as 'an object lesson in … how not to embark upon and pursue a care case' (para 7). He was critical of the lack of clear evidence and analysis, describing the local authority's case as 'a tottering edifice built on inadequate foundations' (para 28) and criticising them for being 'too willing to believe the worst of the father' (para 29). The president accepted some of the authority's concerns about the father but held that '… being an inadequate or even a bad role model is not a ground for making care orders, let alone adoption orders' (para 63). In the judgement, the president went through the local authority's assessment of the father, reading out numerous sections from the social workers' statements, reports and case notes, effectively holding them up to ridicule. He was particularly critical of one of the workers, referred to as 'SW1', calling her work 'seriously flawed' (para 97). Although she is not named, the whole experience must have been crushing and humiliating.

The president does go on to say that ultimate responsibility for the failings lies higher up the organisational hierarchy than the social workers: 'Why, to take her as an example, should the hapless SW1 be exposed to public criticism and run the risk of being scapegoated when, as it might be thought, anonymous and unidentified senior management should never have put someone so inexperienced in charge of such a demanding case?' (para 103). But plenty of people will know, or be able to work out, the identity of SW1 and the other workers referred to by their job titles rather than their names ('jigsaw identification'). And rather than softening the blow to the social worker, the effect of the comment is really just to spread blame further.

To reiterate, in describing these examples I am not trying to defend poor practice; rather, it is to make a point about the culture of the court. Courts are cauldrons of blame. They allocate responsibility, and hold people to account; and in criminal cases, they can send people to prison. But childcare cases are rather different. They are civil rather than criminal law matters, and in theory the focus is on the welfare of the child rather than apportioning blame for what has happened. (There may be separate criminal proceedings.) But in care proceedings, part of the 'threshold criteria' that the court has to consider are whether the harm to the child is attributable to the care given, or likely to be given, not being what it would be reasonable to expect a parent to give them (s. 31 of the Children Act 1989), so there is an element of *attribution* of responsibility. This does not necessarily entail blame, because for many of the parents involved in care proceedings, their own problems and limitations are such that blame would be inappropriate. But that creates a problem for the courts, because they are designed to give out blame; that is one of their routine functions. So there is a lot of frustrated blame bubbling away; and it has to escape, and land on someone. It can't be the parents, so it is very often the person standing next to them, so to speak – the social worker.

Looking back to the earlier discussion about social work's approach to judgement and judgementalism, we can see some of the overlaps and tensions between the social work and legal approaches. Social workers can face criticism for failing to exercise proper judgement, either being too blaming or not sufficiently robust.

Generally, social workers try to understand behaviour and avoid allocating blame. This is a core social value, in notable contrast to the views of the former Conservative Prime Minister John Major, whose advice for dealing with youth offending was to 'condemn a little more and understand a little less' (MacIntyre, 1993). Sometimes personal instinct, professional duty and, it should be remembered, the legal responsibility to support parents in bringing up their children may lead to decisions to leave children in situations which turn out to be harmful (this risk is compounded by poor supervision, heavy workloads and lack of resources). Most social workers try not to be judgemental, but as Brandon et al. (2009: 27) put it, they have to be careful in case 'efforts not to be judgemental become a failure to exercise professional judgement'.

But at times, the frustrations of working with troubled people who may be aggressive, dishonest and uncooperative can lead social workers into less constructive ways of thinking, in which they lose sight of the positives and themselves become blaming (this danger is also compounded by poor supervision, heavy workloads and lack of resources). By the time a child care case gets to court, it is likely that there will have been considerable efforts, perhaps over a period of years, to try to engage the parents and work with them. So it can be a very distressing experience for social workers if the courts are not convinced, and order further assessments or send the child home/refuse to order the removal of the child. In arguing their case strongly, wanting the best for the child, there is a risk that they may come across as judgemental. Social workers have to be, and come across as, 'the epitome of reason' (Dickens, 2005); but it is not always easy to do this under extreme pressure and criticism.

Courts exercise judgement, of course; but the cases we have been discussing give grounds for thinking that they may be rather judgemental in their approach to social workers and local authorities. Why might this be? One reason is that courts inevitably see the hardest cases, the ones where preventive work and alternatives to care have not been successful. It is important not to assume that these represent the majority of cases. The numbers alone suggest this is not so. Although the number of cases entering care proceedings has risen in recent years, it is still considerably less than the number of children who are subject to child protection plans or child in need plans. There were 10,620 care applications in England in the year April 2013 to March 2014, involving just over 18,000 children (Cafcass, 2015). There were about 8,000 children on interim care orders on 31 March 2014 (i.e. ongoing care proceedings: DfE, 2014a: Table A2); but there were 397,600 'children in need' on that day, and 48,300 on child protection plans (DfE, 2014b; and see Dickens and Masson, 2014). In most cases, families and children are helped without going to court.

Both the cases described above involved the use of 'section 20' accommodation for children. This is a provision in the Children Act 1989 that allows local authorities to provide accommodation for children (i.e. usually foster or residential care, or possibly to support kinship placements) without going to court, if the parent(s) agree (agreement is not necessary if the parents are missing or cannot be found). Most children who enter care do so under s. 20; most children who remain in care longer term are on care orders (DfE, 2014a: Tables C3, A2), but there is no time limit on s. 20 and it is possible for children to remain accommodated as long as their parents do not withdraw their agreement. There is often a gulf between lawyers' and social workers' views about s. 20 (see Masson et al., 2013: 201). Lawyers tend to mistrust it, thinking that parents' 'agreement' is often obtained under duress, and it is misused to keep children in care without proper scrutiny by the court. Social workers tend to value it for its flexibility and because it is consistent with their professional values – and indeed, legal requirements – to try to work in partnership with families and not to take cases to court if possible (e.g. the family support provisions of s. 17 and the 'no order principle' in s. 1(5) of the Children Act 1989). Certainly, 'agreement' should not be abused and parents should be fully informed of their rights, but it is proper for social workers to use their powers of reasoning and negotiation to try to reach agreements with parents. And certainly such cases need to be reviewed carefully to ensure that timely action is being taken and they are not allowed to 'drift'; but one should remember that the courts have the luxury of hindsight, and it is all too easy to criticise social workers for delay when they were trying to find constructive, less adversarial ways of working with the family. The court's mistrust of s. 20 should not be allowed to inhibit local authorities from making full use of this provision to support families, trying to work cooperatively with young people and parents (Dickens et al., 2007).

Another reason for the differences of view may be the social class make-up of the judiciary, compared to social workers and, indeed, to the parents. Courts are theatres of social class. The rituals, the ways of speaking and dressing, the expectations of 'proper', respectful behaviour, the necessary levels of literacy and verbal expression – all of these reflect and enhance the power of the assured middle and upper classes. One's professional and social status is exposed very clearly in the court, in details such as where a person sits or stands, who they speak to, even whether they are allowed to speak. The inequalities of educational background, income and social standing are vast. (A survey by the Sutton Trust in 2005 noted that 7 per cent of children in England and Wales attend private schools, but three-quarters of their sample of top judges had done so: Sutton Trust, 2005.) These may be compounded by differences of gender and race. Most senior judges are white men; most social workers are women, and there is a much greater racial diversity in the social care workforce (in December 2012, 83 per cent of employees of local authority children's social care departments in England were female. Overall, 86 per cent were white British, but this varied around the country, and in London, 43 per cent were of Black, Asian or other minority ethnic origin: DfE, 2013: 10–12). This is not to accuse any judge of sex discrimination or racial prejudice, but it is to point out that judges and social workers tend to come from very different worlds. There are risks of misunderstanding and stereotyping on both sides. The danger is if this leads to a breakdown of trust. Courts have to be independent, of course, and have to be satisfied by the evidence and reasoning. 'Trust' is not uncritical acceptance of what is put before one, but is about respect and understanding, appreciating the contribution of the other person and awareness of the larger context in which they operate.

There is evidence that more cooperative approaches can produce better outcomes for children and parents. For example, the combined efforts of local authorities, Cafcass and the courts in a pilot programme to reduce the duration of care proceedings led to significant reductions without reports of impaired thoroughness or justice (Beckett et al., 2014; Dickens et al., 2014). Furthermore, there are encouraging messages from the Family Drug and Alcohol Court, which takes a problem-solving approach in care proceedings, using the authority of the judge and the skills of a specialist multidisciplinary drug and alcohol team (Harwin et al., 2014). Collaborative ways of working need not undermine necessary independence, but can enhance a thorough and proportionate response.

Formal justice and social justice

Let us return to the concept of justice, the second theme in this chapter for exploring the relationships between social work, the law and the courts. Judges and the courts are vital parts of the 'justice system', and people speak of the 'criminal justice system' and the 'family justice system'. As the BASW code showed, justice is also a core principle for social workers, but in a wider sense than the formal justice of the courts. Formal justice is still crucial, and social workers are expected to comply with the duties and powers given by the law, administer them in a fair way, respect the court's procedures and orders, adhere to due process, act on sound evidence and clear reasoning and so on. But on top of this, social workers have a wider understanding and a professional commitment to social justice. The key elements, as summarised in the BASW code, are challenging discrimination, respecting diversity, ensuring the fair distribution of resources, working with others to overcome social exclusion and, as discussed earlier, 'challenging unjust policies and practices'.

The law and the courts can be ways of doing that too, but sometimes laws can be oppressive, and courts might enforce unjust laws and unjust social arrangements. As described earlier, the courts have limited power to challenge democratically passed legislation, particularly with regard to public spending. An example in March 2015 was the Supreme Court's decision to refuse an application against the government's cap on the amount of welfare benefits that a family can receive. The case is *R (on the application of SG and others (previously JS and others)) (Appellants) v Secretary of State for Work and Pensions (Respondent)* [2015] UKSC 16.

One of the reasons for the decision (Lord Reed, para 93 of the judgement) was that the case involved 'issues of social and economic policy, with major implications for public expenditure'. Lord Reed held that such matters are properly decided by democratically elected institutions, and the court should not intervene unless the policy was 'manifestly without reasonable foundation'. Lady Hale spoke out strongly against the policy, highlighting its harsh impact on women and children. She did not consider it a proportionate means of achieving a legitimate aim, and argued that '[i]t cannot possibly be in the best interests of the children affected by the cap to deprive [their parents] of the means to provide them with adequate food, clothing, warmth and housing, the basic necessities of life' (para 226). But she was in the minority, and the appeal was lost.

One cannot rely on the courts for radical social change. The 'haves' usually come out ahead (Galanter, 1974). That is not to say that the courts cannot defend the interests of individuals in some circumstances, and as noted earlier they can influence the way that law and policy is put into practice (whether for good or ill may be a matter of contention); but social change is primarily a matter of campaigning, awareness raising and political activity, not litigation (Cranston, 2007: 316). Courts may respond to these wider forces, but they do not lead them.

The distinction between formal justice and social justice links with ideas about human rights, where a distinction is often drawn between 'first generation', civil and political rights (e.g. not to be subjected to cruel, inhuman or degrading treatment or punishment; freedom of thought and conscience; right to private and family life; freedom from arbitrary or unlawful arrest or detention), and 'second generation', economic, social and cultural rights (e.g. rights to fair wages; safe and healthy working conditions; an adequate standard of living; the highest attainable standard of physical and mental health). Traditionally, first-generation rights have been defended by lawyers in the courts; second-generation rights are promoted through the activities of the welfare state and relevant agencies and social professionals. This is another distinction which is useful but not always clear-cut, and should not be over-drawn. Human rights are indivisible, and lawyers can argue for second-generation rights, just as social workers and their agencies have to uphold first-generation rights (Ife, 2012; Dickens, 2013).

Even so, there is a difference of character between the two sorts of rights. BASW has a human rights policy which makes the point that human rights, as they have been passed into legislation in the UK, often have a narrower meaning than in social work's professional values, where they are linked to wider questions of social justice and equality (BASW, 2015). The question of resources hangs very large over second-generation rights. We have already mentioned some of the questions that arise from the requirement that social workers should bring situations 'where resources are inadequate or where distribution of resources, policies and practice are oppressive, unfair, harmful or illegal' to the attention of their 'employers, policy makers, politicians and the general public'. (Note that this requirement is also in the international statement of ethical principles, not only in the BASW code, although the international version does not include 'illegal'.)

There are three dimensions in this requirement: first, bringing issues of resources and perceived unfairness to the attention of employers; second, to the attention of people outside one's agency; and third, what to do about illegal decisions, policies or practice.

BASW has a policy for employers of social workers to establish effective and ethical working environments (BASW, 2013). It is based on the IFSW policy for employers (IFSW, 2012), but inserts some additional sections to describe the UK policy, organisational and practice contexts. One of its key points is that:

> the most effective social work takes place in environments which balance respect for professional values and standards with organisational accountabilities. An open environment which encourages learning, critical reflection and challenge, fully involving service users/consumers/clients in these processes, is more likely to result in high quality services, public satisfaction and the avoidance of bad practice ...
>
> (BASW, 2013: 8)

So, within agencies, it is important that there is a commitment to high standards, an understanding of social work's professional values alongside proper arrangements for managerial and resource accountability, a culture of openness and willingness to involve and learn from people who use social work services. It is also important that there are effective workload-management policies, a good physical work environment, a commitment to ongoing training and development, good quality social work supervision and systematic reviews of services and practice (BASW, 2013: 12–13).

For all that, many decisions about resources and policies are made above the level of the social worker's organisation; they may not even come from the two central government departments that lead on children's services and adult social care, the Department for Education and the Department of Health, respectively. Decisions about welfare benefit payments, immigration and asylum policy, and NHS or school reorganisations may well have profound implications for people who use social work services. Social workers may have strong views about these matters and may be active in campaigning about them in their own time, perhaps through membership of a political party. However, it is not straightforward to say how far, or by what means, they should raise matters with 'policy makers, politicians and the general public'.

Most social workers in the UK are employed in statutory agencies, such as local authorities and health trusts (although the largest single employer of social workers in England is Cafcass, the body that employs social workers who provide independent reports to the courts in child and family proceedings). They do not have the freedom, or the responsibility, to campaign politically within their occupational role. Social workers in different sorts of organisational settings may have greater freedom, or even specific roles, to do so.

There may be circumstances in which social workers could raise matters with a wider audience as part of their professional activity – for example, through membership of a policy-review working party, or responding to a government consultation, or undertaking and publishing research (with suitable permission and regard for confidentiality). But more vigorous campaigning and direct action are matters which should take place in their own time – and even then, with due regard to the implications for the reputation of the profession and the organisation (the professional integrity dimension, discussed earlier).

What then about the third aspect, if there is something that a social worker considers illegal, or if not illegal, so wrong that they consider they have to take a stand against it directly? In those cases, they should be careful to follow their organisation's whistleblowing procedures, as far as possible, and the law. The Public Interest Disclosure Act 1998 (PIDA, as amended by the Enterprise and Regulatory Reform Act 2013) gives a framework for balancing the duties of employees and employers, together with protection for service users and for staff who decide to whistleblow. So, the law does offer some protection for social workers if they make a disclosure which they reasonably believe to be in the public interest. However, it is well known that it can be a very difficult experience to be a whistleblower, provoking a lot of anxiety and discontent if the person does not think that the right action (or indeed any action) has been taken. Also, despite the legislation, over two-thirds of a sample of 1,000 whistle-blowers said that their own situation had got worse as a result of their action (Public Concern at Work and University of Greenwich, 2013).

The law is an essential backstop, but a better outcome would be that organisations build strong cultures in which it is acceptable for staff to voice their concerns, so that problems are nipped in the bud. This is reflected in BASW's whistleblowing policy, which emphasises the importance of employers encouraging social workers to speak up, and promoting a positive message about this (BASW, 2014b).

Conclusion

This chapter has explored some of the conflicts and dilemmas that arise when social work, the law and the courts come into contact. Despite the challenges, the interdisciplinary encounter also gives opportunities, both to uphold better the rights of people who use social work services and to empower social workers, if it can constructively help them to follow and use the law in the best interests of their service users.

The chapter has given an account of social work values, based on the BASW code of ethics, and explored the themes of judgement and justice. These are key concepts for social work and the law, but there are complexities within each of them, and tensions between the social work and legal approaches. However, there is also potential for the different viewpoints to challenge one another constructively, if this can be done with mutual respect and a genuine will to understand the priorities and challenges facing the other professional. This should be combined with a greater awareness of the contradictions and limitations of one's *own* role, and a readiness to challenge oneself rather than the other person. This sort of reflective and analytic approach, focusing on the implications for practice, is the key to better decision-making and better outcomes for service users.

To conclude, let us revisit the other theme, about the two recent developments in social work thinking, the rediscoveries of radicalism and of relationship-based work. The radical approach gives social work an important vision, so that is not just about passively accepting the existing order and the inequalities and oppression within it (Ife, 2012: 38–39). But it is risky to make overblown claims about challenging oppression and inequality if these cannot legitimately or realistically be achieved (realism is an ethical duty too: Beckett, 2007). However, realistically, much can be: and that takes us back to relationships, and the ways that relationship-based and radical social work can be combined. Good social work starts with a commitment to individuals and families, to treating them with respect and dignity. It starts in the 'small places' (Roosevelt, 1958), the ways that social workers talk to people and talk about people; the ways they keep people up to date with what is happening, even if 'nothing has happened yet'; the ways they show concern for people (service users and other workers), the little acts of thoughtfulness, generosity and calm determination. It looks at people's needs in the bigger picture, but is still clear-eyed about their interests and the interests of others. Good relationship-based social work is a form of quiet radicalism, and many acts of quiet radicalism can make a powerful force for change. If an organisation can tap into this, encourage it and spread it, then the whole agency could be transformed – and it could go beyond that, to contribute to wider social change. This would be relationship-based radicalism, based on a critical, realistic but still ambitious understanding of social work values. This way of changing practice would not be courts lecturing social workers (and other professionals) about what they have done wrong. They have been doing this for years, but it does not work because it does not help to spread *good* practice; if anything, it is counterproductive because it destroys morale and drives staff away from these demanding areas of work. Change would have a better chance of succeeding if it starts from social work values.

References

Banks, S. (2012) *Ethics and Values in Social Work*, 4th edn, Basingstoke: Palgrave Macmillan/BASW.

BASW (2012) *Code of Ethics in Social Work: Statement of Principles*, Birmingham: BASW. Online, available at: www.basw.co.uk/codeofethics.

BASW (2013) *BASW/IFSW Policy on Effective and Ethical Working Environments for Social Work: The Responsibilities of Employers of Social Workers*, Birmingham: BASW. Online, available at: www.basw.co.uk/resource/?id=2027.

BASW (2014a) *Annual Report and Financial Statements, Year Ending 30 September 2014*, Birmingham: BASW. Online, available at: http://cdn.basw.co.uk/upload/basw_114754-10.pdf.

BASW (2014b) *BASW Whistleblowing Policy*, Birmingham: BASW. Online, available at: http://cdn.basw.co.uk/upload/basw_40037-3.pdf.

BASW (2015) *BASW Human Rights Policy*, Birmingham: BASW. Online, available at: http://cdn.basw.co.uk/upload/basw_30635-1.pdf.

Barnard, A., Horner, N. and Wild, J. (eds) (2008) *The Value Base of Social Work and Social Care*, Maidenhead: Open University Press.

Beckett, C. (2007) 'The reality principle: realism as an ethical obligation', *Ethics and Social Welfare*, 1(3): 269–281.

Beckett, C., Dickens, J. and Bailey, S. (2014) *Concluding Care Proceedings within 26 Weeks: Report of the Evaluation of the Tri-borough Care Proceedings Pilot, Updated version*, Norwich: Centre for Research on Children and Families, University of East Anglia.

Online, available at: www.uea.ac.uk/centre-research-child-family/child-protection-and-family-support/evaluation-of-the-tri-borough-care-proceedings-pilot.

Bisman, C. (2004) 'Social work values: the moral core of the profession', *British Journal of Social Work*, 43: 109–23.

Cafcass (2015) *Care Application Demand and Number of Subject Children by Local Authority*, May 2015. Online, available at: www.cafcass.gov.uk/media/244417/may_2015_care_demand.pdf.

Cranston, R. (2007) *How Law Works: The Machinery and Impact of Civil Justice*, Oxford: Oxford University Press.

Dickens, J. (2005) 'Being "the epitome of reason": the challenges for lawyers and social workers in child care proceedings', *International Journal of Law, Policy and the Family*, 19(1): 73–101.

Dickens, J. (2013) *Social Work, Law and Ethics*, Abingdon: Routledge.

Dickens, J. (2016) *Social Work and Social Policy: An Introduction*, 2nd edn, Abingdon: Routledge.

Dickens, J. and Masson, J. (2014) 'The courts and child protection social work in England: tail wags dog?', *British Journal of Social Work*, advance access. DOI: 10.1093/bjsw/bcu144.

Dickens, J., Beckett, C. and Bailey, S. (2014) 'Justice, speed and thoroughness in child protection court proceedings: messages from England', *Children and Youth Services Review*, 46: 103–111.

Dickens, J., Howell, D., Thoburn, J. and Schofield, G. (2007) 'Children starting to be looked after by local authorities in England: an analysis of inter-authority variation and case-centred decision-making', *British Journal of Social Work*, 37: 597–617.

DfE (2013) *The Local Authority Children's Social Care Services Workforce, England, 31 December 2012*. London: DfE. Online, available at: www.gov.uk/government/statistics/the-local-authority-childrens-social-care-services-workforce-england-31-december-2012.

DfE (2014a) *Children Looked After by Local Authorities in England (Including Adoption and Care Leavers), Year Ending 31 March 2014*. Online, available at: www.gov.uk/government/statistics/children-looked-after-in-england-including-adoption--2.

DfE (2014b) *Characteristics of Children in Need in England, 2013-14, Statistical First Release*, London, DfE. Online, available at: www.gov.uk/government/statistics/characteristics-of-children-in-need-2013-to-2014.

Doel, M., Allmark, P., Conway, P., Cowburn, M., Flynn, M., Nelson, P. and Tod, A. (2010) 'Professional boundaries: crossing the line or entering the shadows?', *British Journal of Social Work*, 40: 1866–89.

Family Justice Review (2011) *Interim Report*, London, MoJ. Online, available at: www.gov.uk/government/publications/family-justice-review-interim-report.

Ferguson, I. and Lavalette, M. (eds) (2013) *Critical and Radical Debates in Social Work*, Bristol: Policy Press.

Ferguson, I. and Woodward, R. (2009) *Radical Social Work in Practice*, Bristol: Policy Press.

Galanter, M. (1974) 'Why the "haves" come out ahead: speculations on the limits of legal change', *Law and Society*, 9: 95–160.

Harwin, J., Alrouh, B., Ryan, M. and Tunnard, J. (2014) *Changing Lifestyles, Keeping Children Safe: An Evaluation of the First Family Drug and Alcohol Court (FDAC) in Care Proceedings*, London: Brunel University. Online, available at: www.brunel.ac.uk/chls/clinical-sciences/research/ccyr/research-projects/fdac.

Howe, D. (2008) *The Emotionally Intelligent Social Worker*, Basingstoke: Palgrave.

HM Government (2011) *A New Approach to Child Poverty: Tackling the Causes of Disadvantage and Transforming Families' Lives*, Cm 8061, London: TSO. Online, available at: www.gov.uk/government/uploads/system/uploads/attachment_data/file/177031/CM-8061.pdf.

Ife, J. (2012) *Human Rights and Social Work: Towards Rights-Based Practice*, 3rd edn, Cambridge: Cambridge University Press.

IFSW (2012) *Effective and Ethical Working Environments for Social Work: The Responsibilities of Employers of Social Workers*, Berne: IFSW. Online, available at: http://ifsw.org/policies/effective-and-ethical-working-environments-for-social-work-the-responsibilities-of-employers-of-social-workers-3/.

IFSW and IASSW (2004) *Ethics in Social Work: Statement of Principles*, Berne: IFSW/IASSW. Online, available at: http://ifsw.org/policies/statement-of-ethical-principles.

Lavalette, M. (ed.) (2011) *Radical Social Work: Social Work at the Crossroads*, Policy Press: Bristol.

Macintyre, D. (1993) 'Major on crime: "Condemn more, understand less"', *The Independent*, 21 February. Online, available at: www.independent.co.uk/news/major-on-crime-condemn-more-understand-less-1474470.html.

Masson, J. and Dickens, J., with Bader, K. and Young, J. (2013) *Partnership by Law? The Pre-Proceedings Process for Families on the Edge of Care Proceedings*, Bristol and Norwich, School of Law, University of Bristol and Centre for Research on Children and Families, University of East Anglia. Online, available at: www.uea.ac.uk/ssf/centre-research-child-family/research-fields/children-protection.

Munro, E. (2011) *The Munro Review of Child Protection, Final Report: A Child-Centred System*, London: DfE. Online, available at: www.gov.uk/government/collections/munro-review.

National Adoption Leadership Board (2014) *Impact of Court Judgments on Adoption: What the Judgments Do and Do Not Say*, London, NALB. Online, available at: www.adcs.org.uk/download/resources/adoption/ALB%20-%20Impact%20of%20Court%20Judgments%20on%20Adoption%20-%20November%202014.pdf.

Payne, M. (2006) *What is Professional Social Work?*, 2nd edn, Bristol: BASW/Policy Press.

Public Concern at Work and University of Greenwich (2013) *Whistleblowing: The Inside Story*, London: Public Concern at Work. Online, available at: www.pcaw.org.uk/cms/sitecontent/view/id/127/highlight/greenwich.

Roosevelt, E. (1958) *In Your Hands: A Guide for Community Action for the Tenth Anniversary of the Universal Declaration of Human Rights*, Speech to the United Nations, 27 March. Online, available at: www.gwu.edu/~erpapers/abouteleanor/er-quotes/.

Ruch, G., Turney, D. and Ward, A. (eds) (2010) *Relationship-based Social Work: Getting to the Heart of Practice*, London: Jessica Kingsley.

Social Work Task Force (2009) *Building a Safe, Confident Future: The Final Report of the Social Work Task Force*, London: SWTF. Online, available at: http://webarchive.nationalarchives.gov.uk/+/dh.gov.uk/en/SocialCare/DH_098322.

Sutton Trust (2005) *Briefing Note: The Educational Backgrounds of the UK's Top Solicitors, Barristers and Judges*, London: Sutton Trust. Online, available at: www.suttontrust.com/wp-content/uploads/2005/05/Comparison_educational_backgrounds.pdf.

Turbett, C. (2014) *Doing Radical Social Work*, Basingstoke: Macmillan.

Wilson, K., Ruch, G., Lymbery, M. and Cooper, C. (2011) *Social Work: An Introduction to Contemporary Practice*, 2nd edn, Harlow: Pearson.

2

ANTI-OPPRESSIVE PRACTICE AND THE LAW

Beverley Burke and Jane Dalrymple

This chapter will consider how the law can be used to promote anti-oppressive practice. The reality of contemporary social work is that resources are limited and legalism is a feature of practice. It can be argued that legislation, guidance and regulations prescribing practice promote and encourage good practice since they stress the importance of prevention and support as well as providing legal safeguards when compulsory intervention is needed. However, the controlling and restrictive elements of legislation move social workers away from responding to need to managing risk. The impact of this is the development of a 'defensive and morally timid social work practice' (Stanford quoted in Whittaker and Havard, 2015).

The contradictions that consequently characterise the complex relationship between practitioners, services users and the legislative framework will be examined within this chapter. By encouraging practitioners to critically reflect on the dilemmas they may face when working within restrictive policy and legislative frameworks, while at the same time advocating for people's rights, a more creative and nuanced response to using the law can be promoted. In recognition of the complex relationship which exists between the law and anti-oppressive practice, the authors will demonstrate that using the law alongside professional codes and guidance can contribute to the development of practice that is beneficial, supportive and promotes anti-oppressive values. Readers will be encouraged to address the impact of structural inequalities and legislation which may be experienced negatively by people who use services and to find innovative ways of using the law positively in practice.

The legal and policy context

There is a complex and contradictory relationship between the law, values and power which makes a discussion of the law an interesting one, particularly considering how the law can be used to enhance and support practice which is socially just. The anti-oppressive potential of social work law can be realised only if it is critically interrogated from an ethical perspective, since 'the way values in the law are configured and codified will shape the goals of welfare services' (Preston-Shoot et al., 2001: 2). Practitioners need to be confident in relation to their knowledge and understanding of the law and how it can support practice which is ethically robust.

The law defines the roles and responsibilities of practitioners and directs practice in the areas of prevention, protection and rehabilitation (Clifford and Burke, 2009). Practitioners therefore need to be 'legally literate' (Braye et al., 2011: 92) in their practice in order to be able to manage the complexities that arise when they attempt to manage the diverse and sometimes contradictory elements of practice situations. On the one hand, actions either permitted or required in law can violate ethical standards in social work, while in other circumstances it may be necessary to take actions that are against the law in order to comply with social work values and ethics. Such situations create dilemmas since they lead to conflict with respect to professional values, duties, and obligations and services user's rights to self-determination (Reamer, 2005; Clifford and Burke, 2009). Managing these tensions requires the practitioner to ask challenging and appropriate questions in relation to needs, risks and rights if they are to act appropriately where legal rules and policies are not supportive of actions which are ethically desirable (Braye et al., 2011).

Equally, the law has the potential to be used to challenge decisions that deny people's rights, liberty and equality. The Human Rights Act 1998, for example, is underpinned by values consistent with the humanitarian and democratic ideals of social work and has been used skilfully and responsibly to safeguard the rights of individuals and communities. However, applying legal knowledge to everyday practice situations is fraught with difficulties. Michael Preston-Shoot (2010) points out that there is a disjunction between the law in theory and its implementation by managers and practitioners. Drawing on a range of evidence, including case law and the experiences of service users, he demonstrates how local authorities avoid their legal duties, fail to comply with statutory guidance and take unlawful resource driven decisions. In the case of *R (Goldsmith) v Wandsworth* LBC [2004], the decision to move an older person from a residential home to a nursing home was quashed. The authority made the decision to choose the cheaper option of the nursing home without considering the impact that this decision would have on private and family life (Article 8 ECHR, right to family life) or the proportionality of the decision (Human Rights Act, 1998), given that the older woman could have remained in residential care where she was settled (Preston-Shoot, 2010: 470)

Using legal knowledge and values to inform good practice requires practitioners to have a good knowledge of the law and be able to critically analyse the ideological basis of legislation and social policies, and to evaluate their impact on meeting need without exacerbating inequalities or adding to oppression.

The failure, for example, of practitioners and managers to identify the inherent racism within immigration legislation has resulted in situations where practitioners actively cooperate 'with the removal and deportation of people' (Humphries, 2004: 104) and do not challenge collectively the passing of increasingly restrictive and punitive policies and legislation which has severely limited and removed the provision of welfare services to destitute refugees without status (Preston-Shoot, 2010; Vickers, 2014). People with mental health needs may be treated unfairly because, argues George Szmukler (Szmukler et al., 2014), mental health law can be considered discriminatory. He points out that this discrimination 'seems to be based on deeply embedded (but clearly false) and persistent stereotypes of mental illness being inextricably linked with incompetence (and dangerousness)'. 'Mental health law fails to respect the "autonomy" or right to "self-determination" of the patient in psychiatry in the same way as capacity-based law does for all other patients' (Szmukler, 2014).

The situation facing practitioners, and the families they are working with, is that decisions have to be made to mitigate growing levels of social inequality and poverty within a context of diminishing resources and the increasing privatisation and marketisation of services. Management responses driven by austerity and neo-liberal policy add to the challenges practitioners have to contend with in contemporary social and welfare organisations. Legally aware anti-oppressive and critical practitioners also need to consider how their personal perspectives on welfare and their values are challenged by current neo-liberal discourses which, by focusing exclusively on the individual, promotes an individualistic perspective of self-sufficiency and minimal reliance on the state, an ideological position which fails to take into account the range of structural factors which shape and determine the life chances of individuals. Within this framework, individuals are essentially blamed for the difficulties in which they find themselves, making them responsible for their own well-being. This practice context does not always provide the right conditions for practitioners to positively assert and act on anti-oppressive values such as choice, partnership and respect. Such conditions also provide the circumstances where defensive practice becomes 'part of the culture' of the organisation. This can lead individual practitioners to overestimating risk, sharing or avoiding responsibility, not challenging managers and avoiding supervision (Whittaker and Havard, 2015). Research by Whittaker and Havard found that even before qualifying, final-year social work students were witnessing and experiencing these practice issues. They also recognised that they were effectively being socialised into an ethos and culture of welfare organisations in which they learned to engage in practice which could be described as defensive. Such practice was described by one participant as:

> Sticking overly close to your role and hiding behind legislation – doing what is lawful, not what is ethical (Participant 14, Group 1).

(Whittaker and Havard, 2015: 6)

The reluctance to question managers was identified as an aspect of defensive practice by another participant:

> Defensive practice is about not challenging management decisions and following the procedures in an unreflective and passive way (Participant 6, Group 1).
> (Whittaker and Havard, 2015: 8)

Practitioners therefore have to interrogate and challenge the morality of the legal and social structures within which they work and which structure their practice responses. Holding on to their professional autonomy, creativity and commitment to anti-oppressive values can contribute to the development of practice which is not narrow, legalistic and formulaic but is responsive, relational and supportive. Failure to do so, we would argue, can lead to practitioners failing to focus on social work's social and political mandate to promote humanitarian values and human well-being and the development of social and welfare services which is needs-led, caring and supports social reform (Rogowski, 2015: 33).

A key question to consider is how to ensure that the legal rights and entitlements of the individual inform practice which is person centred, strengths based and ethical (Clifford and Burke, 2009; Bisman, 2014; Saleebey, 2006). Central to this consideration is how the law can be used by practitioners to ensure that the rights, freedoms and well-being of individuals are maximised. We use the following case of Sieta and her familial and social networks to explore the issues and dilemmas of social work in relation to how the law can be used to engage in practice which is anti-oppressive.

Sieta's story

Sieta is an 84-year-old Black woman whose husband, Mark, died a year ago, leaving her on her own. She was born in Jamaica and moved to Manchester to work as a nurse in the 1950s. Mark died suddenly, and Sieta has found it difficult coping with her feelings of loss. Her son Delroy has described her as 'depressed' since her husband died. He does not think his mother is coping since the death of his father. Sieta uses a walking stick to move around the house due to a long-standing back problem. She finds is hard to socialise with others, as she did most things with her husband after he retired. Sieta's neighbour, Jude, has contacted social services because she is worried that Sieta has recently left her flat door open while out shopping and that she is using the gas cooker to keep warm. Sieta is very independent and cooks for herself, although she has had a couple of accidents recently. She also said that she is not sure that Sieta always remembers to eat and commented that she 'enjoys a drink or two'. Jude says that she 'keeps an eye on her' but 'doesn't like to interfere'. Jude is concerned that Sieta is neglecting herself, particularly in relation to personal care, and believes that Sieta's dementia is getting worse.

Sieta

I really like living here and want to try and manage on my own but I miss Mark – he did so much to help me. I do feel very lonely sometimes. I can do a lot for myself but I get a bit muddled especially when I try to make a cup of tea – I seem to get it wrong sometimes. I can't always be bothered to have a wash and it's much too difficult to get in and out of the bath. I worry a bit about the bills even though Delroy tells me there is enough money in the bank. Delroy tells me I shouldn't be here on my own, but this is where I want to be. I've got a nice neighbour, Jude, who pops in and I feel safe having her next door.

Delroy

Mum seems to have gone downhill since Dad died – I do worry about her. I love seeing her, but with my own family and work commitments I don't see her as much as I would like. I'm not sure she is looking after herself, but it is hard to find out exactly what is happening – she keeps a lot to herself and likes me to talk to her about the grandchildren and what I am doing rather than about her. Sometimes I wonder if she is capable of living on her own – it is so hard to know. She has always been such an independent person. Jude has contacted social services now so they can make the decisions.

Jude

Sieta is part of my life – I know she's not family, but I've lived next door to her for over 20 years and watched Delroy and now his young family growing up. She's always been there for others – I don't know what everyone would have done without her over the years. I just worry now that one day she will have a serious accident and no one will be there when she needs them. She is so independent it is difficult to know what to do – but she doesn't look after herself as well as she did when Mark first died. I think he did a lot more than we know. He said she had dementia, which would explain some of the things that she does now. When I phoned social services they asked me if I am her carer – well, Mark used to look after her, and Delroy calls round as much as he can, but really no one cares for her now, that's the problem. Then they asked me if she has capacity. I just said I think she has dementia – I don't know, really.

It is clear from the individual stories that each person has her or his own feelings, experiences and understanding of the situation. It is the practitioner's role to respectfully listen to all viewpoints as part of engaging in a process of dialogue (Powell, 2005). Relationships are critical to effective social work intervention (Ruch, 2010; Wilson et al., 2011; Trevithick, 2012). Through a relational process, the practitioner can work with the Sieta and her family and key people in her life to identify her strengths and needs. A relationship is unique to the professional and the people concerned. It is influenced by a range of factors including the worker's social location, level of experience, understanding of the service user and carers' perspectives and being prepared to act in ways that take their humanity and needs into account, as well as their own, within complex and challenging situations (Clifford and Burke, 2009). The 'use of self' and self-knowledge is a key element within the relational process.

The stories of the various people involved present a number of dilemmas, both for the family members themselves and for any professionals who might be involved with them. The stories can therefore be seen as issues about personal responsibility, structural disadvantage or legal duty (Fook, 2002; Ferguson and Woodward, 2009; Turbett, 2014; Brammer, 2015). If we consider these stories, first, in terms of the *moral obligations* of the people involved, then we have to think about individual rights and responsibilities that people have with each other within personal relationships and communities. Jordan points out that 'moral duties arise out of lives which are interdependent, commitments which are mutual, and communities with common interests' (1990: 21). A morally active and legally literate practitioner (Bisman, 2014; Braye et al., 2011) will consider some key questions, such as:

- Should Sieta be helped to keep her independence?

- What responsibilities does Delroy have in relation to Sieta?

- What role does Jude have?

- What responsibilities do members of the community have towards Sieta? 'How can the strengths of communities, the talents, expertise, and assets of the people who live in them, be harnessed for the benefit of all?' (Ivory, 2015)

- What are the responsibilities of the professionals involved?

- What aspects of the law can be used to support Sieta?

These pose ethical dilemmas for everyone involved, and the perceptions of the people concerned will depend on various personal and social factors (Littlechild and Blakeney, 1996; Clifford and Burke, 2009; Dickens, 2013). Additional questions that therefore need to be thought about include:

- When is it right to make decisions on behalf of someone else when there is a question about their capacity/ability to participate in decision-making?

- Who should decide? What else should be taken into account, and how should the person be worked with?

- At what point should the state use the law to intervene in people's lives?

Legally, there are questions to consider about capacity. Assessing whether or not a person has capacity in relation to the Mental Capacity Act 2005 has been described as a 'powerful act' (Graham and Cowley, 2015: 60). Graham and Cowley suggest that rather than jumping straight in to assessing capacity because we are told to, or because some assumptions have been made based on perceptions of various people, we should begin by maximising a person's capacity and then ask the question:

- What right do I have to assess this person's capacity and why would I even do so?

And, in terms of assessment:

- Who should be involved in the assessment process?

Second, the same stories could be considered in terms of the *structural disadvantages* faced by those involved. As a Black service user, Sieta is likely to find that because racism structures the delivery of health and social care services (Penketh and Ali, 1997; Adams, 2002), mainstream services may not be able to meet her needs; a range of evidence exists which supports the continual failure of the social work profession to provide services that meet the needs of Black and minority ethnic (BME) communities (Chahal and Ullah, 2004; Williams and Johnson, 2010; Lavalette and Penketh, 2014). Despite the growing proportion of older people from BME communities, few attend local authority day centres or care homes. The proportion of older people feeling lonely are higher for some BME communities in Britain than for some White communities. Poor command of English and experience of racism may be factors in this difference (Wisdom in Practice, 2014).

Stereotyping and discriminating against people because they are old has a pervasive influence on the behaviour of professionals. Older people are often perceived as frail or dependent, which means that professionals respond to the social identity they have been assigned. Ageism compounds the discrimination and stereotyping that marginalised groups experience throughout their lives. Older people are often problematised in terms of policy, being regarded, for example, as a drain on limited resources (Gorman, 2005; Bell and Hafford-Letchfield, 2015). Older people may be denied their rights in structural ways such as inequalities with respect to the power and influence that older people have in society (for example, in relation to employment, housing and access to health and social care services). Institutionalised ageism is evident in social structures – legally, medically and through welfare, educational and income policies – as well as being internalised by individuals in society (Crawford and Walker, 2004). Older people consequently have limited access to services and are often treated badly. For people with dementia this is exacerbated, particularly with respect to accessing mental health services which are more easily available to younger adults. Lack of understanding about dementia as an illness continues to be problematic and has led to poor rates of diagnosis and a lack of provision to meet their needs (Andrews, 2015: 18). Furthermore, assumptions are often made that people with dementia lack capacity – the Mental Capacity Act 2005 is clear that a diagnosis such as dementia is not a reason to query capacity. The Alzheimer's Society has expressed concern that the inequality experienced by people with dementia is multifaceted, as they experience discrimination in relation to their age, disability and the stigma attached to their condition (Alzheimer's Society, 2012). Finally, social class and economic position means that older people are likely to have less leverage in terms of the level and nature of care and ability to make choices within the market of care. For Sieta, this could compromise her health and quality of life (Crawford and Walker, 2004; Bell and Hafford-Letchfield, 2015).

Third, the stories could be considered from a managerialist perspective, focusing on *legal duty*. Sieta is entitled to an assessment because she appears to have need for care and support (Care Act 2014). An assessment begins when local authorities start to collect information about the person – first contact – which means that Sieta and her family should be given as much information as possible about the process to ensure a personalised approach to the assessment. The landscape of care provision has been dominated for many years by a care management approach. Social workers had a directive role within a process of managing limited resources and slotting people into available services using bureaucratic and overly cumbersome processes such as resource allocation systems and panels for decision-making. The problem with this was that the assessment focused on what people could not do, with state provision filling any gaps. This dependency approach to meeting need meant that people were expected to highlight their difficulties. It also meant that the natural support and community resources that people might have were often ignored, which, it has been argued, may have made things worse rather than better (Glasby, 2013).

The way in which adults with social care needs are assessed and supported has changed dramatically in the last decade. *Personalisation* has been the key unifying idea in adult social care since at least 2007. It has informed the policies of the previous Labour and Coalition governments and is at the heart of the approach set out in the Care Act 2014. Essentially, personalisation means putting people at the centre of their own care and support planning and recognising their individual strengths and preferences. This has repositioned social

workers in a supportive rather than a directive role, where promoting independent choice and control with 'self-directed support' is an important concept.
Individual 'personal budgets' in particular provide a transparent way for people
to see how much money is available to pay for their care and support, while for
some the provision of a 'direct payment' enables them to employ people to
meet their needs. This has been described as getting away from a 'one size fits
all' approach to care (Shepherd et al., 2008: i) and enables people to develop
personalised packages of support. This could well be helpful for Sieta, although
it is not without its problems (Davey et al., 2007). The aim of personalisation has
been to change social care from a crisis-driven firefighting approach to a preventive well-being service through early intervention and building on social
capital. This involves maximising networks of support between families and
communities. The move to more community-based approaches (including voluntary and informal networks and social enterprise) and increased reliance on
private sector provision has been contentious (Glasby, 2011; Needham and
Glasby, 2014). The argument is that this policy is not based solely on promoting
social inclusion but also clearly lessens reliance on public funds and state responsibility for welfare services, putting the financial burden firmly on communities.
On the other hand, without this, in the current climate of austerity, it is arguably
the only way people can be supported to be independent.

The Care Act 2014 has embedded and extended the personalisation agenda
into social care. Rights to choice, personalised care and support plans, and personal budgets are central to the legislation. The government has responded to
evidence that people want to be more actively engaged as partners, while the
potential impact of harnessing their contribution could be a good economic
way of meeting need and lead to better outcomes. If Sieta is assessed as having
eligible needs for care and support, she should have her support planned and
managed in this way under the Care Act 2014. Focusing on legal duty means
that legislation can be considered a resource to ensure that the rights and
choices of all those involved are respected. Sieta, Delroy and Jude all have rights
and needs. So a practitioner working with Sieta will focus on her needs and try
to ensure that resources are available to meet them. This may seem idealistic,
but anti-oppressive practice is about moving towards the ideal. While the law
cannot make us into good practitioners, it can and should assist and encourage
good practice (Johns, 2005).

Using the law to support Sieta

The starting point for working with Sieta is to have a sound knowledge and
understanding of the law, the assessment process and our own power in this
situation, both in terms of organising our time and using our personal power
to work creatively with Sieta, her family and the community. The statutory

guidance indicates that an initial assessment can be viewed in two ways – either as a process or as a critical intervention (Department of Health, 2014: para. 6.2). Crucially, it states that assessment should not be seen as a gateway to care and support but as an 'intervention', which should help Sieta and her family to understand her situation, the needs she has and how these can be supported. The Care Act 2014 does appear to be underpinned by principles of anti-oppressive practice, and, importantly, the statutory guidance states that assessments must be 'person-centred, involving the individual and any carer that the adult has, or any other person they might want involved' (para. 6.9) and must 'establish the total extent of needs' (para. 6.10). Sieta and her family should be prepared for the assessment process because local authorities are required to 'provide in advance, and in accessible format, the list of questions to be covered in the assessment' (para. 6.38). The Care Act 2014 focuses on a strengths approach – rather than looking at what Sieta cannot do, practitioners are expected to help Sieta to think about her strengths and capabilities, and any support that might be available from her wider support network and within the community. This effectively means focusing holistically on Sieta's life, identifying her needs and agreeing outcomes with her, taking into account her skills, her ambitions and her priorities.

Clearly, any assessment has a power dimension, since power shapes and determines relationships on an individual, group, community, organisational and societal level. Therefore, power issues in social relationships need to be analysed at different levels, 'at the level of political, social and economic structures, and at the level of personal power arising from cultural, institutional and psychological factors' (Clifford, 1998: 685). The practitioner is in control of the process of developing a relationship with Sieta. This means understanding her experience as an individual with her own identity as a Black woman, who as a young woman started a new life in a new country and who has a story to tell about her life. When working with Sieta, practitioners may therefore consider questions such as:

- What is the nature of the power that Sieta has?
- Does this relate to her membership of various social divisions?
- What physical, material and financial resources does the family have?
- What are the cultural and psychological strengths and vulnerabilities of Sieta and her family?

These and other similar questions can assist the practitioner attempting to make a systematic power analysis of situations and will support decision-making regarding levels of vulnerability and potential strengths of Sieta with respect to possible risk. A critical understanding of the process of assessment and the concept of need will help practitioners engage in anti-oppressive practice. This critical perspective should inform an understanding of the relationship between the assessment and the legislation. SCIE reminds practitioners that implementing a strengths approach 'requires cultural and organisational commitment beyond frontline practice' (SCIE, n.d.). Anti-oppressive practice does not just mean understanding and implementing the legislation; it also means that practitioners need to find 'time for research and familiarisation with community resources' (SCIE, n.d.).

Another area of legislation and policy that is relevant in this situation relates to services for BME communities. One of the problems of the Care Act 2014, unlike the Children Act 1989, is that there is no specific reference for the need to take into account race, religion, language and culture in the process of the assessment of care and support needs. However, under the Equality Act 2010, local authorities have to take positive steps to prevent race discrimination. This means that this duty applies to the assessment process, and the planning and provision of services. We have already noted the underuse of services by BME people. This may be compounded by assumptions about extended family support networks (Brammer, 2015; Chahal and Ullah, 2004); note that the experiences of people from BME groups indicate that they can feel ignored by service providers because of myths about family support.

Sieta's personal experiences of being Black, female, ageing and from a particular class must be analysed in relation to understandings gained from an exploration of her experiences of inequality and oppression. Sieta is an older woman who is likely to become increasingly more dependent on the support of her family, friends and significant networks. This position of 'dependency' is not one that Sieta wants, but it is a position that some might see as inevitable. However, Sieta's wishes need to be at the forefront of any action that is taken. The Care Act 2014 expects that all those who have capacity should be involved and influential in the assessment, care and support planning and review processes. Self-respect and autonomy is part of human rights (Gorman, 2005), and the Human Rights Act 1998 supports these principles. The concepts of 'caring', 'dependency', 'need' and 'well-being' therefore have to be critically understood in relation to our work with Sieta and her family if we are committed to engaging in right action in relation to Sieta (Porter, 1999). These terms are 'inextricably bound' together (Watson et al., 2004: 342), although their meanings are contested and context specific. Within the Care Act 2014, the principle of well-being is holistically defined. The local authority has a duty to ensure people's well-being drives its actions in relation to the provision of services which will promote dignity and social inclusion.

The fact that Sieta's powers of decision-making may be impaired by her physical and mental capacities also has to be considered. We need to be aware of the web of power relations in which Sieta is located, as well as relations external to her social and family networks. A detailed understanding of Sieta's life from Sieta and her family and the agencies that she has been involved in is required in order to gain a holistic picture before decisions are made. Our social division membership, knowledge of resources that are available, and experience of working with older people from a particular background will all impact on our work with Sieta.

The potential for Sieta to experience intervention as oppressive is very real. There are a number of factors to think about here. It is possible that any intervention may cause her to worry about losing her independence and her vulnerability is now exposed as a result of the referral. She may feel that she does not need care or want local authority support, and she can refuse an assessment if she has capacity. However, the professional gaze may focus on possible self-neglect, which could be a safeguarding concern, although *Making Safeguarding Personal* (Lawson et al., 2014) means that a practitioner would work with Sieta, respecting her wishes and understanding her need for independence – which is crucial for her overall health and well-being. Workers therefore have to start by thinking about how they listen to Sieta's story in order to develop a trusting relationship. Reports on serious case reviews with reference to self-neglect indicate the importance of a person-centred focus where people decline services. They identify the need to establish a relationship of trust and cooperation over time in order to explore motivation and understand the person and why they have decided to decline services. This may then facilitate greater acceptance of support (Braye et al., 2015). The first principle of the Mental Capacity Act 2005 states that a person must be assumed to have capacity unless it is established that they lack capacity. At this point, there is nothing to indicate that Sieta lacks capacity to make specific decisions. The role of the practitioner is to maximise capacity and ensure that Sieta is supported to be involved and influential in any decision-making about her life.

The suggestion that Sieta has dementia could feed into apparent concerns about her ability to continue living alone. Dementia is described by the World Health Organization as:

> a syndrome – usually of a chronic or progressive nature – in which there is deterioration in cognitive function (i.e. the ability to process thought) beyond what might be expected from normal ageing. It affects memory, thinking, orientation, comprehension, calculation, learning capacity, language, and judgement. Consciousness is not affected. The impairment in cognitive function is commonly accompanied, and occasionally preceded, by deterioration in emotional control, social behaviour, or motivation.
>
> (WHO, n.d.)

It is important to know whether Sieta has a diagnosis of dementia and what form of dementia she has. From an anti-oppressive perspective, practitioners also need to be aware of government policy in relation to dementia and be prepared to contribute towards the aspirations of the current government, stated in the Prime Minister's Challenge on Dementia 2020 (Cabinet Office, Department of Health and Prime Minister's Office, 2015):

> our vision is to create a society by 2020 where every person with dementia, and their carers and families, from all backgrounds, walks of life and in all parts of the country – people of different ages, gender, sexual orientation, ability or ethnicity for example, receive high quality, compassionate care from diagnosis through to end of life care. This applies to all care settings, whether home, hospital or care home. Where the best services and innovation currently delivered in some parts of the country are delivered everywhere so there is more consistency of access, care and standards and less variation. A society where kindness, care and dignity take precedence over structures or systems.

Anti-oppressive practice involves not only being aware of legislation and policy imperatives but being prepared to contribute to aspirations that are clearly intended to improve the lives of people in particular circumstances. It is important also to develop knowledge and understanding about dementia, since no two people with dementia or their carers are the same, and, as in all social work situations, people have unique and differing needs.

We also have to be aware that Delroy believes that Sieta is depressed. While links can be made between depression and dementia (Crawford and Walker, 2005), the causes of Sieta's depression may be linked to other aspects of her life. Sieta has experienced multiple losses, including:

- Her family and country of origin
- Her dignity and respect as a result of racism and ageism
- Her role as an independent person
- The death of her husband
- Her declining mental and physical ability.

For the social worker, understanding Sieta's story means taking time to think about the loss of Mark, which still has a significant impact on her life. His death may also have awakened other losses experienced along her life journey. As practitioners, then, we need to think about issues of grief and loss and its impact on older people, as well as the impact of migration.

We can see from this discussion that Sieta's feelings of anxiety, finding it difficult to remember, problems in looking after herself, finding it hard to socialise with others and low self-esteem are symptoms of both dementia and depression.

Informed by values such as 'the centrality of user need, the importance of good assessment and the benefits of preventive work' (Lymbery, 2004: 169), we therefore need to facilitate the telling of her story in order to complete the assessment and work with everyone involved to put together a care and support plan. In addition, work with Sieta needs to hold at the forefront her right to be self-determining. Gaining knowledge about her experiences will help understand Sieta's fierce desire to maintain her independence – she learned and developed this as a Black woman establishing a new life in Birmingham, a large industrial city in England, with Mark as her main source of support. Recognising and acknowledging changes in her abilities will be difficult and frightening for Sieta. Therefore, together with other professionals and her family, she may need support to be able to maintain her independence. This requires the use of effective communication skills which confirm her sense of self, informed by a strengths perspective that focuses on her capacities and potentialities (Gorman, 2005; Healy, 2005; Saleebey, 2006).

The stories of Delroy and Jude also need to be understood in terms of developing a plan to support Sieta. It is clear that both Delroy and Jude are expecting that social services will take on the responsibility of caring, but both express some ambivalence and lack of understanding about Sieta and how she views her situation. Therefore, careful work needs to be done to enable them to consider how they can support Sieta to maintain her independence. It is interesting to note here that while the principles of the Care Act 2014 are broadly compatible with Article 19 of the UN Convention on the Rights of Persons with Disabilities, the right to live independently and be included in the community and the socio-economic right to support services under Article 19(b), this right does not actually have full legal effect. Nevertheless, it is strongly promoted in the statutory guidance (para. 1.19):

> The wellbeing principle is intended to cover the key components of independent living, as expressed in the UN Convention on the Rights of People with Disabilities (in particular, Article 19 of the Convention). Supporting people to live as independently as possible, for as long as possible, is a guiding principle of the Care Act.
>
> (Collingbourne, 2014; Clements, 2015)

A practitioner would need to build a realistic plan around how Delroy, Jude and other community assets can be utilised to support Sieta. The Care Act 2014 states that local authorities have a general responsibility to promote the welfare of older people.

Intervention at this point could prevent breakdown of the situation for Sieta too quickly. Clearly, Delroy and Jude are thinking about Sieta's inability to manage and the impact of the situation on their lives. Caring has different dimensions which combine feelings and the practical tasks of everyday life. This has been conceptualised as 'caring about' – the feeling part, and 'caring for' – the practical side (Watson et al., 2004). The family may be able to identify some practical ways to reduce the danger of accidents and perhaps alleviate some of the concerns of Jude. There may also be community resources that could be accessed to support Sieta and alleviate any possible depression she may be experiencing. If Sieta is diagnosed as having a form of dementia, then ensuring that the home is dementia friendly and that Delroy and Jude understand the impact of dementia on Sieta's life may help alleviate the stigmatism, exclusion, loneliness and lack of control and empowerment experienced by people with dementia, and enable her to live at home for as long as possible in the early stages of the illness.

Conclusion

Working with Sieta and her family will take time – a problem for managers who need assessments to be completed speedily because of the volume of work. Judgements are likely to be made about the riskiness of Sieta's situation. At the moment, Sieta is happy at home and has a right to private life. Practitioners need to be aware that breaches of the Human Rights Act 1998 can be pursued. Rights of people living with dementia are invariably (and sometimes deliberately) ignored. So the focus when working with people who are living with dementia and their families needs to be on a human rights based approach. Human rights are universal and are intrinsic to human dignity. The PANEL principles (WHO, n.d.) provide a helpful framework to promote the rights of people living with dementia:

- Participation – Everyone has the right to participate in decisions which affect them. Participation must be active, free and meaningful and give attention to issues of accessibility, including access to information in a form and a language which can be understood.

- Accountability – Requires effective monitoring of human rights standards as well as effective remedies for human rights breaches.

- Non-discrimination and equality – A human rights based approach means that all forms of discrimination in the realisation of rights must be prohibited, prevented and eliminated.

- Empowerment – Individuals and communities should understand their rights and should be fully supported to participate in the development of policy and practices which affect their lives.

- Legality - A human rights based approach requires the recognition of rights as legally enforceable entitlements and is linked in to national and international human rights law.

Gorman points out that human rights are about 'acting in an anti-oppressive way, being mindful of the potential for discrimination against older, mentally frail people and making sound judgements that can be evidenced and supported by good recording practices' (2005: 164). Sieta's situation may change, and if in the future Sieta does need to move from her home, then space would need to be allowed for this life transition to take place. This means taking care not to minimise any risk in the future, while at the same time working in ways that respect her dignity rather than being driven by bureaucratic approaches. The skills of the practitioner are about ensuring that Sieta remains central to any decision-making and is involved in subsequent planning. This requires, in particular, skills of partnership working and negotiation – with Sieta, the other key people in her life and other professionals – as well as being able to manage uncertainty, conflict and complexity.

One response to Sieta's story, in a busy day with limited resources, could be to react to pressures from other professionals, the family and the community by taking a bureaucratic approach to the situation. This could lead practitioners to using the law oppressively rather than creatively. The Care Act 2014 provides opportunities for creative practice, but, given the current austerity measures and massive financial cuts most local authorities are having to make to welfare services alongside the lack of any substantial funding to support the implementation of this legislation, it is likely to be a challenge to move beyond a minimal bureaucratic response. However, it is possible to use knowledge values and skills in applying the law and work from an anti-oppressive perspective. The legislation can be used as a resource to support service users and carers to be independent and have an element of choice in how services are provided – but only if the professionally assertive, morally responsible and legally adroit practitioner manages the intricate interaction between legal rules, ethical perspectives, organisational context and budgetary considerations which influence and direct social work decisions and actions.

References

Adams, R. (2002) *Social Policy for Social Work*, Basingstoke: Palgrave.

Adams, R., Dominelli, L. and Payne, M. (eds), *Social Work Futures: Crossing Boundaries, Transforming Services*, Basingstoke: Palgrave Macmillan.

Alzheimer's Society (2012) *Equality, discrimination and human rights*. Online, available at: www.alzheimers.org.uk/site/scripts/documents_info.php?documentID=1674.

Andrews, J. (2015) 'Living with dementia', *Professional Social Work* (September): 18–19.

Bell, L. and Hafford-Letchfield, T. (2015) *Ethics, Values and Social Work Practice*, Maidenhead: Open University Press.

Bisman, C. (2014). *Social Work: Value-Guided Practice for a Global Society*, New York: Columbia University Press.

Brammer, A. (2015) *Social Work Law*, 4th edn, Harlow: Pearson Education.

Braye, S., Orr, D. and Preston-Shoot, M. (2015) 'Serious case review findings on the challenges of self-neglect: indicators for good practice', *The Journal of Adult Protection*, 17(2): 75–87.

Braye, S., Preston-Shoot, M. and Wigley, V. (2011) 'Deciding to use the law in social work practice', *Journal of Social Work,* 13(1): 75–95.

Cabinet Office, Department of Health and Prime Minister's Office (2015) *Prime Minister's Challenge on Dementia 2020.* Online, available at: www.gov.uk/government/ publications/prime-ministers-challenge-on-dementia-2020/prime-ministers-challenge-on-dementia-2020.

Chahal, K. and Ullah, A. I. (2004) *Experiencing Ethnicity: Discrimination and Service Provision,* York: Joseph Rowntree Foundation.

Clements, L. (2015) *Care Act Overview,* Online, available at: www.lukeclements.co.uk/ wp-content/uploads/2015/07/0-Care-Act-notes-updated-2015-09.pdf.

Clifford, D. (1998) *Social Assessment Theory and Practice,* Aldershot: Ashgate.

Clifford, D. and Burke, B. (2009) *Anti-Oppressive Ethics and Values in Social Work,* Basingstoke: Palgrave Macmillan.

Collingbourne, T. (2014) 'The Care Act 2014: A missed opportunity?', *European Journal of Current Legal Issues,* 20(3): online, available at: http://webjcli.org/article/view/ 365/464.

Crawford, K. and Walker, J. (2004) *Social Work with Older People,* 1st edn, Exeter: Learning Matters.

Davey, V., Snell, T., Fernández, J., Knapp, M., Tobin, R., Jolly, D., Perkins, M., Kendall, J., Pearson, C., Vick, N., Swift, P., Mercer, G. and Priestley, M. (2007) *Schemes Providing Support to People Using Direct Payments: A UK Survey,* London: London School of Economics and Political Science, Personal Social Services Research Unit.

Department of Health (2014) *Care and Support Statutory Guidance. Issued under the Care Act 2014.* Online, available at: www.gov.uk/government/publications.

Dickens, J. (2013) *Social Work Law and Ethics,* Abingdon: Routledge.

Ferguson, F. and Woodward, R. (2009) *Radical Social Work in Practice: Making a Difference,* Bristol: Policy Press.

Fook, J. (2002) *Social Work. Critical Theory and Practice,* London: Sage.

Glasby, J. (2011) *Whose Risk Is It Anyway? Risk and Regulation in an Era of Personalisation,* York: Joseph Rowntree Foundation.

Glasby, J. (2013) 'There's no "one size fits all" solution to health and social care integration', *The Guardian,* 28 October. Online, available at: www.theguardian.com/social-care-network/2013/oct/28/solution-health-social-care-integration.

Gorman, H. (2005) 'Frailty and dignity in old age', in R. Adams, L. Dominelli and M. Payne (eds), *Social Work Futures: Crossing Boundaries, Transforming Services,* Basingstoke: Palgrave Macmillan, 154–66.

Graham, M. and Cowley, J. (2015) *A Practical Guide to the Mental Capacity Act 2005: Putting the Principles of the Act into Practice,* London: Jessica Kingsley.

Healy, K. (2005) 'Under reconstruction: Renewing critical social work practices', in S. Hick, J. Fook and R. Pozzuto (eds), *Social Work: A Critical Turn,* Toronto: Thompson Educational Publishing, 219–29.

Humphries, B. (2004). An Unacceptable Role for Social Work: Implementing Immigration Policy. *British Journal of Social Work,* 34: 93–107.

Ivory, M. (2015) 'Can the Care Act deliver on its promises', *The Guardian,* 29 April, p. 3.

Johns, R. (2005) *Using the Law in Social Work,* 2nd edn, Exeter: Learning Matters.

Jordan, B. (1990) *Social Work in an Unjust Society,* Hemel Hempstead: Harvester Press.

Lavalette, M. and Penketh, L. (2014) *Race, Racism and Social Work: Contemporary Issues and Debates*, Bristol: Policy Press.

Lawson, J., Lewis, S. and Williams, C. (2014) *Making Safeguarding Personal: Guide 2014*, London: Local Government Association.

Littlechild, R. and Blakeney, J. (1996) 'Risk and older people', in H. Kemshall and J. Pritchard (eds), *Good Practice in Risk Assessment and Management*, London: Jessica Kingsley, 68–79.

Lymbery, M. (2004) *Managerialism and Care Management Practice with Older People*, Basingstoke: Palgrave Macmillan.

Needham, C. and Glasby, J. (2014) *Debates in Personalisation*, Bristol: Policy Press.

Penketh, L. and Ali, Y. (1997) 'Racism and social welfare', in M. Lavalette and A. Pratt (eds), *Social Policy*, London: Sage, 101–20.

Porter, E. (1999) *Feminist Perspectives on Ethics*, London: Longman.

Powell, J. (2005) '"Value talk" in social work research: Reflection, rhetoric and reality', *European Journal of Social Work*, 8(1): 21–37.

Preston-Shoot, M. (2010) 'On the evidence for viruses in social work systems: Law, ethics and practice', *European Journal of Social Work*, 13(4): 465–82.

Preston-Shoot, M., Roberts, G. and Vernon, S. (2001) 'Values in social work law: Strained relations or sustaining relationships?', *Journal of Social Welfare and Family Law*, 23(1): 1–22.

Reamer, F. (2005) 'Ethical and legal standards in social work: Consistency and conflict', *Families in Society: The Journal of Contemporary Social Services*, 86(2): 163–69, doi: http://dx.doi.org/10.1606/1044-3894.2237.

Rogowski, S. (2015) 'This is no time for neutrality: Critical reflections of an emeritus social worker', *Professional Social Work*, July/August: 33.

Ruch, G. (2010) *Relationship Based Social Work: Getting to the Heart of Practice*, London: Jessica Kingsley.

Saleebey, D. (2006) *The Strengths Perspective in Social Work Practice*, 4th edn, Boston: Pearson Education.

SCIE (n.d.) *Key messages on a strengths-based approach for assessment and eligibility under the Care Act 2014*. Online, available at: www.scie.org.uk/care-act-2014/assessment-and-eligibility/strengths-based-approach/keymessages.asp.

Shepherd, G., Boardman, J. and Slade, M. (2008) *Making Recovery a Reality*, London: Sainsbury Centre for Mental Health.

Stanford, S. (2010) '"Speaking back" to fear: Responding to the moral dilemmas of risk in social work practice', *British Journal of Social Work*, 40(4): 1065–80.

Szmukler, G., Daw, J. and Callard, F. (2014) 'Mental health law and the UN Convention on the Rights of Persons with Disabilities', *International Journal of Law and Psychiatry*, 37(3): 245–52. doi: 10.1016/j.ijlp.2013.11.024. Epub 2013 November 23.

Trevithick, P. (2012) *Social Work Skills: A practice handbook*, 3rd edn, Buckingham: Open University Press.

Turbett, C. (2014) *Doing Radical Social Work (Reshaping Social Work)*, Basingstoke: Palgrave Macmillan.

Vickers, T. (2014) 'Developing an independent anti-racist model for asylum rights organizing in England', *Ethnic and Racial Studies*, 37(8): 1427–47.

Watson, N., McKie, L. Hughes, B., Hopkins, D. and Gregory, S. (2004) '(Inter)-dependence, needs and care: The potential for disability and feminist theorists to develop an emancipatory model', *Sociology,* 38: 331–50.

Whittaker, A. and Havard, T. (2015) 'Defensive practice as "fear-based" practice: Social work's Open Secret?', *British Journal of Social Work,* Advance Access (July 3): 1–17.

WHO (n.d.) *First WHO Ministerial Conference on Global Action Against Dementia.* Online, available at: www.who.int/mental_health/neurology/dementia/en/.

Williams, C. and Johnson, M. R. D. (2010) *Race and Ethnicity in a Welfare Society,* Maidenhead: Open University Press.

Wilson, K., Ruch, G., Lymbery, M. and Cooper, A. (2011) *Social Work: An introduction to Contemporary Practice,* 2nd edn, Harlow: Pearson Education.

Wisdom in Practice (2014) 'Getting older, feeling valued – older people in BME communities', Wisdom in Practice Discussion Paper. Online, available at: www.wisdominpractice. org.uk/minority-ethnic-older-people/.

3

CARE, VULNERABILITY AND THE LAW

Jonathan Herring

This chapter will explore the norms that underpin the law. It will be argued that the law presumes that citizens are autonomous, independent and self-sufficient. The law is designed to promote and protect the values that such a being would want. This works against the interests of those who fall outside the model. In particular, it leads to a devaluing of the importance and impact of care work. It also leads to a sharp divide between those who are labelled as vulnerable and those who are not. This causes particular problems for those in caring relationships who suffer from the lack of respect for care and a misapplication of the notion of vulnerability.

Introduction

Privacy, respect for autonomy and the promotion of independence play a central role in much social work. The British Association of Social Workers (2012), in its *Code of Ethics for Social Workers*, emphasises the values of autonomy. That means allowing service users to determine for themselves how to live their lives, unless there is a risk of serious harm to others. The opening principle is:

> Social workers should build and sustain professional relationships based on people's right to control their own lives and make their own choices and decisions. Social work relationships should be based on people's rights to respect, privacy, reliability and confidentiality.

The second principle states that:

> Social workers should support people to reach informed decisions about their lives and promote their autonomy and independence, provided this does not conflict with their safety or with the rights of others. Social workers should only take actions which diminish peoples' civil or legal rights if it is ethically, professionally and legally justifiable.

These principles very much reflect a particular understanding of the self and the ethical principles that should govern our behaviour – an understanding that is based on the image of the self as a bounded, unencumbered, autonomous person, whose freedom is under challenge and needs to be protected.

That is an understanding which is reflected in legal principles too. The right of bodily integrity, the right to respect for private life and the importance of autonomy are some of the most important rights in law. Lorraine Code (1991: 78) argues that for supporters of individualism:

> Autonomous man is – and should be – self-sufficient, independent, and self-reliant, a self-realizing individual who directs his efforts towards maximizing his personal gains. His independence is under constant threat from other (equally self-serving) individuals: hence he devises rules to protect himself from intrusion. Talk of right, rational self-interest, expedience, and efficiency permeates his moral, social, and political discourse.

The role of the law, under this model, is to keep others out, to preserve independence and to enable self-sufficiency. Such an approach is based on a particular understanding of the self. As Clapton (2003: 541) argues, much legal and philosophical discussion 'assumes a prototypical disembodied person – that is, typically a male characterized by independence and the presence of rationality and reason'.

In this chapter I want to argue against using such a norm as the starting point of legal analysis for social work intervention. I will argue for a norm which starts with what I would argue is a more accurate understanding of the self, One where the self is deeply vulnerable, profoundly relational and utterly interdependent with others (Herring, 2013). At the end of the chapter I will mention a few practical consequences of taking this approach. I will start by exploring three key aspects of the nature of the person.

We are vulnerable

Vulnerability is an inherent part of being human (Shildrick, 2002; Beckett, 2006). Admittedly, this is generally not how people understand themselves. We like to puff ourselves up with our talk of capacity, independence and autonomy.

If we simply take a list of characteristics of those labelled 'vulnerable people', it is soon apparent that they describe a large portion of the population. Samia Hurst (2008), for example, after looking at existing international guidelines on research ethics, has produced a list of vulnerable groups. This includes the following:

- Racial minorities

- The economically disadvantaged

- The very sick

- The institutionalised

- Children

- Prisoners

- Pregnant women and foetuses

- Incompetent persons

- Persons susceptible to coercion

- Persons who will not derive direct benefits from participation

- Persons for whom research is mixed with clinical care

- Junior or subordinate members of a hierarchical group … [such as] medical and nursing students, subordinate hospital and laboratory personnel, employees of pharmaceutical companies, and members of the armed forces or police

- Elderly persons

- Residents of nursing homes

- Patients in emergency rooms

- Homeless persons

- Refugees or displaced persons

- Patients with incurable disease

- Individuals who are politically powerless

- Members of communities unfamiliar with modern medical concepts

- Patients with incurable diseases

She acknowledges that more could be added to that list. But there can be few people who do not fall into one category or another, at least at some point in their lives. But my argument is not simply to suggest that vulnerability is more common than is often presented – rather, that we are all vulnerable (Fawcett, 2009).

We are vulnerable because our bodies are vulnerable. We are corporeal beings. This corporality creates vulnerability. Death itself is the ultimate sign of that, but more can be said. While the popular image is of our bodies as static, immutable self-contained entities, in fact our bodies are constantly changing. New material is continually being added to them and old material being discarded (Herring, 2014a). They are profoundly leaky (Shildrick, 2002). Our bodies are dependent on a wide range of internal organisms and external forces for survival. Our health is frail. Sickness, illness and accidents are but a breath, a slip, a sneeze away (Matambanadzo, 2012). As Fineman (2013a) puts it: 'we are born, live, and die within a fragile materiality that renders all of us constantly susceptible to destructive external forces and internal disintegration'. We should notice, however, that these vulnerabilities affect not only us, but also those we are in relationships with. Not only are we at risk of harm to our own bodies, the bodies of those we are in relationships with are at risk of harm, and injuries to their bodies impact on ours.

Not only are we dependent in biological terms, so too are we for our physical and psychological well-being. We rely on others to a far greater extent than is commonly acknowledged. We tend to take for granted the many social structures and forms of assistance which disguise our vulnerability. Indeed, there is considerable societal pressure to mitigate or disguise our vulnerability and to claim self-sufficiency. It is striking how much is made of the need to make special accommodations for disabled people, in order to minimise the impact of their disabilities, when contrasted with the many provisions that society makes for the 'able bodied' to meet their disabilities. Hence, the lift is promoted as an accommodation that enables wheelchair users to get to the second floor, with no notice being paid to the provision of steps which performs the same function for others. In a powerful article, Kate Lindemann (2003) writes:

> Colleagues, professional staff members, and other adults are unconscious of the numerous accommodations that society provides to make their work and life style possible. ATM's, extended hours in banks, shopping centres and medical offices, EZpass, newspaper kiosks, and elevators are all accommodations that make contemporary working life possible. There are entire industries devoted to accommodating the needs of adult working people. Fast food, office lunch delivery, day time child care, respite care, car washing, personal care attendants, interpreters, house cleaning, and yard and lawn services are all occupations that provide services that make it possible for adults to hold full time jobs.

As this observation highlights, we are keen to emphasise the vulnerabilities of others, and to downplay our vulnerabilities and the provisions made to meet them (Dodds, 2012).

We are dependent on others not only for the most basic physical needs of food, shelter and sewerage, but also for emotional support. As Mary Neal (2012) puts it:

> I am vulnerable because I am penetrable; I am permanently open and exposed to hurts and harms of various kinds. These two sources of vulnerability – reliance on others for co-operation, and openness to positive harm – are simply two means by which I might come to experience suffering; thus, it is suffering, and the capacity for

suffering, that is definitive of this negative aspect of vulnerability. ... [N]one of us can meet her basic needs and satisfy her core desires without the co-operation of others; and even the most capable adult is vulnerable to hurt and harm, both physical and emotional.

Neal goes on to accept that the extent of the vulnerability may vary from person to person and at different points in a person's life, in a large part depending on the extent to which there is social provision to meet people's needs during their life course. As Fineman (2013b) expands on that observation:

> Throughout our lives we may be subject to external and internal negative, potentially devastating, events over which we have little control – disease, pandemics, environmental and climate deterioration, terrorism and crime, crumbling infrastructure, failing institutions, recession, corruption, decay, and decline. We are situated beings who live with the ever-present possibility of changing needs and circumstances in our individual and collective lives. We are also accumulative beings and have different qualities and quantities of resources with which to meet these needs of circumstances, both over the course of our lifetime and as measured at the time of crisis or opportunity.

We are relational

From our very beginnings, we live in relationships with others. From within our mothers, to our early stages of self-awareness, to our steps to self-understanding, we are in relationships. It is our relationships which give us the words we use to understand ourselves. And it is our relationships which give us our sense of identity – whether that be: I am a daughter; I am a Hindu; I am a Geordie. These relationships form ourselves and come to define who we are. It is only in response to others that our selves have meaning. This understanding of the self means we are in constant danger of our self being challenged by others rejecting us, not accepting us as members of a group, not providing the support we expect or using our relationships to harm us (Gergen, 2009; Sugarman and Martin, 2011).

This relational understanding of the self is complex, and much more argumentation would be required to flesh it out fully. However, if it is correct, or even partly correct, is becomes clear that the emphasis on individual autonomy and promotion of independence is deeply misguided. We do not, we do not want to, indeed we cannot, make decisions 'on our own'. I do not possess the power to make decisions about 'my life' because no such thing exists. 'My life' is deeply embedded in the lives of those around me and those with whom I am in relationship (Baier, 1994). There may be some sense in talking about us making decisions about our lives, but individualised autonomy is a fantasy, a dangerous fantasy. Similarly, talk of independence and self-sufficiency is as foolish as mooting that we should try and live without eating or drinking. An assessment of a person's skills in isolation from others cannot be done. If you were to ask me, 'Are you a good parent?', I could not answer that question. I parent with my partner and cannot understand my role as separate from theirs. My parenting is in relation to my children, and I cannot understand how it might operate with different children. So, too, in legal and social work interventions can we only really analyse people in terms of their relationships and those around, and not as some kind of atomised individual.

Caring relationships are core to humanity

It flows from the two points already made (that we are vulnerable and that we are relational) that caring relationships are the glue that meets our needs, gives us our identity and enables us to live (Donchin, 2000). As Elizabeth Frazer and Nicola Lacey (1993: 178) argue:

> The notion of the relational self, in contrast to both atomistic and inter-subjective selves, nicely captures our empirical and logical interdependence and the centrality to our identity of our relations with others and with practices and institutions, whilst retaining an idea of human uniqueness and discreteness as central to our sense of ourselves. It entails the collapse of any self/other or individual/community dichotomy without abandoning the idea of genuine agency and subjectivity.

It is true that there will be times in our lives when, in a very obvious way, we will be dependent on others for our most basic needs. In early years and in times of sickness, perhaps particularly towards the end of life, we will need care. On other occasions, we may imagine ourselves primarily providing care, be that as parents or carers for others. However, the marker between care giver and care receiver is a false one, I would argue. Careful studies of caring relationships indicate that in fact both parties receive and give in such relationships (Herring, 2014b). Only the most superficial of observations will conclude that there is a 'carer' and a 'cared for'. Further, many who regard themselves as carers require for others to carry out that role (Kröger, 2009). As Fiona Williams (2000: 477) argues, we need to recognise 'us all as interdependent and as having the potential and responsibility to be caring and cared for'.

I now move to consider some of the practical implications of adopting this understanding of the vulnerable, interdependent, caring self.

Centring on caring relationships in law and social work

The way we understand the self and the norms which we use as the basis for our approaches has a profound impact on what we see as the role of law and social work (Baier, 1994). We are portrayed as independent self-interested people (Sevenhuijsen, 1999). For the individualised understanding of the self, we have a James Bond type figure: an isolated, lone man fighting against the power of darkness to find his path to freedom. For him the rights he will need will be those of bodily integrity (he must not be touched, unless he so wishes), privacy (he must not be looked at, unless he so wishes) and autonomy (his decisions must not be interfered with). In short, he wants to be left alone.

Yet those kinds of rights make no sense in the context of an intimate relationship of care. There must be touching; the looking is constant; and life is chaotic, marked not by freedom, but by obligations. Here we need legal responses that enable the care to be given, that ensure the obligations of care are fairly shared, that care is valued and acknowledged, and that the costs of care do not fall disproportionately. We aim to promote and uphold caring relationships – not the freedom of them. We need protection for our vulnerabilities; our responsibilities need to be acknowledged, rather than our freedoms. We ned legal regimes that uphold caring relationships as at the core of society. Susan Dodds (2007) argues:

> Attention to vulnerability ... changes citizens' ethical relations from those of independent act so carving out realms of right against each other and the state, to those of mutually-dependent and vulnerability-exposed beings whose capacities to develop as subjects are directly and indirectly mediated by the conditions around them.

For every social work and legal intervention, the key questions include: does this promote a caring relationship? Does it acknowledge our mutual vulnerability? Does this uphold our interdependence?

Mutual vulnerability

One of the dangers of emphasising vulnerability and care, as this article has done, is that these concepts are open to misuse. I want to highlight two dangers and show how, in fact, the arguments presented here argue against them.

The first error is to separate out particular groups as 'vulnerable'. It is common in political and social work discourse to identify a particular person or group as vulnerable and that doing so justifies paternalistic intervention. As Fineman (2013a) puts it:

> The designation of vulnerable (inferior) populations reinforces and valorizes the ideal liberal subject, who is positioned as the polar opposite of the vulnerable population. This liberal subject thus constructed is invulnerable, or at least differently vulnerable, and represents the desirable and achievable ideals of autonomy, independence, and self-sufficiency.

However, if we accept that we are all vulnerable, this mitigates the vision into 'them and us'; 'the competent and the not competent'; the 'vulnerable and the non-vulnerable'. Yes, the provisions of society may mean that some people's needs are less well met than others, but there is no inherent vulnerability in any group that justifies them being singled out in need of special treatment due to their vulnerability. It means that in providing protection, we need to recognise our own fallibility, weakness and vulnerability, and that must influence what is the correct response. This is not to say that it is improper to recognise that social provision has rendered one group's vulnerability a particular source of harm to them, but in doing so we must acknowledge our mutual vulnerability and the role of the state in causing particular vulnerability to be a source of loss.

Let me give two examples of this. The first is *R (McDonald) v Kensington and Chelsea* (2013). In short, the case concerned the provision of carers for a woman with continence issues and whether the supplying of adult nappies was an adequate alternative. While not wanting to belittle the complex legal issues, one point receives no attention in the judgement. We all have continence problems. Virtually everyone in England benefits from the sewerage system at considerable public expense. So what Ms McDonald was claiming was not some unusual provision for a unique need. It was a provision for the continence issues we all have. It was found the local authority were entitled to withdraw payment for her carers. The continence needs of the majority are met without argument. Ms McDonald's needs were seen as unusual. Our mutual vulnerability was not acknowledged here.

Another example is children. There is a mass of social structures which push children towards a passive, non-autonomous role, and a mass of social structures which enable adults to live apparently independent and autonomous lives. These often go unnoticed and assumed as normal (Peterson and Wilkinson, 2007). The division between the adults and children becomes reinforced and ignored. Children are presented as ignorant and vulnerable, and by contrast adults are capacitous and self-sufficient. Yet this overlooks the important role of children as carers of their parents. It overlooks the knowledge children have – their capacity to wonder; to be delighted; to throw themselves utterly into something; to see anew; their idealism; their ability to make electronic equipment work! Are adults wiser, better decision-makers, than children? I am not so sure. Children are typically presented as vulnerable, yet parents are often the vulnerable ones. Ironically, the worry of parents about their vulnerable children renders the parents vulnerable. We recognise that the truth is that we adults, like the children, understand little, make terrible decisions and are utterly dependent on others. We flee from that mirror and render children different as 'the vulnerable' because we recognise our own vulnerability in them (Herring, 2012).

Another error in law and social practice is that it is common to divide 'the carer' from the 'cared for'. Yet, in caring relationships the division between bodies and selves becomes blurred, so that a harm to one body is a harm to another. In caring relationships the 'me' and 'you' becomes dissolved. Each party benefits and suffers together. They each give and receive care for the good of the relationship. This is why I think it is so important to seek to promote caring relationships, rather than promoting 'carers' (Herring, 2014a; Hughes et al., 2005). As Carol Gilligan (1982: 73) writes, 'The ideal of care is thus an activity of relationships, of seeing and responding to need, taking care of the world by sustaining the web of connection so that no one is left alone.' The relational view of care would emphasise interdependence over dependency, and mutual vulnerability over the frailty of one person. The relational approach is likely to see care in the context of the relationship between two people in which each is contributing care to the other: be that in terms of the psychological, emotional or physical sense. Michael Fine and Caroline Glendinning (2005) capture this importance of the relational aspect of care in these words:

> Recent studies of care suggest that qualities of reciprocal dependence underlie much of what is termed 'care'. Rather than being an unidirectional activity in which an active care-giver does something to a passive and dependent recipient, these accounts suggest that care is best understood as the product or outcome of the relationship between two or more people.

The danger is that the language of carer and cared for creates an image of the person 'needing care' as having a problem, which is solved by the 'carer'. The 'carer' can become glorified and given power (Orme, 2001). It is not surprising with such an image that disability advocates have grave concerns over the concept of carer (Herring, 2014a). Further, it creates social work and welfare interventions that seek to deal with the problems facing the 'cared for' or the 'carer'. Instead we need to be looking at way which can promote the well-being of the caring relationship.

This relational aspect is important because it puts the activities within their context, a context which provides those acts with meaning (Daly and Lewis, 2000). The provision of care only makes sense and can be properly understood when placed in the context of the parties' relationships (Schwarzenbach, 1996). That action of caring for the parties can have a meaning well beyond the here and now. It may reflect a long-standing commitment or a mutual responsibility. The act may have overtones recalling aspects of the relationship many years ago.

There is another important point here, and that is that the division of 'carer' is not only false because it imagines that one party to the relationship is the provider of the care, it also overlooks the point that the 'carer' may themselves be receiving care from others (Herring, 2014b). Notably, 378,000 carers are themselves registered as permanently sick or disabled, according to official statistics (Carers UK, 2015). Thus it is more accurate to acknowledge the networks of care that we live in, rather than dividing us up into providers of and recipients of care (Beckett, 2007). All of us fall into both categories.

Vulnerability and care as private

There is a real danger of care of the 'vulnerable' being downgraded in modern legal and social thought. It is seen as a private matter for individuals and their families to organise. Care is largely ignored and under-valued by the state and legal system (Herring, 2013). This is challenged by an acknowledgement that vulnerability is universal and care is essential for the welfare of all society. To quote Fineman (2013a):

> Privatization of dependency masks it, along with the other implications of human vulnerability and allows us to indulge in fantasies of independence, self-sufficiency, and autonomous agency. In an autonomous liberal subject analysis, if individuals or their private institutions fail, it is perceived as reflecting their weakness and incapacity, because the divide between public and private leaves them outside of general public or state responsibility-they occur in a separate sphere.

The failure to acknowledge the importance of care means that its burdens are unequally distributed and vulnerabilities are inadequately met. As Joan Tronto (2002) argues, the distribution of care is an exercise of power:

> Relatively more powerful people in society have a lot at stake in seeing that their caring needs are met under conditions that are beneficial to them, even if this means that the caring needs of those who provide them with services are neglected. More powerful people can fob caregiving work on to others: men to women, upper to lower class, free men to slaves. Care work itself is often demanding and inflexible, and not all of it is productive. People who do such work recognize its intrinsic value, but it does not fit well in a society that values innovation and accumulation of wealth.

A society which recognised the promotion of caring relationships as central to its well-being would never accept the situation Tronto identifies.

The dangers of relationships

Of course, not all relationships are good. Relationships and social structures can be oppressive. A central aspect of relational approaches must be in protecting people from the harms that abusive relationships can cause. A relational approach should not seek to support all relationships. Care ethicists would seek to promote relationships marked by mutual care and respect.

Eva Feder Kittay (2007: 468), writing from an ethic of care perspective, is aware of the dangers of promoting any relationship marked by care. She argues:

> Total self-sacrifice, the annihilation of the self in favor of the cared for, is neither demanded by the practice of care nor is it justifiable, for one can see that a relationship requires two selves, not one self in which the other is subsumed and consumed. A care ethic is not a mere reaction to individualism, but it tempers individualism by insisting that the relationships in which we stand help to constitute the individual we have become, are now and will be in the future.

The tensions between promoting care and protection are highlighted in the care ethicist literature by the distinction between an ethic of care and an ethic of justice. Carol Gilligan, the grandmother of care ethics, distinguished an ethic of care from an ethic of justice (Gilligan, 1982). Virginia Held (2006: 15) explains the difference:

> An ethic of justice focuses on questions of fairness, equality, individual rights, abstract principles, and the consistent application of them. An ethic of care focuses on attentiveness, trust, responsiveness to need, narrative nuance, and cultivating caring relations. Whereas an ethic of justice seeks a fair solution between competing individual interests and rights, an ethic of care sees the interest of carers and cared-for as importantly intertwined rather than as simply competing.

However, Held (2006: 15), arguably the leading contemporary care ethicist, argues that an ethic of care includes justice:

> There can be care without justice. There has historically been little justice in the family, but care and life have gone on without it. There can be no justice without care, however, for without care no child would survive and there would be no persons to respect.

Held is correct to emphasise that justice must be included with an effective ethic of care, although its role should be to support caring relationships.

Indeed, it is only in appreciating the importance of caring relationships to the self that we can recognise the severity of the wrong in abuse within intimate relationships and the importance of preventing it (Herring, 2011). Abusive relationships involve not just harm, but the turning of what should be a tool for self-defining and meaning into a tool of self-destruction. It turns what should give life meaning into something that deprives life of its joy.

Relationships involve responsibilities

We must recognise the importance of responsibilities. In traditional liberal thought, obligations arise through the choice of a person to undertake them. Relational supporters see responsibilities arising not from choice but from the relationship that develops (Leckey, 2007). Parenthood would be a good example of this. One cannot escape the responsibilities of parenthood by claiming one did not choose to be a parent. The responsibilities of a relationship must be recognised to enable the relationship to work and flourish.

Typically, in traditional liberal thought we start with a premise of freedom: we are free to act as we wish unless there is a particular obligation or duty that arises. The burden is on those who seek to claim there is a duty. A relational approach starts with responsibilities and connection as a norm. The question is not, 'Is there a good reason to restrict my freedom', but rather, 'Is it possible to have some freedom, given the responsibilities of those I am connected to?' (Leckey, 2007). This causes concern to some. Should we not start with a presumption we are free, rather than starting with obligations? However, I think a presumption of freedom is misguided. First, it is simply unrealistic for most people. Our lives our not marked by the freedom to do as we choose, but our responsibilities to others. Second, we do not mind that, because responsibilities are necessary so that relationships flourish. As Polona Curk (2011: 67) puts it: 'We take responsibility for each other because we continue to need each other and because we establish meaningful relationships through taking responsibility for each other.' Responsibilities therefore can be seen not as the corollary of rights, but rather, rights are the tools we need to be able to carry our responsibilities. It is the performance of our relational responsibilities which should be key, not the maintenance of our freedoms (Williams, 2000).

Conclusion

Mary Becker (1999: 52) writes: 'patriarchy values power, control, autonomy, independence, toughness, invulnerability, strength, aggressiveness, rationality, detachment (being non-emotional), and other traditionally masculine attributes that have proven effective in the battle against other men'. This chapter has argued that such values should have no place in the law or modern social work practice. We need to set aside the norms of the isolated independent male, bolstered by legal rights of autonomy, freedom and privacy. We should replace them with a model that values caring relationships as central to a good society – that seeks to acknowledge our mutual vulnerability, our profound interdependence and our responsibilities to each other.

References

Baier, A. (1994) *Moral Prejudices. Essays on Ethics*, Cambridge, MA: Harvard University Press.

Becker, M. (1999) 'Patriarchy and inequality: Towards a substantive feminism', *University of Chicago Legal Forum,* 21: 21–52.

Beckett, A. (2006) *Citizenship and Vulnerability*, Basingstoke: Palgrave.

Beckett, C. (2007) 'Women, disability, care: Good neighbours or uneasy bedfellows?', *Critical Social Policy,* 27: 360–89.

British Association of Social Workers (2012) *Code of Ethics for Social Workers*, London: BASW.

Carers UK (2015) *Facts About Carers*, London: Carers UK.

Clapton, J. (2003) 'Tragedy and catastrophe: Contentious discourses of ethics and disability', *Journal of Intellectual Disability Research,* 47: 540–62.

Code, L. (1991) 'Second persons', in L. Code (ed.), *What Can She Know? Feminist Theory and the Construction of Knowledge*, Ithica: Cornell University Press).

Curk, P. (2011) 'Passions, dependencies, selves', in C. Lind, H. Keating and J. Bridgeman (eds), *Taking Responsibility, Law and the Changing Family*, Aldershot: Ashgate, 51–67.

Daly, M. and Lewis, J. (2000), 'The concept of social care and the analysis of contemporary welfare', *British Journal of Sociology,* 51: 281–303.

Dodds, S. (2007) 'Depending on care: Recognition of vulnerability and the social contribution of care provision,' *Bioethics,* 21: 500–20.

Donchin, A. (2000) 'Autonomy, interdependence, and assisted suicide: Respecting boundaries/crossing lines', *Bioethics,* 14(3): 187–212.

Fawcett, B. (2009) 'Vulnerability: Questioning the certainties in social work and health', *International Social Work,* 52: 473–93.

Feder Kittay, E. (2007) 'Searching for an overlapping consensus: A secular care ethics feminist responds to religious feminists', *University of St Thomas Law Journal,* 4: 468–88.

Fine, M. and Glendinning, C. (2005) 'Dependence, independence or inter-dependence? Revisiting the concepts of care and dependency', *Ageing and Society,* 25(4): 601–21.

Fineman, M. (2013a) '"Elderly" as vulnerable: Rethinking the nature of individual and societal responsibility', *Elder Law Journal,* 20: 71–104.

Fineman, M. (2013b) 'Feminism, masculinities, and multiple identities', *Nevada Law Journal,* 13: 1–47.

Frazer, E. and Lacey, N. (1993) *The Politics of Community: A Feminist Critique of the Liberal Communitarian Debate*, Hemel Hempstead: Harvester Wheatshear.

Gergen, K. (2009) *Relational Being*, Oxford: Oxford University Press.

Gilligan, C. (1982) *In a Different Voice*, Cambridge, MA: Harvard University Press.

Held, V. (2006) *The Ethics of Care*, Oxford: Oxford University Press, 2006.

Herring, J. (2011) 'The serious wrong of domestic abuse and the loss of control defence', in A. Reed and M. Bohlander (eds), *Loss of Control and Diminished Responsibility*, Aldershot: Ashgate.

Herring, J. (2012) 'Vulnerability, children and the law', in M. Freeman (ed.), *Law and Childhood Studies*, Oxford: Oxford University Press.

Herring, J. (2013) *Caring and the Law*, Oxford: Hart.

Herring, J. (2014a) 'Why we need a statute regime to regulate bodily material' in I. Goold, K. Greasley, J. Herring and L. Skene (eds), *Persons, Parts and Property*, Oxford: Hart.

Herring, J. (2014b) 'The disability critique of care', *Elder Law Journal*, 8: 1–18.

Hughes, B., McKie, L., Hopkins, D. and Watson, N. (2005) 'Love's labours lost? Feminism, the disabled people's movement and an ethic of care', *Sociology*, 39: 259–75.

Hurst, A. (2008) 'Vulnerability in research and health care: Describing the elephant in the room?', *Bioethics*, 22: 191–202.

Kröger, T. (2009) 'Care research and disability studies: Nothing in common?', *Critical Social Policy*, 29: 398–420.

Leckey, R. (2007) 'Contracting claims and family law feuds', *University of Toronto Law Journal*, 57: 1–41.

Lindemann, K. (2003) 'The ethics of receiving', *Theoretical Medicine and Bioethics*, 24: 501–534.

Matambanadzo, S. (2012) 'Embodying vulnerability: A feminist theory of the person', *Duke Journal of Gender Law and Policy*, 20: 45–83.

Neal, M. (2012) '"Not gods but animals": Human dignity and vulnerable subjecthood', *Liverpool Law Review*, 33: 177–200.

Orme, J. (2001) *Gender and Community Care*, Basingstoke: Palgrave.

Peterson, A. and Wilkinson, I. (2007) *Health, Risk and Vulnerability*, Abingdon: Routledge.

R (Macdonald) v Kensington and Chelsea [2013] UKSC 33

Rogers, W., Mackenzie, C. and Dodds, S. (2012) 'Why bioethics needs a concept of vulnerability', *International Journal of Feminist Approaches to Bioethics*, 5: 11–38.

Schwarzenbach, S. (1996) 'On civil friendship', *Ethics*, 107: 97–112.

Sevenhusen (1998) Too Good to be True? Feminist Considerations about Trust and Social Cohesion, IWM Working Paper no. 3, Institute for Human Sciences, Vienna.

Shildrick, M. (2002) *Embodying the Monster: Encounters with the Vulnerable Self*, Abingdon: Routledge.

Sugarman, J. and Martin, J. (2011) 'Theorizing relational agency', *Journal of Constructivist Psychology*, 24: 283–89.

Tronto, J. (2002) 'The value of care', *Boston Review*, February 2002.

Williams, F. (2000) 'The presence of feminism in the future of welfare', *Economy and Society*, 31: 502–19.

4

COERCION IN SOCIAL CARE

Robert Johns

Introduction

The very idea of coercion in social care seems contradictory, and, to many, even abhorrent. How can someone be compelled to accept care? How can someone who is an adult be forced to comply with the decisions that someone else is making for them? How can someone be obliged to stay living in a care home where they do not wish to be? This surely is an infringement of their basic rights, a true deprivation of liberty.

The answer, in brief, is when someone has lost the 'capacity' to make decisions for themselves, so they are legally considered to have lost the right to self-determination. This raises a whole host of legal, policy, practice and ethical issues which this chapter aims to highlight. The intention here is to analyse how these interact and intersect, rather than offer detailed advice about how practitioners should apply the law in specific cases (for which see Barber et al., 2012; Brown et al., 2015; Department for Constitutional Affairs, 2007; Johns, 2014; Mandelstam, 2013; Ministry of Justice, 2008; SCIE, 2015; Williams and Evans, 2013).

The first part of the chapter connects coercion to the legal notion of 'capacity' and locates this aspect of social work law within the wider legal framework of adult social care. This is then connected to ethics and the operation of social work principles where compulsory intervention is authorised by the law. The majority of the chapter is then given over to an analysis of relevant parts of the Mental Capacity Act 2005, including developments in relation to the statutorily defined Deprivation of Liberty Safeguards and the various interpretations by the courts. This analysis will include reference to some implications for social work practice and ethics, and changing views of the relationship between the individual and the state.

The specific question which this chapter addresses is how and why is it justified to take over people's rights to make decisions for themselves in their own 'best interests'? This is an important aspect of social work law often overlooked in the discipline's inevitable preoccupation with compulsory intervention in child safeguarding and protecting the public in youth justice or mental health cases.

Capacity

Put very simply, capacity refers to people's ability to reason, thereby using cognitive powers through which people can gain knowledge, interpret information and assess potential outcomes of certain kinds of decisions. One might also refer to it as rationality. On this basis, the law can justifiably hold people responsible for the consequences of their reasoning process. A decision to commit a crime is assumed to be on the basis of a conscious decision to do so, which results in consequences in terms of sanctions imposed – usually referred to as a 'sentence'. A decision to enter into a contract likewise is assumed to be on the basis of a conscious choice, and failure to meet obligations under the contract through, for example, not paying the requisite amount of money at the appropriate time also has consequences – debt enforcement procedures and the like under legal civil proceedings.

However, the law has always recognised that this assumption of rationality or capacity is not reasonable in some cases. It has long been accepted as not appropriate for young children, although when children cease to be young is a debatable point. Currently, in England and Wales the law assumes that under 10s cannot be held responsible for actions that would, in the case of an adult, be regarded as criminal offences. Higher age limits apply in other scenarios, such as agreeing contracts. Likewise, the law has accepted that where someone has a serious disability of the mind, they cannot reasonably be expected to be held accountable for their (otherwise criminal) actions (Criminal Procedure (Insanity) Act 1964).

Yet, what if the concern is not so much the issue of holding someone accountable for their actions, but protecting someone from decisions or actions that could cause harm to themselves?

In the case of children this is very straightforward: parents have a duty to protect them. If, for whatever reason, parents are unable to do so, then the state will involve themselves in their welfare –currently in England and Wales principally through the operation of the Children Act 1989. Social workers are clearly very much involved in this, and the ethical basis for it is relatively unproblematic, although there are obviously going to be debates about the extent to which the state should intervene in family welfare and at what point that action should end. One predictable answer to this boundary question is age 18, but in cases where the state provides substitute care, should that responsibility extend beyond that age? Also, what should be the threshold for state involvement? These are all highly contested issues, and there is a welter of case law in which two cases stand out: re *B (Children) (Care Proceedings: Standard of Proof)* (2008) and re *B (A Child) (Care Proceedings: Threshold Criteria)* (2013). Although direct parallels with vulnerable adults should not be drawn, deliberation of the threshold for state intervention is very much a concern in this area as well.

In the case of adults, protecting the vulnerable is far from straightforward. For there is not only the issue of personal safeguarding, there is also the question of what to do when someone becomes incapable of managing their own personal or property affairs. Originally deriving from the royal prerogative powers concerning the property of people who lack capacity, this aspect of law has surprisingly had quite a long history. Yet only in the last 50 years or so has there been any attempt to codify the exercise of the royal prerogative (parens patriae) and common law, beginning with the Mental Health Act 1959 (Bartlett, 2008: 23–32). This at least clarified the arrangements for property by setting out a range of responsibilities for the Court of Protection, but the gap still remained in relation to personal care and treatment. Creative use of common law attempted to address this, as, for example, in cases such as *Norfolk and Norwich Healthcare Trust v W* (1996), *R (Adult: Medical Treatment)* (1996), *C (Adult, refusal of treatment)* (1994) and *Ms B v an NHS Hospital Trust* (2002), all of which concerned consent to medical treatment in one way or another – either compelling people to accept it in their own best interests, or allowing them to refuse it.

One significant gap in legal provision was revealed in the celebrated *Bournewood* case (*R v Bournewood Community and Mental Health NHS Trust*, 1998) in which a hospital took upon itself to detain a man who appeared not to have capacity. This was deemed in his own 'best interests', notwithstanding the wishes of professional carers. While UK courts held this kind of protection and promotion of best interests to be lawful, being compliant with common law, the European Court took a different view, holding that there was a lack of clarity as to who qualified to lose rights to self-determination, in what circumstances, and with what appeal rights (*HL v UK*, 2004). This decision partially influenced the move to codify deprivation of liberty best interests decision-making procedures in those cases where someone falls outside the admission and detention categories allowed for in mental health legislation.

Consequently, it is now possible to draw a distinction between two interrelated sets of legislation that potentially apply to adults who are deemed unable to make decisions for themselves:

- Mental health legislation, principally the Mental Health Act 1983, as amended by the Mental Health Act 2007, which makes provision for compulsory detention in psychiatric hospital and compulsory community supervision (guardianship) of people who pose a danger to themselves or others or need such oversight (sections 2, 3, 4 and 7 Mental Health Act 1983);

- The Mental Capacity Act 2005, amended by the Mental Health Act 2007 to include Schedule A1, that now allows for someone who has lost the ability to understand their own best interests to be compelled to remain somewhere. In cases involving social workers as Best Interest Assessors, 'somewhere' can only be a hospital or registered care home; for the Court of Protection it can be anywhere approved by the court.

It is important to understand that there is now no other statutory legislation that compels someone to accept treatment, care or supervision, given the abolition of removal powers that existed in section 47 of the National Assistance Act 1948 (section 46 Care Act 2014). The tenor of the welter of legislation that comprises the framework of adult social care law is assessment for potential provision of services. Adult social care law also refers to arrangements for service delivery and, more generally, empowerment in the form of choice of services with, latterly, prevention of need that reflects a 'strengths' approach to adult care (section 1 Care Act 2014). Significantly, the Care Act 2014 safeguarding provisions (sections 42–45) cannot be imposed in the same way as the protective orders incorporated into Part IV, Children Act 1989 (emergency protection orders, police protection orders, care and supervision orders, sections 44, 46, 31–39 Children Act 1989). Nor is it possible to compel someone to accept support services.

Indeed, this provision is regarded as quite distinct from any local authority duty to safeguard. In *A and C* (2010) the court held that in cases where someone is possibly deprived of their liberty in their own home, the local authority has two distinct and quite separate duties: to investigate and, if necessary, to report to the Court of Protection; and to provide support and care services. Unless there was an immediate threat to life or limb, local authorities did not have the power to regulate, control or coerce without the agreement of the court.

Ethics and coercion in social care

A challenging question, and one rarely posed in social work law literature, is how is compulsory intervention ethically justifiable? One obvious riposte is to cite 'common sense', presumably implying it is clear that in some cases someone is so vulnerable that they cannot look after their own interests. Yet the demarcation between those occasions when intervention is justified and those when it is not is by no means certain, and definitely not 'common sense'. For the degree to which benign coercion, if it can be called that, is acceptable depends on different interpretations of ethics and justice.

For the purpose of this discussion, ethics will be divided into two broad categories, the second being subdivided. The fundamental ethical consideration revolves around whether something is right or wrong because the action itself is simply right or wrong, or whether the degree to which it is right or wrong depends on who carried out the action, in what circumstances, with what intent and for what purpose. In other words, is the consideration principle based (absolutist) or purpose based (teleological, determined by ends or goals)?

For more detailed consideration of these theories in relation to social work see Banks (2012), Beckett and Maynard (2013), Gray and Webb (2010), Johns (2016) or Parrott (2015). Note also in passing that there is a fourth approach, or a variation of the third approach, that asserts the importance of relationships

Table 4.1 Distinguishing approaches to ethics and decision-making

principle-based approaches to ethics	purpose-based approaches to ethics	
non-naturalistic	teleological, naturalistic	
deontological, based on nature of duty (derived from Kant)	utilitarian, based on consequences (derived from Bentham, Mill)	virtue based (derived from Aristotle)
universal, categorical, objective	relative, depends on circumstances, subjective	
social workers act out of a sense of duty or obligation	social workers judged by the consequences of actions	Social workers judged by whether they themselves are virtuous
legal judgements principle based	legal judgements look to potential consequences	legal judgements evaluate characteristics of decision-makers
what matters is the character of the act itself	what matters is the outcomes of the act	what matters is the character of the agent

as being central to ethics, which some have labelled the ethics of care approach (for consideration of how this approach applies to adult care and personalisation see Lloyd, 2010).

A detailed consideration of ethical theory would be out of place here, but, nevertheless, it would be useful to explore briefly how the different broad approaches relate to the notion of coerced social care, before considering the operation of the Mental Capacity Act 2005.

A principle-based deontological approach to capacity, consent and compulsory intervention would emphasise rights and principles in the sense that these declared formal principles come first in any consideration in any given case.

Ada Phelps, in her early 90s, is now living on her own having been recently widowed, and is not eating. She refuses all social care and support services. Her health is beginning to suffer, and her relatives are becoming seriously worried.

Whether social workers can intervene in this situation depends on which principles apply. Following Kant, there are first principles that social workers would have an absolute duty to obey, the so-called categorical imperatives. These should be universal and objective. It may be that the categorical imperative is that people have absolute rights to self-determination without exception, in which case unless Ada is willing to agree to have social care services, nothing can be done. Or it may be that the categorical imperative is that no one should be allowed to die, which means that at the point where medically it is proven that someone is at risk of dying through self-neglect, then the absolute insistence on preserving life overrides personal wishes and compels action.

It does not matter for the time being what the law actually says in this regard, since the concern here is to connect ethical theory to behaviour by analysing the precise way in which practitioners decide how to act. What matters from a deontological perspective is that rules or principles can be universalised, so that people would be willing for a rule to be followed by everyone at all times and in all places. Even more importantly, what matters is that rules or principles come first, a priori, and that once having decided a course of action in accordance with the principles, it cannot then be revised if there are unfortunate consequences. So in Ada's case, the fact that, if the self-neglect continues, it may lead to her death cannot trump any absolute principle that she has to agree to the action. On the other hand, if the absolute principle is preservation of life, then compulsory intervention can be justified at the point when she is at risk of dying. The implications for this in terms of Ada's feelings of self-worth and dignity then become irrelevant, even though the research evidence suggests that the mortality rates of older people admitted to care is significantly higher that the equivalent age group in the community (Shah et al., 2013).

This approach to ethics stands in strong contrast to utilitarianism, which anchors all considerations to potential most likely consequences. In order to determine whether something is right or wrong, a utilitarian simply has to look at the results of the action. So in Ada's case, if the results of her being left on her own and being allowed to refuse care services is that she might die, then that might be regarded as unethical from a utilitarian perspective – and any steps to avoid this justified – if that keeps the majority happiest. True, compelling her to accept services or leave her home might have devastating consequences in terms of her emotional well-being, but if the consequence would be that she would survive physically, then that might be considered a better outcome, and the disadvantages therefore outweighed by the overall advantages. Hence there is a complex calculation going on, and this calculation lies at the heart of utilitarian thinking, sometimes referred to as the principle of utility. Utility here means which course of action serves the needs of the greatest number of people, is of use in promoting the happiness of the greatest number.

Naturally it is not always going to be possible to gauge accurately what any consequences might be. However, it would be feasible to devise some rules whereby, in cases where people met certain criteria, compulsory intervention would be permitted because in such cases it has generally been found that the end result is better than allowing people to suffer. While this is a rule, note that such a rule is devised on the basis of potential consequences, not on first principles. So it is quite different from a deontologically formulated rule.

Under the same umbrella of purpose-based ethics is virtue ethics, which approaches ethical and legal dilemmas somewhat differently. In Ada's case, what matters is the calibre of the professionals caring for her, and relatives supporting her. If they are committed and reliable, they can be safely entrusted with making the right decision. There is no way of predicting whether they would impose a solution on Ada or not, since what matters is that they would be conscientious people, scrupulous in their care and concern for her, who would be bound to make an appropriate decision on her behalf. Any legal over-sight of that decision-making process would simply confine itself to considera-tion of the motives of decision-makers. It may be that there are disputes between decision-makers to be resolved, in which case courts would focus on decision-makers' motivation and competence, evaluating who has the strongest claim to best promote the service user's interests. This might include assessing the qual-ity of the relationship, a consideration that is central to the ethics of care approach which has some parallels with virtue ethics.

Relating law to ethical theory

It would arguably be simplistic to connect any one ethical theory to one piece of legislation, for laws are devised for a whole number of disparate reasons, reflecting a whole range of influences. Furthermore, laws can also often be related to different ethical theories at one and the same time. Penalising peo-ple who break the speed limit, for example, serves the interests of the majority who want vehicle speeds controlled. At the same time, speed limits are rules devised to minimise the chances of people dying on the roads, and preserva-tion of life is an absolute principle, a categorical imperative. So here there is a combination of principle-based and purpose-based considerations operating simultaneously.

It would also be fair to say that no legislation truly represents the application of one specific approach consistently. In social work law there is a good exam-ple of law reflecting different ethical approaches in mental health legislation. Here, there appears to be an assumption that it is in the interests of the majority for there to be some means of protecting society from the implied threat posed by people who refuse to accept that they need to be admitted to hospital, surely a utilitarian argument – hence the provision for someone to be removed from their homes and taken to hospital against their will, and detained there for certain maximum periods (section 2 Mental Health Act 1983 for maximum 28 days, and section 3 for maximum six months initially, to be precise). The justi-fication for these rules is made explicit in sections 2(2)(b) and 3(2)(c) which both refer, inter alia, to 'health or safety' of the patient or 'protection of other persons'. This implies a calculation that it is in the overall interests of society (serves the greatest interest of the greatest number of people) for there to be protection against the threat allegedly posed by people with serious mental health problems. On this basis, a general rule has been devised that looks to the potential disastrous consequences of people being allowed to refuse psychiatric treatment.

At the same time, responsibility for actual decisions in relation to detained patients is delegated or entrusted to specific professionals who have a wide discretion as to how they control patients' freedoms; for example, the Responsible Clinician can impose Community Treatment Orders on certain detained patients, as well as decide on the appropriate form of medical treatment (sections 17A–G Mental Health Act 1983). Limited appeal rights against that professional's decisions implies a strong element of trust, reinforced by the strong reluctance of courts to review purely 'clinical' decisions, indicating a virtue ethics approach.

The Mental Capacity Act 2005 also represents an example of a mixture of different ethical approaches, both in what the law says and how it is interpreted. To demonstrate this, the discussion now turns to the Deprivation of Liberty Safeguards (section 4 Mental Capacity Act 2005, as amended) focusing on the interpretation of those safeguards in a landmark legal judgement, delivered by the Supreme Court in March 2014.

Capacity, ethics and the Mental Capacity Act 2005

One absolute, a priori, principle implied in the Mental Capacity Act 2005 is that adults have the right to make their own decisions unless it can be demonstrated that they do not have capacity. Capacity is to be assumed unless there is evidence to the contrary (section 1(2) Mental Capacity Act 2005). What exactly lack of capacity means is defined in section 2, and in section 3 this is further clarified in relation to decision-making. This part of the Act is strongly deontological in its assertion of key principles, for example, not making assumptions about people's capacity on the basis of 'age or appearance' (section 2(3)(a) Mental Capacity Act 2005).

When it comes to section 4, as amended, the analysis becomes more complex. It is tempting to conclude that, providing the principles are observed, decision-making is delegated to trusted professionals, suggesting a virtue ethics approach. However, in determining what is in the service user's best interests there is a welter of relevant subsections, supplemented and complemented by the Mental Capacity Act 2005 Code of Practice (Department for Constitutional Affairs, 2007), that imply considerable legislative fettering of professional decision-making. There is certainly not the same degree of discretion afforded to professionals as there is to the Responsible Clinician under the Mental Health Act 2007, even though mental health decisions could be even more dramatically life-changing than the best interest decisions under mental capacity legislation.

Section 4 Mental Capacity Act 2005 now includes the Deprivation of Liberty Safeguards, technically introduced by section 4A added by virtue of section 50 Mental Health Act 2007. This in turn refers to Schedule A1, an additional schedule to the original Mental Capacity Act 2005, which is in effect the Deprivation of Liberty Safeguards themselves. These were introduced in order to meet the objections of the European Court in *HL v UK* (see above) by putting what were previously common law decisions on a statute basis. In order to do this, legislation adapts existing structures so that there is now reliance on local authorities taking responsibility as Supervisory Bodies with clear responsibilities to oversee and implement the safeguards. Supervisory Bodies can authorise deprivation of liberty only where this is the recommendation of a Best Interest Assessor, the majority of whom are social workers with additional training. The Best Interest Assessor must make the recommendation on the basis of six assessments, at least one of which has to be determined by a professional from another discipline. This is in order to meet the quite complex and detailed requirements that must be complied with before the deprivation of liberty can be authorised.

Some have severely criticised this system, in one case describing it as 'tortuous and complex' (*AJ (Deprivation of Liberty Safeguards)* 2015: para 26). In 2014 the House of Lords went so far as to describe the Deprivation of Liberty Safeguards as 'not fit for purpose' and urged the government to undertake a comprehensive review of them (House of Lords, 2014: paras 257–58). This task was delegated to the Law Commission who reported back in 2015 (Law Commission, 2015).

Interpreting the Mental Capacity Act 2005

For the purpose of this analysis, it needs to be noted that the first task of the Best Interest Assessor or, indeed, the Court of Protection when investigating cases is whether someone is being deprived of their liberty or simply subject to a number of restrictions. (Best Interest Assessors are only involved in cases where someone is compelled to remain in a care home or hospital.) Restrictions as such would not fall within the ambit of the Deprivation of Liberty Safeguards; rather, the test is whether the person is subject to continuous supervision or control and not free to leave. Only once this definition of deprivation threshold is crossed can the Best Interest Assessor or Court of Protection go on to consider whether the other criteria are met: evidence of 'mental disorder', lack of capacity in relation to relevant decisions, no advance decisions already registered as binding, no conflict with mental health legislation compulsory detention grounds and, finally, whether the deprivation of liberty is truly in someone's 'best interests'.

So the definition of deprivation of liberty is crucial, but should this definition be absolute or relative? Is it determined by reference to objective principles, or subjective in the sense that deprivation will be experienced more keenly by some people than others? In ethical terms, do deontologically derived absolute principles apply, or is it the purpose of the deprivation that really matters, and therefore would a utilitarian or virtue ethics approach be more justifiable?

That is precisely the issue that came to the fore in the landmark legal case finally determined by the Supreme Court in 2014. This has become known as the 'Cheshire West' case, although the Supreme Court actually heard another case alongside it (*Cheshire West and Chester Council v P, P and Q (MIG and MEG)*, 2014). Briefly, the facts were:

> *P, in his 30s, had cerebral palsy and Down's syndrome, and was living under close supervision in a residential environment in which it was sometimes necessary to restrain him. The degree of control over his life was such that the Court of Protection concluded that he was being deprived of his liberty, for which there had to be legal justification given that he was unable to give informed consent.*

> *The Court of Appeal disagreed. Legal justification was not required since he was not being deprived of his liberty. Necessary restrictions were being imposed, such as would be used for anyone in a similar situation.*

> *The Supreme Court ultimately overrode this and reverted to the Court of Protection view. Deprivation of liberty was an absolute concept in the sense that allowances could not be made for disabilities. Either he was being deprived of his liberty or he was not. In this case he was.*

This is necessarily a very truncated summary of the case and the plethora of legal issues that the courts had to consider, but what matters in terms of ethics is the way in which the Appeal Court and the Supreme Court came to their divergent conclusions, for this reveals markedly different approaches to the whole issue of ethics and rights, differences that are paralleled in social work practice.

The Court of Appeal considered that the degree of control which P encountered would be normal for anyone with those disabilities – it was 'the inevitable corollary' of them, as the judge put it, and the control had to be assessed by reference to the 'relevant comparator', who was someone with the same condition 'or suffering the same inherent mental and physical disabilities and limitations' (*Cheshire West and Chester County Council v P*, 2011, judgement paras 86, 110). These controls would be necessary regardless of the environment. The comparison should not be with an 'ordinary adult going about normal life' (paragraph 86).

The Supreme Court rejected this comparator test as it was essentially a circular argument: if someone with this kind of disability is normally restricted in this way, then this is acceptable for everyone with that kind of disability. It would then be difficult to see when the full safeguards of the law in relation to deprivation of liberty would apply, for restrictions could always be considered 'normal'.

In the Supreme Court's view, the deprivation of liberty definition had to be objective and absolute, that is, applicable to anyone and not relative to the degree of disability. Interestingly, the Supreme Court criticised the line of argument that confuses benevolent justification for a course of action with the objective interpretation of what constitutes deprivation of liberty. In other words, deprivation of liberty cannot be condoned simply because the decision-makers are virtuous – an explicit rejection of the virtue ethics approach of deciding legal cases in this context. Human rights were considered universal and objective, and, moreover, what constitutes 'deprivation of liberty for a non-disabled person is also a deprivation for a disabled person'. Life may be comfortable and enjoyable but one can still be deprived of one's liberty. 'A gilded cage is still a cage' (*Cheshire West and Chester Council v P, P and Q*, 2014, judgement paras 45–46).

So much for the interpretation of the Mental Capacity Act 2005. How does this relate to ethics?

Ethics and interpretation of social work law: Deontological, utilitarian or virtue ethics?

Adopting the distinction between principle-based and consequentialist purpose-based approaches to ethics illustrates the difference between the approaches of the two courts.

The Appeal Court was prepared to apply relative concepts, and seemed to have in the back of its mind concern for the implications of a decision that P was being deprived of his liberty. The line of reasoning adopted appears to imply that staff were doing their best, and it was difficult to see how they could do otherwise given the degree of P's disabilities – just as they would for anyone else in his situation. So long as staff were dedicated, committed and well-intentioned, the court would presumably be satisfied. It would be fair to conclude that this line of reasoning is primarily utilitarian (being consequentialist), although potentially strongly laced with virtue ethics. For, after all, the court seems to be implying, there must be hundreds of people in the same position as P cared for by hard-pressed staff. Surely it is not in the overall interests of the 'country' for each case to have to be assessed under the Mental Capacity Act 2005 section 4 Deprivation of Liberty Safeguards. Indeed, it may not be in anyone's interests, since it is a foregone conclusion that the action is justified.

The Supreme Court would have none of this line of reasoning. The only issue to be determined was objectively whether or not P was being deprived of his liberty. Since this was a universal concept, it should be determined by absolute considerations, those that apply to everyone. This is a matter of principle, and the consequences are irrelevant as ethical or legal considerations.

Predictably, the consequences of this decision by the Supreme Court were quite dramatic, for the number of referrals to Supervisory Bodies with requests for assessments by Best Interest Assessors under the Deprivation of Liberty Safeguards increased eightfold in the six months following the Supreme Court decision. At the end of April 2014, there were 359 applications for assessments outstanding with recommendations awaited, whereas at the end of September 2014 this figure had risen to 19,429 (Care Quality Commission, 2015: 6). The Deprivation of Liberty Safeguards system means Best Interest Assessors and the Court of Protection are having to adjust to a new reality, in which their workload may well permanently increase, but at least, in the view of the Supreme Court, the law will be applied fairly and equitably to all, regardless of disability.

Connecting this aspect of social work law to social work practice

This analysis of the *Cheshire West* case offers a useful illustration of differences of approach to the whole issue of rights and ethics of actions. By using this example from social work law, parallels can be drawn with the challenges facing social work practitioners, for many of the daily dilemmas confronting them are ethical just as much as they are legal. Analysis of ethics and law together enables practitioners to reflect more deeply on how and why they act as they do. Do practitioners always act on the basis the principles are unassailable, and cannot be varied in any circumstance? Or are they more inclined to look to the potential consequences of their actions, to see what might be the greatest good that can be achieved? Or do they believe that what really matters is the quality of the relationships they engender with service users, the degree of trust that builds up between them, and through that come shared meanings and shared decision-making?

It is not being suggested that any one of these approaches is right or another is wrong. However, it is certainly worth pausing to reflect on how these different ways of applying social work law might translate in the context of working with vulnerable adults, especially in relation to issues of capacity and consent.

Primarily, the saga of *Cheshire West and Chester* teaches that this is a complex area of practice where ethics really matter, in which the courts grappled with the mode of achieving the best outcome but eventually concluded that concepts such as deprivation of liberty had to be universal and applied across the board. Accommodating people's needs within a paternalistic framework in which professionals know best, with differential standards applied to disabled people and non-disabled people, was firmly rejected.

Thus, for social workers this reinforces and underlines that service users' rights must always be respected, even if it is 'obvious' what should happen. For residential care homes, this judgement has major implications, since it may well mean that a far greater proportion than hitherto of their residents will be subject to the Mental Capacity Act 2005 Deprivation of Liberty Safeguards provisions in future. To those who object to this, on the grounds that this involves using intrusive legal procedures unnecessarily, the counterargument has now been forcefully asserted: people have certain rights that are absolute.

Finally, it is also valuable to reflect on social workers' relationship with the law. Students on qualifying courses have a mixture of attitudes to law, positive and negative (Preston-Shoot and McKimm, 2012). What this summary of recent developments in capacity and consent law demonstrates is that law is constantly subject to interpretation and review, the meaning of terms is often contested, and so the law can never be used as a substitute for reflecting on ethical practice. What the law does is set a framework, but even that framework can sometimes change. The importance of keeping up to date with the ways in which the courts interpret the law has never been greater, for different ethical interpretations of the law can have a major impact on practice.

References

Cases

A and C [2010] EWC 978 (Fam)

AJ (Deprivation of Liberty Safeguards) [2015] EWCOP 5

B (A Child) (Care Proceedings: Threshold Criteria) [2013] UKSC 33

B (Children) (Care Proceedings: Standard of Proof) [2008] UKHL 35

C (Adult, refusal of medical treatment) [1994] 1 All ER 819

Cheshire West and Chester Council v P; P and Q (MIG and MEG) [2014] UKSC 19

Cheshire West and Chester County Council v P [2011] EWCA Civ 1257

HL v the United Kingdom [2004] 40 EHRR 761

Ms B v an NHS Hospital Trust [2002] EWHC 429 (Fam)

Norfolk and Norwich Healthcare (NHS) Trust v W [1996] 2 FLR 61

R (Adult: Medical Treatment) [1996] 2 FLR 99

R v Bournewood Community and Mental Health NHS Trust, ex parte L (Secretary of State for Health and others intervening) [1998] 3 All ER 289

Secondary sources

Banks, S. (2012) *Ethics and Values in Social Work*, 4th edn, Basingstoke: Palgrave.

Barber, P., Brown, R. and Martin, D. (2012) *Mental Health Law in England and Wales*, 2nd edn, London: Sage.

Bartlett, P. (2008) *Blackstone's Guide to the Mental Capacity Act 2005*, 2nd edn, Oxford: Oxford University Press.

Beckett, C. and Maynard, A. (2013) *Values and Ethics in Social Work*, 2nd edn, London: Sage.

Brown, R., Barber, P. and Martin, D. (2015) *The Mental Capacity Act 2005: A Guide for Practice*, 3rd edn, London: Sage.

Care Quality Commission (CQC) (2015) *Monitoring the use of the Mental Capacity Act Deprivation of Liberty Safeguards in 2013/14*, Newcastle: Care Quality Commission.

Department for Constitutional Affairs (2007) *Mental Capacity Act 2005 Code of Practice*, London: The Stationery Office.

Gray, M. and Webb, S. A. (2010) *Ethics and Value Perspectives in Social Work*, Basingstoke: Palgrave.

House of Lords (2014) *Mental Capacity Act 2005 Post-Legislative Scrutiny*, London: The Stationery Office.

Johns, R. (2014) *Capacity and Autonomy*, Palgrave: Basingstoke.

Johns, R. (2016) *Ethics and Law for Social Workers*, London: Sage.

Law Commission (2015) *Mental Capacity and Deprivation of Liberty, A Consultation Paper* (consultation paper 222), London: The Stationery Office.

Lloyd, L. (2010) 'The individual in social care: The ethics of care and the "personalisation agenda" in services for older people in England', *Ethics and Social Welfare*, 4(2): 188–200.

Mandelstam, M. (2013) *Safeguarding Vulnerable Adults and the Law*, 2nd edn, London: Jessica Kingsley.

Ministry of Justice (2008) *Mental Capacity Act 2005 Deprivation of Liberty Safeguards*, Norwich: The Stationery Office.

Parrott, L. (2015) *Values and Ethics in Social Work Practice*, 3rd edn, London: Sage.

Preston-Shoot, M. and McKimm, J. (2012) 'Tutor and student experiences of teaching and learning law in UK social work education', *Social Work Education*, 31(7): 896–913.

SCIE (2015) *The Deprivation of Liberty Safeguards*. Online, available at: www.scie.org.uk/publications/ataglance/ataglance43.asp.

Shah, S. M., Carey, I. M., Harris, T., DeWilde, S. and Cook, D. G. (2013) 'Mortality in old care home residents in England and Wales', *Age and Ageing*, 42: 209–15.

Williams, P. and Evans, M. (2013) *Social Work with People with Learning Difficulties*, 3rd edn, London: Sage.

5

CHILD PROTECTION

Kim Holt

Introduction

The term 'reform', with particular reference to family justice and child protection, continues to be used indiscriminately. There are associated terms that are almost as pervasive: modernise, timely, quality, timeframes and deadlines. These terms have been deployed routinely within the last decade with procedures that have been introduced with the aim of ensuring that court proceedings in respect of children are concluded more quickly, while at the same time reducing the resources that are required to deal with these complex matters. The introduction of the Public Law Outline (PLO) (Ministry of Justice, 2008) in 2008, the revised PLO 2010, 2013 and 2014 and the Children and Families Act 2014 has set in train further instrumental approaches to dealing with complex child protection cases by requiring local authorities to demonstrate compliance with pre-proceedings protocols prior to an application to court being made, when in many instances the families have been known to children's social care for several years (Broadhurst and Masson, 2013).

Debates continue between the modernisers who are seeking reform through legislation and protocols that have introduced further procedural elements to achieving justice for children and their families, and the more conservative approach that advocates a holistic approach to decision-making (*Re B (A child) (Care Proceedings: Threshold Criteria)* [2013] UKSC, 33; *Re B-S (Children)* [2013] EWCA Civ 1146; *Re A and B v Rotherham Metropolitan Borough Council* [2014] EWCF 47; *Re J and S (Children)* [2014] EWFC 4; *Re C (A Child)* [2013] EWCA Civ 431; *Re R (a child)* [2014] EWCA Civ 1625; *M P-P (Children)* [2015] EWCA Civ 584; *Re W (Adoption Application: Reunification with Family of Origin)* [2015] EWHC 2039; *Re H* [2015] EWCA Civ 583; *Re B and E (Children)* [2015] EWFC B203). These differences could be perceived as a simple clash between pro- and anti-reformers, but this chapter highlights that the landscape is far more complex. There is an inherent tension between achieving positive outcomes for children and their families, while achieving compliance with procedures that are principally aimed at reducing costs and resources (Broadhurst et al., 2010).

Regardless of the complexity, these terms never shed any light on the detail of how professionals work with families who turn to a system when they are most in need and at times of crisis. There has been widespread uncertainty following the call for holistic assessments following the judgements in *Re B* [2013] and *Re B-S* [2014] that appear to clash with the 'reform' agenda that is driving a 26-week deadline for the completion of care proceedings. This chapter explores the need to revisit the importance of placing the child and their family at the heart of the family justice and child protection system. Achieving positive outcomes through detailed therapeutic interventions with adequate resources is more likely to resonate with the kind of reform that practitioners and families will embrace (Broadhurst and Mason, 2014). Fundamentally, child protection needs to move away from being a system that is process and assessment driven, to providing interventions that prevent the revolving-door syndrome, whereby practitioners and families *tick the box* but no real change occurs (Featherstone et al., 2014). The recent child sexual exploitation inquiries in Rochdale, Rotherham and Oxfordshire highlight the increasingly sophisticated world of perpetrators that requires an equally strategic response from front-line practitioners who need more than ever to be engaging with children, young people and their families, rather than adopting an all-too-frequent remote control response to child protection that permits moral judgements that feed into the populist and oppressive social attitudes towards children on the edge of care (Jay, 2014).

However, with severe cuts to the front-line services that are so very crucial to the protection of children and young people, and the need for professionals to increasingly *feed the beast* with information that organisations require to demonstrate quality and response targets, professionals are increasingly prone to professional ignorance as they are essentially removed from front-line practice where they are able to elicit the rich narratives that protect children (Holt and Kelly, 2014a).

The modernisation agenda – the remote control approach to child protection

'Reform' implies a repositioning of power from the centre to the users of public services. There is evidence to suggest that this is indeed what the government intends, but the drive to achieve quality within shorter timescales with no corresponding resources is arguably not conducive to facilitating this aim. The Family Justice Review (Ministry of Justice, 2011) set in train changes within the system of justice that protects children, which have resulted in further instrumental procedures that may indeed shift cases away from the court into a preproceedings protocol; however, without a significant rethink of policy, this places decision-making increasingly within an administrative rather than judicial space that will merely shift power from one arm of the state to another (Holt and Kelly, 2014b). Local authorities hold considerable power when working with families in the context of child protection, and any notion of partnership working in the current context is becoming increasingly illusive (Broadhurst and Holt, 2010). Achieving alternative forms of dispute resolution outside of the court in public law cases where children are on the edge of care is risky, particularly when the local authority is operating within a climate of austerity and targets and is increasingly focused on data inputting to satisfy the regulatory requirements, as the consequences for not doing so are high (Holt and Kelly, 2015a). Practitioners are reporting that if recordings are not completed, they are placed on report – there are no corresponding sanctions for not undertaking detailed work with families, as this is increasingly considered a luxury that the local authority cannot afford. Social workers and lawyers are operating between a rock and a hard place; the practice reality of a remote control approach to child protection is so radically at odds with the rhetoric that is supporting a modernisation agenda (Holt and Kelly, 2015b).

The timetable for the child or the deadline for parents

Further significant changes were introduced with the Children and Families Act 2014 that purport to address the timetable for the child with the imposition of a deadline for the completion of the majority of care cases within 26 weeks. This timeframe, introduced with no research evidence to support, leaves very little scope for families to make changes following the local authority making the application to court when the clock begins to tick (Holt and Kelly, 2015c).

There is an assumption built into the revised PLO 2014 that all cases apart from emergency situations should be properly prepared with all assessments that are required to inform the decision-making undertaken before a case proceeds to court. There is an acknowledgement that due to severe cuts within public sector services, the application of the protocol nationally is at best patchy, and this is highly problematic when the family justice system is built on the premise of achieving alternative forms of dispute resolution without the oversight of the court (Holt and Kelly, 2015d).

However, following the plethora of cases during 2014 and 2015 that followed the landmark judgements regarding permanency planning in *Re B (A Child) (Care Proceedings: Threshold Criteria)* [2013] UKSC and *Re B-S (Children)* [2013] EWCA Civ 1146, social work and legal practitioners have faced further confusion and there has been widespread uncertainty.

Re B and *Re B-S* reinforce the need for a detailed understanding of the child and their family that requires more than a cursory assessment, which lacks the depth of analysis required for a deeper understanding of the alternative options for the child. The facts of *Re B-S* are well rehearsed, but, briefly, the children in this case were placed for adoption in April 2012, and the mother applied for leave to oppose the adoption orders in 2013.

The Court of Appeal, on hearing this matter, took the opportunity to reinforce the key points from the recent Supreme Court decision in *Re B*. In brief, the child's interests are paramount, and those interests include living with their birth family. Furthermore, the court must consider all the *realistic* available options, and in assessing the birth family's capacity to care for a child, judges must consider the support the family could be offered (Luckock, 2008).

Not surprisingly, there followed a plethora of cases that have sought to challenge the making of care and adoption orders during 2014. In *Re A and B v Rotherham Metropolitan Borough Council* [2014] EWFC 47, the child was placed with potential adopters and Mr Justice Holman made the decision that it was positively better for the child not to be adopted but to move to live with a maternal aunt. The facts in this case were unprecedented, attracting strong opinion on either side. In *Re M'P-P (Children)* [2015] EWCA Civ 584 (June 2015) and *Re W (Adoption Application: Reunification with Family of Origin)* [2015] EWCA 2039, there were further developments, and the court arrived at a different conclusion from the original court, with the decision that the children should remain living with their foster carers. The decision has been published as *Re B and E (Children)* [2015] EWFC B203.

Regardless of whether there is a meaningful legal right to challenge an adoption order at this late stage (judgement of Lord Justice Munby in *Re J and S (Children)* [2014] EWFC 4), the consequences are significant in respect of the importance of achieving a holistic understanding of the child and their family, together with a view about permanency options, at the earliest opportunity (Holt and Kelly, 2015a).

Furthermore, the widespread uncertainty among professionals operating within the family justice system during 2014 prompted the President of the Family Division to take the opportunity in the case of *Re R (a child)* [2014] EWCA Civ 1625, 16 December 2014, to calm the chorus of concern among professionals following the judgement in *Re B-S*, but it has highlighted the tensions and contradictions within a system that is seeking speedy resolutions but requiring a complex understanding of the child and their family. These tensions mirror the administrative space of social work practice whereby practitioners are juggling the demands of increased bureaucracy leaving little time for the level of detail required to satisfy the court (Holt, 2013).

There has always been a duty on local authorities to keep rehabilitation of a child to its family at the forefront and to routinely consider all options for the child's permanency when care planning. Recent changes introduced with the PLO (2008), the Practice Direction 36C 2013, the revised PLO (2014) and the Children and Families Act 2014 have placed increased emphasis on diverting cases away from court wherever it is safe and possible to do so – thereby family and kin placements should, with the exception of emergency situations, have been fully explored long before an application to court is made. However, there has been nothing more than a cursory consideration as to how these cases can be diverted away from court when there continues to be a front-loading of resources into assessments that are generally of a poor quality and therapeutic interventions are generally unavailable unless privately funded (Holt, 2014).

The concern for the author is that the changes ushered in with the Family Justice Review (Ministry of Justice, 2011) have undoubtedly introduced delay for children at the pre-proceedings stage and long before. In many instances, children will have been left holding the risk for long periods while the local authority effectively gathers evidence through an instrumental set of protocols and procedures. The pre-proceedings protocol is frequently introduced following a lengthy period of local authority involvement with the child and their families. A study by Holt et al. (2013) found that in the majority of cases, children had been the subject of a child protection plan for up to 18 months, and had been known for up to three years from the initial point of referral. There was clear evidence of a revolving-door syndrome, with families seeking support, an initial assessment being undertaken and the case closed at the earliest opportunity, only to be reopened when the concerns escalated. The pre-proceedings protocol was simply adding another layer of procedure with scarce resources employed to effectively 'tick the box' rather than undertake the detailed work necessary to effect the change required. The author remains concerned that despite the rhetoric that the child should remain the priority, children are becoming increasingly lost in a system that is adult focused and target driven (Parton, 2014).

The hegemonic concern with the welfare of the child

The welfare of the child should indeed remain the paramount consideration of the court, a principal enshrined in the Children Act 1989 and difficult to dispute. However, while ensuring the welfare of the child remains the central focus in all decision-making concerning the child is indeed laudable, it is the author's contention that recent developments in policy and practice ushered in by the previous Coalition government, and no doubt reinforced by the subsequently elected Conservative government, have introduced an instrumental approach to child welfare (Featherstone et al., 2013).

Furthermore, the instrumental approaches to parents may be failing to recognise the potential of many parents, if offered appropriate support, to care safely for their children. The impact of austerity measures in the context of the now hegemonic concern with the timetable for the child have further contributed to a strained relationship between the local authority and parents (Featherstone et al., 2014). Achieving timely decision-making for children is of course important and legitimate, as we have seen the consequence of delay and poor planning in respect of outcomes for children (Luckock and Broadhurst, 2013); the concern is when the timetable for the child is used to support a modernisation agenda (Ministry of Justice, 2011) which is principally aimed at reducing costs when a case goes to court – which indeed supports timely decision-making but lacks the flexibility to respond to less instrumental approaches (Holt and Kelly, 2014(a)).

The family justice review set in train a direction of travel that is not readily reversible, and it places the emphasis on achieving a holistic assessment of the child and their family to a pre-proceedings stage. Given the deadline for the completion of cases following an application to court, the pressure is on to achieve both timely decisions and to build in the flexibility required before a case proceeds to court. The author remains unconvinced that achieving flexibility within a formal pre-proceedings protocol when parents have received a letter informing them of the local authorities' intention to initiate care proceedings is conducive to achieving the level of detail that is required. Increasingly, each stage of the family justice system is adopting an instrumental approach, reinforcing a culture whereby timescales for working with families are being reduced and more tightly defined. Achieving holistic assessments, never mind therapeutic interventions within a target-driven context, remain illusive (Featherstone et al., 2011).

Furthermore, there is an urgent need for a fundamental rethinking of the dominant paradigm in policy and practice in child protection (Lonne et al., 2009). The emergence of procedures, protocols and policies that are principally focused on the need to assess and respond to risk is premised on assumptions that these will highlight both quality and shortcomings in practice that will ultimately protect all children. This approach needs radical change; it is the rich narratives of children and their families that tell a story that no assessment tool can achieve. Professionals need to be released from the iron cage of data inputting and a culture of cut and paste to fill in the boxes with descriptive words that may prevent blame for not complying with reporting deadlines in the short term, but will do nothing to improve the lives of children and their families, as most of this information is second- and third-hand, resulting in a not surprising approach that is risk-averse and reactionary (White et al., 2008).

The decision to remove a child from their parents has to be balanced with 'considering the effectiveness of help available to children and families' (Munro, 2011: 36, para 2.25). It is imperative that we move away from a culture of assessment that is driven by prescriptive tools and is largely descriptive, towards achieving a holistic view of the child and their family and identifying how distress within the family can be supported and risk reduced; removing a child from their parents and kin, particularly for very young children, will inevitably result in permanency planning that also holds risks for the child (Hunt and Waterhouse, 2013). In order to achieve the level of analysis suggested in *Re B and Re B-S*, there needs to be a radical rethink of how professionals intervene with children and their families, as the current system is not conducive to achieving what is effectively good practice. The core activity of child protection practice must be about making sense in the context of contested meanings and conflicting paradigms (Buckley, 2009). Within a context of regulation and procedure, and without the time allowed to explore the complexities, practitioners have become reactive, defensive, narrow and arguably oblivious to the complex factors that influence professional judgement.

Furthermore, a suspicious and forensic approach to child protection discourages a holistic focus on the complexity of relationships (Sykes, 2011). It is imperative that practitioners move away from a disembodied relationship with children and their families that fails to capture the interconnectedness of relationships. In response to the judgements in *Re B* and *Re B-S*, there is an urgent need for a more explicit engagement and understanding of the philosophical literature on ethics, where there is considerable attention given to decision-making based upon weighing up of a range of often competing needs and interests (Gray and Webb, 2010).

The hegemonic concern with the timetable for the child reinforces that children 'cannot wait' for parents to change, particularly where parental problems are deemed to be entrenched – lamentably failing to respond to the timetable for their child (Holt and Kelly, 2014a). There is little or no scope in this context for ongoing long-term intervention, and the culture within social work practice focuses on a quick turnaround with off-the-shelf packages of care rather than a recognition for some families that managed dependency and that long-term support may be in the best interests of the child (Turney, 2005). Time is of the essence within local authorities where there has been a move from depth to surface in order to achieve procedural imperatives, resulting in time-limited interventions/programmes that are off the shelf (Howe, 1997).

The important area of practice that focuses on developing relationships and making sense of conflicting narratives, which elicit a deeper understanding of the strengths and risks within the family, has been eroded. Where information is being relied upon from a secondary source, the rich narratives are lost and what is left is descriptive texts that afford very little insight to what the child or their families need (Holt and Kelly, 2012).

Ferguson (2011) highlighted the importance of the helping alliance formed between professionals and families that is being eroded as the skills in developing effective relationships within a context of crisis are lost in an increasingly digital world. Instead, personal contact is replaced by suspicious, time-limited approaches when relationship-based work is eroded due to the value placed on the standardisation of assessment and response in a climate of austerity and targets (Munro, 2011).

It order to reverse the trend of standardisation and response, it is imperative that we move away from a culture of assessment with no follow-up therapeutic interventions, as the rich detail shared during this work helps to form the back-cloth to the local authority decisions about risk.

Conclusion

The legislative changes introduced with the Children and Families Act 2014 and recent decisions from the Supreme Court and Court of Appeal serve as a reminder of how the state gains but rarely gives up power over individuals, and the relative ease with which significant changes are introduced without ques-tion or challenge, and then become permanent features over time that are rehearsed and reinforced. The move to a front-loading of cases to the adminis-trative space of a pre-proceedings stage may appear to be a less draconian approach to dealing with complex child protection matters; however, this approach relies upon the rights of children and their families remaining a prior-ity above the need for local authorities to reduce costs and resources. In a cli-mate of austerity, targets and timescales, the rights of children and their families can often be lost (Holt and Kelly, 2012).

It is important to note that human rights are universal, and a right to a fair trial when the state intervenes in family life should be central in a democratic society, and that protection under the law should not be dependent upon an accident of birth or economic power. Legislative changes that have been intro-duced with little resistance can be seen as a direct attack on welfare, and are counterproductive in terms of achieving justice for children and their families (Byrom, 2013). There has been mounting concern regarding the cost of welfare on the state, but the scenes observed in courtrooms in twenty-first-century Britain, and in circumstances where there are child protection concerns and parents who lack capacity, portray a shameful picture on a society that purports to hold the welfare of the child as the paramount consideration. When the state intervenes to remove children, it is unforgivable that parents are left in a posi-tion where they are powerless to defend the action, as they have no right to legal representation in private law and there is a deadline imposed for the con-clusion of proceedings in public law (*Re H* [2014] EWFC B127 (14 August 2014)).

Moreover, in *Re D (A Child)* [2014] EWFC 39, where the matter related to the removal of a child from parents with significant learning difficulties by Swindon Borough Council, Justice Munby gave the following judgement:

> What I have to grapple with is the profoundly disturbing fact that the parents do not qualify for legal aid, but lack the financial resources to pay for legal representation in circumstances where, to speak plainly, it is unthinkable that they should have to face the local authority's application without proper representation.

(para. 3)

The landscape in the most complex of child protection cases has changed considerably during the last decade, with the aim of diverting cases away from court through a front-loading of cases to a pre-proceedings stage. However, the children and families who face pre-proceedings protocols and processes have often been known to children's social care for at least three years, and this process often only introduces further delay to effectively allow the local authority to 'tick the box' (Holt and Kelly, 2014a). While achieving just and fair outcomes for children and their families without the need to involve the court is of course desirable, often the oversight of the court in the most complex of cases is necessary. It is a travesty of justice given the complexity of these cases that either a deadline for the completion of the case is given at the outset, or in complex private matters there is no right to legal aid, and therefore legal representation, when state intervention can, and often does, result in children permanently living away from their birth parents and family.

There needs to be an urgent rethink about child protection practice at the interface with the court; however, the previous Coalition government and the present Conservative government show little sign of moving away from what has been a sustained attack on welfare and the children and families who turn to a system at times of crisis and when they are most in need.

References

Broadhurst, K. and Holt, K. E. (2010) 'Partnership and the limits of procedure: prospects for relationships between parents and professionals under the Public Law Outline', *Child and Family Social Work*, 15(1): 97–106. (First published online 23 September 2009, DOI: 10.iii/j.1365-2206.209_00648x)

Broadhurst, K., Wastell, D., White, S., Hall, C., Peckover, S., Thompson, K., Pithouse, A. and Davey, D. (2010) 'Performing "initial assessment": Identifying the latent conditions for error at the front door of local authority children's services', *British Journal of Social Work*, 40: 352–70.

Broadhurst, K. and Mason, C. (2013) 'Maternal outcasts: Raising the profile of women who are vulnerable to successive, compulsory removals of their children', *Journal of Social Welfare and Family Law*, online, available at: http://dx.doi.org/10.1080/09649069.2013.805061

Broadhurst, K. and Mason, C. (2014) 'Social work beyond the VDU: Foregrounding co-presence in situated practice – why face-to-face practice matters', *British Journal of Social Work*, 44: 578–99.

Buckley, H. (2009) 'Reforming the child protection system: Why we need to be careful what we wish for', *Irish Journal of Family Law*, 12(2): 27–32.

Byrom, N. (2013) *The State of the Sector: The Impact of Cuts to Civil Legal Aid on Practitioners and Their Clients*, Warwick: University of Warwick.

Featherstone, B., Broadhurst, K. and Holt, K. E. (2011) 'Thinking systemically – thinking politically: Building strong partnerships with children and families in the context of rising inequality', *British Journal of Social Work*, 42(4): 618–33.

Featherstone, B., Morris, K. and White, S. (2013) 'A marriage made in hell: Early intervention meets child protection', *British Journal of Social Work* (Advanced Access).

Featherstone, B., White, S., Morris, K. (2014) *Re-Imagining Child Protection Towards Humane Social Work with Families*, Bristol: Policy Press.

Ferguson, H. (2011) *Child Protection Practice*, Basingstoke: Palgrave Macmillan.

Gray, M. and Webb, S. (2010) *Ethics and Value Perspectives in Social Work*, Basingstoke: Palgrave.

Holt, K. and Kelly, N. (2012) 'Administrative decision making in child-care work: Exploring issues of judgment and decision making in the context of human rights, and its relevance for social workers and managers', *British Journal of Social Work*, 44(4): 1011–26.

Holt, K. E. Kelly, N. Doherty, P and Boradhurst, K (2013) 'Access to justice for families? Legal advocacy for parents where children are on the "edge of care": an English case study', Journal of Social Welfare and Family Law, 35 (2) 163–177.

Holt, K. E. (2013) 'Territory skirmishes with DIY advocacy in the family courts: A Dickensian misadventure', *Journal of Family Law*, 43(9): 1150–59.

Holt, K. E. (2014) *Child Protection*, Basingstoke: Palgrave.

Holt, K. E. and Kelly, N. (2014a) 'Why parents matter: exploring the impact of a hegemonic concern with the timetable for the child', *Child and Family Social Work Journal*, 21(2): 156–65.

Holt, K. E. and Kelly, N. (2014b) 'The emperor has no robes: Why are members of the judiciary in the most complex of child-care cases, abandoning a sinking ship?', *Journal of Family Law*, 44(10): 1424–33.

Holt, K. E. and Kelly, N. (2015a) 'When adoption without parental consent breaches human rights: Implications of *Re B-S (Children)* [2013] EWCA Civ 963 on decision making and permanency planning for children', *Journal of Social Welfare and Family Law*, 37(2): 228–40.

Holt, K. E. and Kelly, N (2015b) 'Access to justice: The welfare of children and their families lost in a target focused and cost driven system', *Journal of Family Law*, 45(2): 167–74.

Holt, K. E. (2015c) 'What has happened since the Family Justice Review: A brighter future for whom?', *Journal of Family Law*, 45(7): 807–13.

Holt, K. E. and Kelly, N. (2015d) 'When is it too late? An Examination of A and B v Rotherham Metropolitan Borough Council [2014] EWFC 47', *Journal of Family Law*, 45(4): 403–10.

Hunt, J. and Waterhouse, S. (2013) *It's Just Not Fair! Support, Need and Legal Status in Family and Friends Care*, Oxford: FRG/Oxford University Centre for Family Law and Policy.

Howe, D. (1997) 'Psychosocial and relationship-based theories for child and family social work: political philosophy, psychology and welfare practice', *Child and Family Social Work,* 2: 161–69.

Jay, A. (2014) *Independent Inquiry into Child Sexual Exploitation in Rotherham 1999–2013*. Online, available at: http://www.rotherham.gov.uk/downloads/file/1407/independent_inquiry_cse_in_rotherham

Lonne, B., Parton, N., Thompson, J., and Harries, M. (2009) *Reforming Child Protection*, London and New York: Routledge.

Luckock, B. (2008) 'Adoption support and the negotiation of ambivalence in family policy and children's services', *Journal of Law and Society*, 35(1): 3–27.

Luckock, B. and Broadhurst, K. (2013) *Adoption Cases Reviewed: An Indicative Study of Process and Practice*, Project Report, London: Department of Education.

Ministry of Justice (2008) *Public Law Outline*, London: Ministry of Justice.

Ministry of Justice (2010) *Practice Directions 12A – Public Law Proceedings Guide to Case Management*, London: The Stationery Office.

Ministry of Justice (2011) *Family Justice Review: Final Report*, London: Ministry of Justice.

Ministry of Justice (2013) *Practice Direction 36C – Pilot Scheme: Care and Supervision Proceedings and Other Proceedings Under Part 4 of the Children Act 1989*, London: The Stationery Office.

Munro, E. (2011) *The Munro Report of Child Protection: Final Report – A Child Centered System*, London: Department for Education.

Parton, N. (2014) *The Politics of Child Protection: Contemporary Developments and Future Directions*, London: Palgrave Macmillan.

Sykes, J. (2011). 'Negotiating stigma: Understanding mothers' responses to accusations of child neglect', *Children and Youth Services Review*, 33(3): 448–56.

Turney, D. (2005) 'Who cares? The role of mothers in cases of child neglect', in J. Taylor and B. Daniel (eds), *Child Neglect Practice Issues for Health and Social Care*, London: Jessica Kingsley, 249–1217.

White, S., Hall, C. and Peckover, S. (2008) 'The descriptive tyranny of the common assessment framework: Technologies of categorisation and professional practice in child welfare', *British Journal of Social Work*, 39(7): 1197–217.

6

HASTENING SLOWLY: DOES THE LAW PROMOTE OR FRUSTRATE TIMELY ADOPTION FROM CARE?

Her Honour Judge Sally Dowding

> *There is a public perception ... that local authorities/adoption agencies are target-driven, and are seeking adoption orders simply to meet their quotas, without any reference either to the well-being of children or the ... Convention rights of the parents.*
>
> Wall LJ in *Re B (Placement Order)* [2008] 2 FLR 1404 at 1408.

Non-consensual adoption from care will always be controversial, and these wise words of the former President of the Family Division acknowledge the concerns of the general public, encouraged by certain sectors of the press. Bullock (2011) expresses another side of the coin:

> while there are undoubtedly a lot of abused and neglected infants entering care, for most of them adoption does not leap out as the automatic solution for all kinds of reasons, not just the stupidity, stubbornness and prejudices of social workers and judges.

For good or ill, successive governments in recent years, beginning with Tony Blair's Labour administration, have generated a flurry of initiatives both to speed up and to increase adoptive placements. This enthusiasm has to be considered within the legal context of the hierarchy of placement choice, as prescribed by section 22C Children Act 1989, which requires consideration first of rehabilitation to birth parents, and then placement within the wider family: only if safe family placement cannot be achieved should consideration be given to permanency elsewhere. As Lord Templeman famously stated in *Re KD (a Minor)* [1988] 1 All ER 577 HL:

> The best person to bring up a child is the natural parent. It matters not whether the parent is wise or foolish, rich or poor, educated or illiterate, provided the child's moral and physical health are not endangered. Public authorities cannot improve on nature.

While acknowledging the importance of using all reasonable endeavours to preserve the child's place within the family of origin, this chapter is predicated upon the assumption that all kinship options have been fully explored and the local authority plan is for permanency outside the family.

One very striking fact about adoption is that whereas in most areas of life, processes have accelerated over the years, the opposite is true of adoption. There is nothing new in the concept of children being brought up by someone other than their parents, and the earliest, informal adoptions could be achieved virtually instantly – the adoption of Moses by Pharaoh's daughter provides an early and striking example. Relinquished babies in the first half of the last century were often placed at little more than a few weeks old and adopted well before the first birthday. The process is now very much slower, and the object of this chapter is to consider the extent to which the law assists or hinders the expressed political aim of increased and speedier adoptions.

Formal adoption within England and Wales has a surprisingly short history, with the first adoption statute coming into force in 1926 as a measure designed primarily to address the problems associated with orphans created by World War I. In the first part of the twentieth century, the emphasis within adoption policy was upon finding babies for childless couples, while simultaneously meeting the needs of relinquished babies. The Adoption Act 1976 effected significant change in law and policy by permitting the court to dispense with parental consent to adoption where such consent was found to be unreasonably withheld. That legislation was superseded by the Adoption and Children Act 2002, which permits a court to dispense with parental consent to adoption if the child's welfare so requires. Statistics released by the Office for National Statistics show that in 1975, babies accounted for 21 per cent of all adoptions; this figure remained relatively constant over the next ten years, before dipping to 15 per cent in 1990 and to 5 per cent by 1999. There remains a trickle of babies relinquished for adoption each year, but the majority of children now adopted are either adopted by a step-parent or have been through the care system in some shape or form.

Beginning the adoption process

It is fair to say that social workers and the courts are castigated in varying degrees by various interest groups for creating or permitting delay, and there have been many recent innovations seeking to address this. The Department for Education's Action Plan for Adoption (2012) set out a number of initiatives; since 22 April 2014, we have the unified Family Court, rather than a three-tier system, which should at least facilitate allocation of cases to appropriate judicial oversight, and we also have a statutory deadline, enshrined within the Children and Families Act 2014, of 26 weeks for care and supervision proceedings, extendable only exceptionally. However, the first and most obvious point to make is that a court can do nothing until an application is issued – and thus if children are to be adopted at a younger age, thought must be given to expediting the process which brings such children to the attention of the courts.

Once a child is accommodated, voluntarily (Children Act 1989, s. 20) or otherwise, the Care Planning, Placement and Case Review (England) Regulations 2010 (as amended) should provide a robust mechanism for preventing drifting in care. A care plan is required, containing a comprehensive assessment of the child's needs and how the local authority intends to establish legally secure arrangements for the child. It also requires regular reviews, first within four weeks, then within three months and thereafter at six-month intervals. Despite the requirements of the regulations, children may remain in section 20 accommodation for long periods with little obvious planning for rehabilitation or for permanency elsewhere. Statistics published by Department for Education (2014) show that, as at 31 March 2014, 68,840 children were looked after by local authorities, with a national average of 11 per cent of such children experiencing three or more placements in the year ending with that date – suggesting that some children are drifting within the system rather than being the beneficiaries of clear and coherent plans for their future. There have been a number of recent cases in which the extended use of section 20 accommodation has been rigorously criticised – notably including *Re A (a Child)* [2015] EWFC11, in which the President of the Family Division said:

> There is, I fear, far too much misuse and abuse of section 20 and this can no longer be tolerated.

Further criticism of the misuse of section 20 is contained within the judgements in *Re W (Children)* [2014] EWCA Civ 1065 and *Northamptonshire County Council v AS and ors* [2015] EWHC 199 Fam.

The best safeguard against such drift should be the Independent Reviewing Officer (IRO), but the limitations of reliance upon the IRO were starkly illustrated by the case of *A and S (Children) v Lancashire County Council* [2012] EWHC 1689 (Fam), recounting the sorry tale of two brothers who had entered the care system at the ages of two years and six months, respectively, had been made the subject of freeing orders under the Adoption Act 1975, and had drifted in and out of multiple placements, notwithstanding no fewer than 35 IRO-chaired statutory reviews. Peter Jackson J, in making declarations of human rights violations against both the Local Authority and the IRO, quoted the IRO's description of the obstacles to doing the job properly, including a 'tick-box system, driven by mandatory performance indicators, creating the illusion of action without any evidence of the quality of the achievement'. This reflects concern expressed within the Munro report (2011) that performance and inspection systems do not assure *quality* of work and should give pause to those who, by implication at least, promote quantity before quality in the placement of children for adoption.

It follows that the first imperative, where proceedings are required, is a timely application: commonly, a care application first, followed by an application for a placement order. However, if from the outset the plan is single-track adoption, and if there has been compliance with the pre-issue formalities, there is no legal obstacle to the local authority issuing placement proceedings without concurrent care proceedings, or to issuing both at the same time. As I will discuss, the pre-issue formalities have the potential to create significant delay for the child.

Progressing a plan of adoption

The possibility of permanency by way of adoption should be considered from the outset of every case. As long ago as 1999, the late Bracewell J highlighted, in *Re D and K (Children) (Care Planning: Twin Track Planning)* ([1999] 2 FLR 872), the need to consider adoption at an early stage, holding that once a local authority appreciates that adoption is a viable option, it must twin-track plan to ensure that the court has the fullest possible information to facilitate the choice between adoption and rehabilitation. This requires consideration as to how the local authority should 'satisfy' itself that a child should be placed for adoption, as stipulated by section 22 Adoption and Children Act 2002. The original framework associated with the 2002 Act required both reference to an adoption panel and ratification of the panel's recommendation by the local authority's decision-maker as a prerequisite to local authority satisfaction that the child ought to be placed for adoption. A placement application made in advance of ratification of panel recommendation is premature: this was so held in *Re P-B (a Child)* [2006] EWCA Civ. 1016. However, the Adoption Agencies (Panel and Consequential Amendments) Regulations 2012 gave effect from 1 September 2012 to the Family Justice Review proposal that panel referral be abolished for those cases which are already the subject of court scrutiny, with the intention of reducing the delay which panels may create – despite OFSTED's findings (2012) that there is no evidence of panels contributing to delay.

Whether the 2012 regulations have the effect of reducing delay is an interesting question. Superficially, it is attractive to remove from the process the need to convene a panel and then minute its recommendations, before referral to the local authority decision-maker for ratification. However, this removal does not detract from the local authority's obligation pursuant to Adoption Agencies Regulations 2005 regulation 19 (as modified by the 2012 Regulations) to satisfy itself as to whether the child should be placed for adoption, taking into account all information including the child's permanency and health reports. Consequently, the potential for delay reduction depends upon the effectiveness of the procedures adopted by the local authority in order to reach its regulation 19 decision, and in particular upon an adequate supply of decision-makers with sufficient time at their disposal to give these cases the anxious and detailed attention which they will require. Inevitably, the smaller the local authority, the smaller the number of decision-makers, and the greater the risk that sickness of other absence will build delay into a process designed to reduce it. It is also noteworthy that there can be difficulties in securing a timely permanency medical, although this is a problem with NHS provision and not necessarily within the control of the local authority. Early reference for an adoption medical carries the disadvantage that the parent may perceive adoption to be a foregone conclusion, however carefully it is emphasised by the court that all options remain open until the final hearing.

If delay is to be avoided, the local authority must take expeditious steps to secure the decision-maker's approval of any adoption plan. Local authorities are sometimes reluctant to seek ratification of an adoption plan because a party proposes a different option – for example, a family member who seeks to displace the local authority's adverse assessment before the matter goes any further. This view is usually justified by reference to the decision of *Re B (Placement Order)* [2008] 2 FLR 1404, where the Court of Appeal found that the procedure before the adoption panel was fatally flawed, thus making it impossible for the decision-maker to make a decision based upon the panel's recommendation. The essence of the problem in that case was a failure to provide the panel with expert reports already in existence, and a misrepresentation of the experts' views. It was nowhere suggested that the procedure was flawed because another party might wish to commission a further assessment, notwithstanding the local authority's primary plan being one of adoption. In the guidance given in the course of *Re B*, the court emphasised that reports which have been filed and served within the proceedings must go to the Panel (now the decision-maker), or at very least an accurate summary of those reports. Wall LJ went on to state:

> a panel's decision is a recommendation and a pre-requisite to the application for a placement order. In these circumstances, the panel will thus almost always have to make its recommendation in the light of the fact that the proceedings are contested, and that the expert evidence before the panel may be neither complete nor that which is ultimately placed before the court. It is for this reason, of course, that the final decision about adoption rests with the court.

In other words, once the local authority comes to a clear view that adoption is the way forward, it should make sure that all is in train to present the case to the decision-maker, even if other parties may seek to adduce additional evidence at the final hearing.

The placement application

Once a placement application has been issued, it is passed to an adoption judge for scrutiny and initial directions. The application should be accompanied by a report in the format prescribed by PD14 to the Family Procedure Rules (FPR) 2010 – an Annex B report, which stands as evidence within the placement proceedings, and is a formal document requiring the information prescribed by PD14. Only those who meet very specific criteria are permitted to prepare adoption reports: the Restriction on the Preparation of Adoption Reports Regulations 2005 make it a criminal offence, punishable by up to six months in prison or by fine, to prepare an adoption report unless qualified to do so, or supervised by a person who is qualified to do so. Most courts insist upon full, accurate and literate adoption reports because the child may well access the report in later life and is entitled to expect that time and trouble has been taken in its compilation – so, not infrequently, amendments are required, often at short notice to fit in with the proceedings timetable. If the reports are accurate and comprehensive when filed, the potential for delay is reduced. The British Association for Adoption and Fostering has spearheaded a project to align the Annex B report with the Child Permanency Report required by the Agency Decision-Maker (ADM) in order to tell the child's story and bring the child alive for the ADM. There is much overlap between the reports, and the rationale for the project is to reduce duplication of effort, although it is pertinent to remember that when the adoption application is issued, the local authority is required to file an Annex A report, the first part of which replicates, with appropriate updating, much of the information contained within the Annex B report. It follows that remodelling the Annex B report to conform to the Child Permanency Report may reduce delay at the placement application stage, but will create additional work when the Annex A report is required. A possible solution to this would be the recasting of the first part of the Annex A report to facilitate easier reproduction of information from the Annex B report.

Hopefully, the paperwork will be in order, enabling a decision to be made at the final hearing without the need for adjournment. As indicated earlier, the court may dispense with parental consent only if the welfare of the child so requires. A 'parent' for the purpose of giving consent to adoption is defined by section 52(6) of the 2002 Act as a parent *with* parental responsibility: the consent of those without parental responsibility is not required, presumably upon the assumption of limited involvement.

It is important to recognise that it is unusual within the wider European community, Australia and many other jurisdictions to permit the making of non-consensual adoption orders, and there have been a number of recent authorities within this jurisdiction highlighting the extreme nature of an order facilitating a child's adoption in the face of parental opposition. The most important of those cases is the Supreme Court decision of *Re B (A Child) (Care Proceedings: Threshold Criteria)* [2013] UKSC 33 in which the Supreme Court pronounced such orders a 'very extreme thing, a last resort ... the most extreme option' and a last resort when all else fails, to be made only in exceptional circumstances where the child's welfare dictates that nothing else will do. McFarlane LJ, in the case of *Re G* [2013] EWCA Civ 965, described the decision in *Re B* as a 'very clear wake-up call'. That theme continued in the landmark case of *Re B-S* [2013] EWCA Civ 1146, in which the President of the Family Division refers to real concerns about what he describes as a recurrent inadequacy of analysis and reasoning advanced in support of a case for adoption, ascribing those failures to social workers, to guardians and to judges. Judges are required to insist upon proper evidence, addressing all options realistically possible, and analysing the arguments for and against each option in a non-linear, holistic fashion. *Re B-S*, while clearly very important in highlighting the essential precursors to the making of adoption orders, did not change the law: it merely reminds judges and practitioners alike of what is already required. However, it was the catalyst for changes to the templates used by social workers and guardians in writing their reports, to ensure that all realistic options receive attention. The emphasis is of course upon the word 'realistic': this was explained by Pauffley J in *Re LRP (a Child)* [2013] EWHC 3974 (Fam) as a reference to 'the sensible and practical possibilities rather than every potential outcome, however far-fetched'. Additionally, Baker J observed in the case of *Re HA (s Child)* [2013] EWHC 3634 (Fam) that, in *Re B-S*:

> The Court of Appeal is simply emphasising the need for a rigorous analysis and comparison of the options for the child's future, having regard to the advantages and disadvantages of each option.

As at 31 March 2014, there was a 14 per cent reduction in placement orders (Department for Education, 2014), accompanied by a perceived increase in applications for further assessment. This inspired the National Adoption Leadership Board, chaired by Martin Narey, to produce a document in November 2014 entitled *Impact of Court Judgments on Adoption: What the judgments do and do not say*. The President of the Family Division confirmed in *Re R (a Child)* [2014] EWCA Civ 1625 that this 'myth-buster' did not have judicial endorsement, adding:

> I wish to emphasise, with as much force as possible, that *Re B-S* was not intended to change and has not changed the law. Where adoption is in the child's *best* interests, local authorities must not shy away from seeking, nor courts from making, care orders with a plan of adoption, placement orders and adoption orders. The fact is that there are occasions when nothing else will do, and it is essential in such cases that a child's welfare should not be compromised by keeping them within their family at all costs.

In deciding whether to seek a placement order, the feasibility of finding an adoptive family should form part of the local authority's deliberations, but there is a distinction to be drawn between children who ought to be placed for adoption but may be difficult to place, and children in respect of whom there is doubt as to whether adoption is the optimum plan. The authorities as to both sets of circumstances were reviewed by the court in *Re F (a child)* [2013] EWCA Civ 1277 – where a placement order was found to have been inappropriately made because, at the point of it being made, the outcome of proposed interventions was unclear and therefore it was not known whether adoption was the appropriate course to pursue. However, if adoption is considered to be in the child's best interests, then a placement order should be made even though it may be difficult to find adopters: this was confirmed in *Re T (Children): Placement Order* [2008] EWCA Civ 542. The opposite finding was made in the case of *NS-H v Kingston-upon-Hull City Council and MC* [2008] EWCA Civ 493, where a 3-year-old boy has been made subject to care and placement orders on the basis of failure to thrive, but then failed to thrive in foster placement, raising the possibility of organic rather than imposed cause. Wilson LJ took the view that there was a real prospect that the child's mother could persuade the court that it was not appropriate for the placement order to remain in force, and held that the necessary foundation for a placement order was that the child is in a condition to be adopted, and is *ready* to be adopted. In *Re P (Children: Parental Consent)* [2008] EWCA Civ 535, the local authority's plan was to seek adoptive placements for the children, but with a fall-back of long-term fostering if adoptive placements proved impossible of achievement. The Court of Appeal upheld the principle of pragmatic dual planning, and emphasised that the perceived difficulty of finding adopters was not a reason not to make placement orders in respect of children who ought to be placed for adoption. Unfortunately, there is a significant difficulty if placement proceedings do not take place in tandem with care proceedings: in *Re F* (supra), Black LJ expressed herself horrified by the discovery that a parent within such proceedings may not be entitled to legal aid – a theme taken up in subsequent cases, but with no solution yet advanced by either government or the Legal Aid Agency.

Matching

After the making of a placement order, the next step is to identify a 'forever family'. Section 1(5) Adoption and Children Act 2002, as originally enacted, required an adoption agency, in placing a child, to give due consideration to the child's religious persuasion, racial origin, and cultural and linguistic background – commonly interpreted as requiring promotion of the child's identity by securing the closest possible match. Seeking the elusive perfect match has obvious potential for delay: Narey (2011) laments 'a continued, unjustified obsession with ethnicity'. This was addressed in the statutory guidance (2011 revision), which stipulates:

> If the prospective adopter can meet most of the child's needs, the social worker must not delay placing the child with the prospective adopter because they are single, older than other adopters or do not share the child's racial or cultural background.

Section 3 Children and Families Act 2014 repeals section 1(5) of the 2002 Act in England, thus rendering the former section 1(5) factors of secondary importance to speed of adoption. Whether such policy is superfluous, or indeed a new policy at all, is an interesting question. LAC (98)20, published by the Department of Health in 1999, indicates:

> The Government has made it clear that it is unacceptable for a child to be denied loving parents solely on the grounds that the child and adopters do not share the same racial or cultural background.

It follows that headlines such as *'Cameron to Outlaw Race Barrier in Bid to Speed up Adoption'* (Times, 24 February 2012) are referring to little more than a recycling of established guidance, although that does not guarantee that such guidance is faithfully followed. The dilemma for social workers is, as ever, balancing optimum placement against minimum delay. Ethnicity is unlikely to be the only issue to take into account: the child may have a number of different needs, depending upon age, health and care history to date, and it may well be that the only placement available offering the specific skills to deal with these additional needs cannot meet the child's racial or ethnic profile. Research – such as that of Walker (2008) – acknowledges the need to balance the benefits of cultural matching against the imperative of selecting carers appropriate to the child's specific attachment needs. Moreover, in multicultural societies, children present with complicated ethnicities which may be difficult to replicate: this was recognised by Wilson J (as he then was) in *Re C (Adoption: Religious Observance)* [2002] 1 FLR 1119, where he commented that it will rarely be possible to find a home which reflects all elements of a very mixed cultural heritage. Even without these additional difficulties, research undertaken by Farmer et al. (2011) found that 70 per cent of Black and minority ethnic (BME) children in a (small) study sample incurred placement delay. The phrasing of section 1(5) never suggested that precise matching trumped all other considerations, but if a placement is cross-cultural, it would be helpful both to the court and ultimately to the child if the Annex A report sets out in some detail why this is the placement of choice, notwithstanding that it is not wholly consistent with the child's own background.

Another facet of the Action Plan (supra) is earlier use of the Adoption Register. Additionally, the 2014 Act permits searching and inspection of the register by prospective adopters, in order to encourage swifter matches. Stott and Hocking (2012), reporting on a pilot designed to maximise use of the adoption register, note that the register is not a quick fix: matching more children with less delay is a complex issue, and availability of suitable adopters is a national resource issue rather than one of local practice. In other words, there is little substitute for greater recruitment as a route to faster adoption. The Schools and Adoption Bill 2015 proposes power to oblige adoption agencies to work together to increase the pools of available adopters and thus expedite matching children with their new families.

The adoption application

Hopefully, the child is placed, all goes well, and in due course the prospective adopters issue their application to adopt. The application triggers notice to the birth parents, which in itself can be problematic. If the accuracy of the birth parents' addresses cannot be confirmed, the court should invite disclosure by HMRC. Failure to give the birth parents notice can result in an adoption order being set aside, as occurred in the case of *Re W (a Child) (Adoption Order: set Aside or Leave to Oppose)* [2011] 1 FLR 215. Many parents assume that the placement order is the end of the road: suddenly learning that the child remains not formally adopted can raise hopes that the child might yet return to them. Section 47(5) 2002 Act prevents any application by the birth parents to oppose the making of an adoption order without the permission of the court. The test for permission is set out in *Re P (a Child) (Adoption Order: Leave to Oppose Making of Adoption Order)* [2007] 1 WLR 2556 – namely whether there has been a change in circumstances of sufficient nature and degree to open the door to the second stage, requiring the court to consider whether it is in the welfare interests of the child to grant the parent permission to challenge the making of the adoption order. Interestingly, when the House of Commons Standing Committee scrutinised the bill which became the 2002 Act, the British Association of Social Workers (2001) submitted a memorandum calling for section 47(5) to be removed from the bill. Its rationale for this was as follows (para. 24):

> Clause 47 (5) precludes the court from giving leave unless it is satisfied that there has been a change of circumstances. We think this restriction is unnecessary and undesirable. There may for example be grounds for opposing the particular adoption application. It would not look reasonable for a court to refuse a parent leave to oppose an application which the court itself was minded to refuse.

In *Re W*, a placement order had been made in 2008, the child placed for adoption in February 2009, and an application for adoption made in August 2009. The adoption order was granted in March 2010, without any word from the birth mother: it later transpired that notice had been sent to the wrong address. The court held that setting aside for procedural defect must not be conflated with the test for permission to oppose pursuant to section 47(7) 2002 Act. In a triumph of legal gymnastics which doubtless bewildered the birth mother, the court set aside the adoption order as being procedurally flawed and then promptly regranted an adoption order because the birth mother's challenge fell short of the test described in *Re P.* Thorpe LJ emphasised that an application for permission to oppose was an 'absolute last ditch opportunity', likely to be successful only in 'exceptionally rare' circumstances, while Coleridge J observed that during the time in which the birth parent had been sorting out her life, the child's life had moved on in her absence. Sympathy and admiration for the mother's efforts were held insufficient to open the door to reversing the child's adoption journey.

Since *Re P*, there have been a number of important cases addressing the issue of permission to oppose, including *Re B-S*, in which it was held that the hurdle should not be set too high, and that judges should avoid reference either to a 'stringent test', or to 'exceptionally rare circumstances'. The President of the Family Division observed that Parliament intended section 47(5) to provide a real remedy, cautioning that 'unthinking reliance upon the concept of "exceptionally rare" runs the risk – a very real and wholly unacceptable risk – of rendering s. 47 (5) nugatory and its protections illusory'. In particular, the child having settled with adopters does not automatically justify refusal of leave to oppose. Mostyn J sought within the case of *Re SSM* [2015] EWHC 327 (Fam) to put a gloss on the term 'change of circumstances', indicating that 'what Parliament clearly contemplated was proof of an unexpected change in the basic facts and expectations on which the court relied when it made the placement order'. In evaluating the parents' application, the court must consider the prospect of successfully opposing the making of an adoption order, not the prospect of rehabilitation. If the court decides that it is in the welfare interests of the child to give the parent permission to oppose, then when hearing the adoption application, it must consider whether the child's welfare demands that the court dispenses with the parents' consent in the circumstances which *then* prevail – not the circumstances at the time of making the placement order. It is very rare for a parent to be legally represented in making an application for permission to oppose – another casualty of the restrictions upon public funding – and many parents are disappointed to learn that the grant of permission to oppose does not equate to a fast-track rehabilitation of the child to parental care.

The facility to seek permission to oppose has potential to create delay and uncertainty for the child and adopters, coupled with the cruelty of potentially false hope for the birth parents. Against that background it is tempting to propose that the door should close upon the parent once the child is placed for adoption, and that any application by a parent for leave to revoke a placement order prior to placement must be made within a specific period after the granting of the placement order – perhaps one year. The contrary argument is that adoption plans are not always fulfilled, as amply demonstrated by the case of *A and S v Lancashire* (supra), and excluding the birth parents from all prospect of regaining the care of a child who is not yet a legal member of another family is unlikely to be human rights compliant and risks a return to the 'statutory orphans' created by the freeing order regime.

Adoption by foster parents

Concurrent planning and fostering for adoption formed part of the 2010/2015 Coalition government's adoption strategy, although neither is, in reality, a new initiative and no amendment to the law is required to implement the policy. If the prospective adopter is also an approved foster carer, the child can be placed as a fostered child in advance of any placement order. More interesting legal questions may arise where a foster parent wishes to adopt a child without the local authority's blessing. Coventry City Council became embroiled in two cases on this point. In *Re A; Coventry City Council v CC and A [2008] 1 FLR 959,* Wilson LJ addressed delay created by a foster-parent application:

> were a judge to consider that there was a real prospect that in adoption proceedings a court would find that it would serve the welfare of the child, throughout her life, to be adopted by her foster mother rather than by anyone else, it would ... rarely be a proper exercise of ... discretion for questions of delay to precipitate a refusal to allow the foster mother's application to be made.

In other words, constructive delay should still be countenanced – although admittedly that decision predated the current emphasis upon very rapid decision-making. That said, it is consistent with the current policy, as demonstrated by the now-amended Adoption Scorecards, that the date of permanent placement is more significant than the date of adoption, even if the original placement was not for adoption.

In *Re A,* prospective adopters had been identified but introductions had not begun. This contrasted with *O v Coventry City Council* [2012] 1 FLR 302, in respect of which a partial appeal was reported as *Coventry City Council v PGO* [2011] EWCA Civ 729. At first instance the judge granted an injunction to restrain removal of two young children from their foster placement, notwithstanding that the foster parents had cooperated with well-advanced introductions to prospective adopters, and had made a very late application. The Court of Appeal confirmed the jurisdiction to grant such an injunction, but held that the correct test was whether there was a real prospect that the foster carers would establish that the local authority's wish to remove the children was irrational, disproportionate, otherwise unlawful or in breach of the Article 8 rights of the foster carers or children. A negative answer should have led to dismissal of the injunction application, and a positive one to further examination of issues of promptness in bringing proceedings, impact of delay, and the possibility of jeopardising the candidacy of the identified adopters – a point which proved sadly prophetic when the prospective adopters withdrew their application.

Ultimately, the court refused the foster carers' *Re O* adoption application, holding that the risks of maintaining the children in the foster placement out-weighed the risks of moving them. The court rejected the immediate attraction of leaving the children in their current placements: this complied with its duty (2002 Act, s.1(2)) to afford paramount consideration to the child's welfare throughout life, but of course resulted in delay before the children could be permanently placed.

Challenging adoption orders

Adoption is intended to be permanent and life-long, and it follows that adoption orders should rarely be susceptible of challenge – and thus due process must not be compromised by the imperative of expedition. The President of the Family Division reminded judges in *Re W and Re H* [2013] EWCA Civ 1177 at 31 of the importance of allowing the prescribed appeal period to elapse between indicating a decision in favour of adoption and pronouncing the order:

> ... I can see no reason why the *hearing* of the adoption application, if the judge thinks this appropriate, should not immediately follow the dismissal of the parent's applica-tion ... Nor do I see any problem if the judge then and there announces his decision that there should be an adoption order. The problem arises if the judge proceeds then and there to *make* the formal adoption order. For the future, judges should postpone *both* the making of the formal adoption order and the holding of the cel-ebratory event until after the parent's time for applying to this court for permission to appeal has expired.

It is extraordinarily difficult to challenge an adoption order once the period for appeal has elapsed. This is well demonstrated by the irremediable injustice reported in the case *Webster v Norfolk CC* [2009] 1 All ER 106, where parents failed to overturn the adoption of their birth children, although retrospectively exonerated from causing the perceived harm which led to that adoption. One of the very few exceptions can be found in the sad case of *Re M (Minors)* [1991] 1 FLR 458, in which the natural father of two girls was given permission to appeal out of time the making of a step-parent adoption order, made with his consent but in ignorance of the girls' mother's terminal cancer: she died within three months of the adoption. The Court of Appeal described the case as wholly exceptional, setting no precedent for the future. This contrasts with the rejection of mistake of fact as a basis for setting aside an adoption order in the case of *Re B (Adoption Order: Jurisdiction to Set Aside)* [1995] 3 WLR 40 which concerned a Kuwaiti Arab Muslim who had been adopted by a Jewish couple, believing the child to be of Syrian Jewish descent. After the adopters' death, the 'child' applied to set aside the order, claiming that he felt welcome in neither the Jewish nor the Arab community. The Court of Appeal held that the adoption could not be unscrambled, Simon Brown LJ indicating that there were 'compelling reasons for treating adoption orders as being of peculiar finality'.

Adoption outcomes

A study by Biehal and colleagues in 2010 estimated that 20 per cent of children adopted beyond infancy will experience placement breakdown. The more recent research undertaken by Selwyn et al. (2014) suggests a rather lower disruption rate, but also highlights the difficulties of obtaining accurate statistics. The realities of placement breakdown were vividly illustrated by the harrowing case of *Re K (A Child: Post Adoption Placement Breakdown)* [2012] EWHC B9 (Fam), where a local authority was obliged to seek a care order in respect of a girl of 15 who had been adopted years earlier. HHJ Bellamy commented:

> The message from research evidence, such as it is, is that the later a child is placed for adoption the greater the risk of the placement disrupting ... these parents have encountered the same difficulties which have defeated so many families of late adopted children. For these parents, what began with high hopes, borne out of a desire to provide a loving home to a disadvantaged child, has ended in tears.

Proposals to reduce the risk of placement breakdown include the Narey (2011) recommendation of a Social Impact Bond to finance post-adoption services, and the Adoption Action Plan suggestion of an Adoption Passport to guarantee access to services. Rushton and Upright (2012) propose a one-to-one parenting programme specifically to assist adoption support workers in providing advice and assistance to adopters struggling with a child's challenging behaviour. The impact of the recently announced Adoption Support Fund on post-adoption services remains to be evaluated.

Conclusion

Adoption is a draconian order which is life-changing for the birth parents, the adoptive parents and the child. It is right that any application which has the effect of permanently severing a child's connection with their family of origin should be rigorously scrutinised. That takes time, which has to be balanced against all the research which points to the early adoption as having the greatest prospect of success. Research published by Ward et al. (2014) points to most children being 2 or older before reaching their adoptive placements. That same research also cites the findings of Van den Dries et al. (2009) that children adopted after their first birthdays show less attachment security than non-adopted children – and thus the sooner a decision can be made, the better for the child.

Thomas (2013) opines that the 2002 Act is seen as having stimulated cultural change and a determination to find adoptive placements for a broader range of children, but cites Biehal et al. (2010) who note a perception of failure on the part of the adoption enthusiasts within the then Coalition government to appreciate the real difficulties in attracting suitable adopters for older or more difficult children. Sadly, every initiative designed to create a legal and policy framework which facilitates timely adoption is of limited utility without the resources required to encourage prospective adopters to come forward and to support them in their efforts to parent some of the most troubled young members of society, but it is right to conclude by noting that 5,050 children were adopted in the year ending 31 March 2014 (Department of Education, 2014), representing, even after a modest reduction in 2014, an increase of 26 per cent from 2013, and 58 per cent from 2010. The continuing challenges include supporting those placements, searching for suitable adopters for children who wait and ensuring that birth families' rights to fair and human rights compliant hearings are not jeopardised by the imperative of faster adoption: as Pauffley J indicated in the case of Re NL [2014] EWHC 270 (Fam), 'Justice must never be sacrificed upon the altar of speed.'

The law, policy and practice described in this chapter were accurate at the time of writing. Inevitably there have been further developments since that time.

References

Biehal, N., Ellison, S., Baker, C. and Sinclair, I. (2010) *Belonging and Permanence: Outcomes in Long-Term Foster Care and Adoption*, London: BAAF Publications.

Bullock, R. (2011) 'Think of a number, double it, add on ten', *Adoption and Fostering*, 35(4): 2–3.

British Association of Social Workers (2001) *House of Commons Standing Committee – Adoption and Children Bill 'Memorandum to Committee from the British Association of Social Workers*. Online, available at: www.publications.parliament.uk/pa/cm200102/cmstand/special/sto11128/11128501.htm.

Department for Education (2012) *An Action Plan for Adoption: Tackling Delay*, London: Department for Education.

Department for Education (2014) *Children Looked After in England (Including Adoption and Care Leavers) in the Year Ending 31 March 2014*. Online, available at: www.education.gov.uk/researchandstatistics.

Department of Health (1999) *Care Proceedings and Adoption: Amendment to LAC (98) 20.*

Farmer, E., Ouwejan, D. Dance, C., Beecham, J. and Bonin, E. (2011) *An Investigation of Family Finding and Matching in Adoption, Adoption Research Initiative.* Online, available at: www.adoptionresearchinitiative.co.uk.

Munro, E. (2011) *Review of Child Protection, Final Report: A Child-Centred System,* London: Department for Education, Cm 8062.

Narey, M. (2011) 'The Narey Report', *The Times,* 5 July.

National Adoption Leadership Board (2014) *Impact of Court Judgments on Adoption: What the Judgments Do and Do Not Say.* Online, available at: www.adcs.org.uk/resources/adoption.html.

OFSTED (2012) *Right on Time: Exploring Delays in Adoption.* Online, available at: www.ofsted.gov.uk.

Rushton, A. and Upright, H. (2012) *Enhancing Adoptive Parenting: A Parenting Programme for Use with New Adopters of Challenging Children,* London: BAAF.

Selwyn, J., Wijedasa, D. and Meakings, S. (2014) *Beyond the Adoption Order: Challenges, Interventions and Adoption Disruption,* University of Bristol School for Policy Studies – Hadley Centre for Adoption and Foster Care Studies.

Stott, A. and Hocking, L. (2012) *Maximising the Use of the Adoption Register Pilot January 2011–January 2012: Evaluation Report.* Online, available at: www.adoption register.org.uk.

Thomas, C. (2013) *Adoption for Looked After Children: Messages from Research: An Overview of the Adoption Research Initiative,* London: BAAF.

Van den Dries, L., Juffer, F., Van Ijzendoorn, M. H. and Bakermans-Kranenburg, M. J. (2009) 'Fostering security? A meta-analysis of attachment in adopted children', *Children and Youth Services Review,* 31(3): 410–21.

Walker, J. (2008) 'The use of attachment theory in adoption and fostering', *Adoption and Fostering,* 32(1): 49–57.

Ward, H., Brown, R. and Hyde-Dryden, G. (2014) *Assessing Parental Capacity to Change when Children are on the Edge of Care: An Overview of Current Research Evidence,* London: Department for Education.

7

THE CHANGING FACE OF YOUTH JUSTICE

Martin Wasik

Introduction

In this chapter we are concerned with the operation of the criminal justice system as it applies to defendants under 18 years of age. This group includes children (10–13) and young persons (14–17), collectively referred to as 'juveniles' and, in this context, 'young offenders'. While youth justice is certainly part of the wider criminal justice system, it is a highly distinctive area in which many of the rules, guidelines and conventions are different from those which apply to young adult (18–20) and adult (21 and over) defendants. This reflects a long-standing policy choice to deal with young offenders separately from their older counterparts as far as possible. As we will see, the reality of criminal justice is that few youngsters who break the law are prosecuted and taken to court. The great majority are dealt with more informally, through youth cautioning, the latest form of diversionary measure designed to avoid the stigma and labelling associated with bringing young defendants before the courts. Youth is an important factor in deciding criminal justice outcomes because offending may, in large part, reflect immaturity and inexperience. Young offenders often suffer from a range of social disadvantage and difficulty. It is important to remember that the majority of youngsters 'grow out of crime' (Rutherford, 1986), and that while criminal justice intervention may sometimes help to reinforce social boundaries, provide support and assist in promoting desistence from crime, it may also have the unintended effect of reinforcing delinquency. Minor criminality in early years may be a natural testing of the rules rather than evidence of a settled pattern of antisocial activity (see further Pickford and Dugmore, 2012: 61–86).

Those young offenders who are prosecuted appear in youth courts (a form of magistrates' court), which have a different ethos and markedly different procedures and powers than adult magistrates' courts and the Crown Court. While the sentencing of adults tends to focus on passing a punishment which is proportionate to the seriousness of the crime committed, the principal aim of the youth justice system as a whole (including sentencing) is to 'prevent offending' (Crime and Disorder Act 1988, s. 37) while at the same time having regard to the 'welfare of the child' (Children and Young Persons Act 1933, s. 44). Even in serious cases which need to be marked by punishment, sentencing guidelines make it clear that a juvenile aged 15, 16 or 17 should normally receive a reduction of between 25 and 50 per cent on the sentence which an offender of 18 or over would receive for the same offence (Sentencing Guidelines Council, 2009: para. 11.16). The great majority of young offenders who are dealt with in the youth court receive non-custodial penalties. While this pattern of dealing with young offenders has been a familiar one for many years, there have been important political changes over the last 30 years, from an interventionist and more punitive stance taken towards young offenders in the New Labour years to a more measured policy of reductionism since then. Most strikingly, over the last 20 years there has been a very significant fall in the overall numbers of youngsters coming into the youth justice system. Between 2006 and 2015, the number of first-time entrants into the youth justice system fell by nearly 80 per cent. This dramatic change carries the implications that youngsters now within the system often present with a more entrenched and complex range of social and psychological problems. Youth justice professionals refer to these juveniles as having very challenging and ingrained behaviour and greater and more complex needs than before (Carlile, 2014: 6; Bateman, 2014: Ministry of Justice, 2016: para. 2).

The most significant modern statutory changes in the area of youth justice were brought about by the New Labour government in the Crime and Disorder Act 1998. Some aspects of that Act are dealt with in following sections of this chapter. It is important first to appreciate the major organisational and managerial changes which were made by the Act and which are still in place today. It established youth offending teams (known as YOTs). These are multidisciplinary bodies, one for each local authority area, 156 in all across England and Wales. Precise membership of YOTs varies from one area to another, but normally includes police, probation and youth social workers, as well as representatives from health, education, employment and housing. Central to the rationale of each YOT is the multidisciplinary approach to tackling youth offending (see Fox and Arnull, 2013: chapter 3; Pickford and Dugmore, 2012: chapter 5; Souhami, 2008). Reflecting the fall in numbers of juveniles entering the youth justice system, the statutory caseload of YOTs has fallen by 74 per cent since 2006 (Ministry of Justice, 2016: para. 24). YOTs operate under the umbrella of the Youth Justice Board (YJB), also established under the 1998 Act. The YJB came close to being abolished in the early days of the Coalition government but, in the end, it survived with a new and varied remit. Its formal responsibilities are now to advise the Secretary of State for Justice on matters relating to youth justice, to encourage consistency through a National Framework for youth justice and the production of national standards in practice. It also oversees the provision of services, including the commissioning and management of custodial places for young offenders. The YJB oversees youth justice in England and Wales, though some of the arrangements are different in Wales (Field, 2015). The youth justice system operates quite differently in Scotland. For a useful comparison of the two systems see Souhami (2013).

Diversionary measures

The police are the 'gatekeepers' of the youth justice system, and are influential in deciding how to deal with lawbreaking by juveniles. They have long been accorded discretion in this role. A police officer may, for instance, decide to take no further action. Or they may decide to arrest the juvenile and pass the matter to the Crown Prosecution Service (CPS) with a view to prosecution. The decision whether to prosecute or not is a matter for the CPS and not the police, although in practice the two organisations work together closely. The third, middle, option is to issue a youth caution, a formal disposal of the case but which does not amount to a conviction. Cautioning is largely a matter for the police, subject to national guidelines, though the CPS will advise where necessary. There are many advantages to cautioning instead of prosecuting young offenders, and cautioning has become a widespread and important practice. The New Labour government took the view that cautioning practices were too variable and lax around the country, and the Crime and Disorder Act 1998 introduced a 'three strikes' model for cautioning, involving (in general terms) a 'reprimand' for the first infraction, a 'final warning' for the second and prosecution for the third. These arrangements were replaced by a system of 'youth cautions' and 'youth conditional cautions' introduced by the Coalition government in the Legal Aid, Sentencing and Punishment of Offenders Act (LASPO) 2012. A police officer may give a person under the age of 18 a youth caution if the officer decides that there is sufficient evidence to charge the juvenile, the juvenile admits that they committed the offence, and the officer does not consider that prosecution or the issuing of a youth conditional caution is appropriate (Legal Aid, Sentencing and Punishment of Offenders Act 2012, s. 66ZA). There is no requirement of consent to this course of action by the juvenile, or by their parent or guardian, but if the juvenile is aged under 17 the caution can only be given if an appropriate adult (AA) is present (see the section of this chapter entitled 'The role of the appropriate adult', below). In the year ending March 2015, the police issued 20,080 youth cautions, a decrease of 22 per cent from those given the year before, and a decrease of 81 per cent from ten years ago (Ministry of Justice/Youth Justice Board, 2016). As explained above, this does not mean that young offenders are being prosecuted instead; the reduction in cautioning must be seen in the context of the high-percentage reduction in young offenders coming in to the youth justice system as a whole, including those cautioned. In the year ending March 2015, the total number of juveniles who were cautioned or convicted was down by 70 per cent from ten years ago (Ministry of Justice/Youth Justice Board, 2016).

The officer must explain to the juvenile, and to the AA, in ordinary language the meaning and effect of the caution. When a youth caution has been given, the officer must refer the juvenile to the local YOT as soon as possible (Legal Aid, Sentencing and Punishment of Offenders Act 2012, s. 66ZB), and a member of that team, who will often be a social worker, will assess the juvenile and may arrange for them to take part in a locally available rehabilitative or reparative programme. While a youth caution is more likely to be appropriate for a first offence, there is no prohibition on giving a youth caution to a juvenile who has had one before, or to one who has earlier been convicted before the youth court. It is important to appreciate that while a youth caution is not a conviction, it is recorded by the police and, if the juvenile is prosecuted and convicted for a later offence, the caution will be cited in court. It can be taken into account, for instance, when deciding if the juvenile is a 'persistent offender' (see 'Custodial sentences', below). Also, if the offence which is the subject of the youth caution is a qualifying sexual offence under part 2 of the Sexual Offences Act 2003, the juvenile will be placed on the sex offender register for a period of 30 months. Finally, alongside the youth caution is the alternative of the youth conditional caution. The main difference from the standard youth caution is that conditions are imposed, which usually involve the making of reparation to the victim of the offence. The relevant guidance states that conditions must be appropriate, proportionate and achievable. Failure to comply with a condition means that the juvenile can be prosecuted for the original offence (Crime and Disorder Act 1998, s. 66E).

The role of the appropriate adult

A juvenile must not be interviewed by the police or asked to sign any written statement unless an AA is present. This applies to voluntary interviews as well as interviews following an arrest and the issuing of a youth caution (above). Until recently, the requirement for an AA to be present applied to any person aged under 17, but Code C to the Police and Criminal Evidence Act (PACE) 1984 now extends that to anyone who appears to be under the age of 18 (para. 1.5A, with effect from June 2014). A juvenile should normally be interviewed at a police station, where the interview will be recorded, so that interviews at other places (e.g. at school) should occur only very exceptionally. The role of the AA is not that of a passive observer, but is to advise the person being interviewed, assist with communication and make sure that the interview is being conducted properly and fairly in accordance with PACE (para. 11.17). If a parent or guardian is not available, or is unwilling or deemed unsuitable to act in this capacity, a local authority social worker will usually be called on to fulfil the role, and proper training of the AA in police procedure and the rights of a suspect is essential in order to ensure that the young person understands what is happening. This includes the meaning of the police caution before interview ('you have the right to remain silent but it may harm your defence if you do not mention something which you later rely on in court; anything which you do say may be given in evidence') and a full awareness of the young person's rights (in particular, the right to legal advice). An AA can, for example, insist that a juvenile is not interviewed without a solicitor being present, even if the juvenile does not want legal advice. The AA's function is to 'safeguard the interests of children and young persons detained or questioned by police officers' (Police and Criminal Evidence Act 1984, s. 38(4)). They must be allowed to converse privately with the juvenile at any time, and must be present during any search or identification procedure. It is not, however, the function of the AA to give legal advice, nor to sit in on a discussion between the young person and their solicitor. Local authorities have a legal duty under the Crime and Disorder Act 1988 to ensure provision of an AA for children via the YOT. National standards require that AAs are properly trained and vetted. Their role is 'critical to ensure that children receive the advice and protection that they need' (Ministry of Justice, 2016: para. 38). AAs have no role to play in supporting a juvenile in court, nor do they have any role in relation to victims of crime, or witnesses. It is possible that a social worker who has acted as an AA may later be required to write a report on the juvenile for the youth court. The report must refer only to offences admitted by the juvenile, and not to matters discussed in police interview but not charged in court (see further Fox and Arnull, 2013: 86).

Youth courts

As mentioned above, youth courts are a specialised form of magistrates' courts, designed for dealing with those under 18 who are prosecuted rather than receiving a youth caution. In every magistrates' courts centre one court will be designated as the youth court. It is designed and furnished in a less intimidating and confrontational style than the traditional adult court. Usually the court is presided over by a bench of three lay magistrates. They will also sit as magistrates in the adult court, but will have chosen to receive additional training to sit in the youth court. There must always be at least one man and one woman magistrate on the bench. Occasionally, however, instead of three lay magistrates there may be a single district judge. The bench is always advised and assisted by a court clerk. The decline in the number of juveniles entering the youth justice system, which was mentioned above, is reflected in the population of young people sentenced at court, which has been declining year on year over the last ten years, and fell by a further 10 per cent in the year to March 2015, in which year 30,960 young people were sentenced by the courts (Ministry of Justice/ Youth Justice Board, 2016).

There is a clear policy that, wherever possible, juveniles should be dealt with in the youth court. That is the specialist venue. Accordingly, youth court magistrates have a more extensive range of powers than their colleagues in the adult magistrates' court. In particular, the maximum custodial sentence which can be imposed in the adult court is normally six months' imprisonment, whereas the youth court magistrates are empowered to pass a detention and training order (DTO) for up to two years. This may seem an odd differential, given that young offenders generally receive significantly lower sentences than adults for equivalent offending. It should be understood that, in cases of serious offending, it is the Crown Court (and not the magistrates) who will deal with the case. In the case of a young offender, however, the case must appear to be serious enough to attract a sentence of at least two years on conviction before it can be transferred to the Crown Court. This threshold ensures that the youth courts deal with the great majority of young offenders. Apart from the Crown Court dealing with juveniles where the anticipated sentence is above two years, that court must deal with any juvenile charged with a homicide and any case in which the juvenile is jointly charged with an adult whose case is to be heard in the higher court.

There has recently been criticism of youth courts as a specialist venue for juveniles, especially in a review conducted by Carlile (2014). It was pointed out in that report that few lawyers appearing in the youth court have any specialist training in cases involving young people and, in general, they tend to be newly qualified advocates who are 'learning the ropes' before representing adult defendants. One effect of the fall in numbers of young defendants has been that youth courts have less work and are sitting less frequently. Some youth courts have closed, and the remaining courts may receive defendants from different YOT areas on a rotational basis (Carlile, 2014: 5). There is therefore concern over a further erosion of judicial and advocacy experience (Wigzell and Stanley, 2015). For discussion of the practical working relationship between the YOT and the local youth court see Fox and Arnull (2013, chapter 8) and Staines (2015, chapter 3).

The role of the responsible officer

In those cases which come before the youth court, most juveniles admit the offence. A plea of guilty attracts a proportionate reduction in sentence (up to a maximum of one-third) for an admission at 'the first reasonable opportunity' (Sentencing Guidelines Council, 2007: para. 4.2 and Annex 1). Since in those circumstances there is no contested trial, only a short sentencing hearing, the magistrates rely upon sentencing guidelines and on information provided in a pre-sentence report (PSR) to assist them. The PSR is produced by the 'responsible officer', who for offenders aged under 18 will usually be a local authority social worker assigned to the YOT, so in the remainder of this chapter it can be assumed that 'responsible officer' means 'social worker'. There is a structured framework for assessment of young people who have admitted or been convicted of an offence, known as the Asset assessment tool, which was introduced in 2000. Asset is designed for use in *diversionary measures* (see above), in the youth court for bail and sentencing decisions, and in supervision under a youth rehabilitation order or following release from a DTO. The framework is based around the presence or absence of a range of risk factors statistically associated with offending and reoffending. These risk factors have been identified from criminological research, especially longitudinal studies. They include poor parenting, family conflict, family involvement in crime, low intelligence, delinquent peer group, truanting or low educational achievement, social and economic disadvantage, and substance or alcohol misuse (Pickford and Dugmore, 2012; Fox and Arnull, 2013: chapter 5). Of course there is no inevitable connection between these factors and youth offending. Nor should the completion of Asset become a tick-box exercise (see Baker, 2004). Any assessment within the PSR must 'adopt an individualised approach ... that draws out the specific needs, circumstances, priorities, abilities and attributes of the young person ... This can be a challenge when assessments are required to be completed within specified times-scales, where the temptation may be to use the assessment tool as a means of gathering information without ... analysing it to try [to] understand what is underlying the offending behaviour' (Pickford and Dugmore, 2012: 151). A report assessment employing Asset will typically involve the officer meeting on more than one occasion with the young person concerned, and a range of other people including the young person's parent(s) and perhaps with others, such as a teacher or a family social worker. The assessment should be a collaborative exercise, building on the multidisciplinary strengths of the YOT. For further practical advice on undertaking an effective assessment see Pickford and Dugmore (2012: 154–57). Of course, apart from the needs of the juvenile, in the youth justice context it has to be remembered that the reason for the young person's involvement in the system is their commission of an offence, which may need to be marked by a proportionate punishment (Sentencing Guidelines Council, 2009: para, 1; von Hirsch and Ashworth, 2004: chapter 3). Apart from the PSR prepared on a young offender, there are other situations in which the court will request a report from the responsible officer. These include a report on the willingness of the victim of the offence to take part in reparative activities within a reparation order, and the suitability of the offender's home environment for the practical working of requirements in a youth rehabilitation order. These specific examples are referred to where appropriate, below.

Referral orders

Where a young offender is prosecuted, is before the youth court for the first time and admits the offence, there is a very high chance that the outcome will be a referral order. If the youth court does not propose to pass a custodial sentence, a hospital order or a discharge, then it is in effect *required* to make a referral order. There is also discretion to make a referral order in other circumstances, including where this is not the young offender's first appearance before the court (Powers of Criminal Courts (Sentencing) Act 2000, s. 16 and s. 17). The referral order is a unique form of sentence, because it transfers responsibility for setting conditions to govern the young offender's future behaviour to a *youth offender panel* established by the local YOT. The youth court simply sets the duration of the order, the minimum being three months and the maximum twelve months. The youth offender panel consists of volunteer members of the local community, steered by a member of the YOT. The young offender must attend. The parent or guardian of the young offender should also attend (and may be so ordered by the court). Wherever possible, the victim of the offence should also be there, provided that they agree to be involved. After discussion, at which everyone is encouraged to put forward their point of view, the panel will draw up an agreement, known as a 'youth offender contract', in which the juvenile agrees to a programme of activity. The contract usually includes a clear reparative element, and lasts for the period set by the court. If the juvenile does not engage with this process, fails to agree a contract within a reasonable time or fails to comply with its terms, the youth offender panel can refer the case back to the youth court, which will revoke the order and sentence the juvenile in a different way. If a juvenile commits a new offence during the period of a referral order the court dealing with the new offence may revoke the referral order and re-sentence (Powers of Criminal Courts (Sentencing) Act 2000, schedule 1).

While the referral order in principle provides an important measure of reparative justice, there have been persistent problems in its practical implementation. In particular, there have been disappointingly low levels of attendance and involvement by victims at youth offender panels meetings. There has also been criticism of the lay membership of panels, as being amateur, socially unrepresentative and having procedures which lack due process and produce inconsistent outcomes (Crawford and Newburn, 2003). While these criticisms need to be taken seriously, it must be understood that the panel is not a court, and the reparation order has been established in order to provide a form of inclusive, socially rooted and less confrontational form of justice. The low level of involvement of victims does, however, go to the heart of the reparative model of criminal justice, and is the principal shortcoming of referral orders are they currently operate (see further Haines, 2000).

Non-custodial sentences

The youth court has power to deal with an offence by imposing an *absolute or conditional discharge* (Powers of Criminal Courts (Sentencing) Act 2000, s. 12). In either case, the young offender walks free from court with no immediate penalty, save for the fact that they now have a criminal conviction. In the case of a conditional discharge, the discharge is conditional upon no further offence being committed within a specified period of time, up to a maximum of three years but more commonly for six or twelve months. There is no supervision, nor any involvement of the YOT. If a new offence is committed within the discharge period, then the juvenile will receive an additional punishment for that breach as well as the sentence for the new offence. There are certain restrictions on the use of the conditional discharge in relation to young offenders. In particular, if the young offender has received two or more youth cautions and is convicted within two years of the last caution, the court cannot deal with the offence by a conditional discharge unless there are 'exceptional circumstances' for doing so (Crime and Disorder Act 1998, s. 66ZB).

If the youth court decides to *fine* a juvenile for the offence, the amount of the fine is limited (to a maximum of £250 for those aged 10 to 13, inclusive, and to a maximum of £1,000 for those aged between 14 and 17, inclusive), and in general the court will order the parent or guardian of the young offender to pay (see 'Orders against parents', below). If a compensation order to the victim of the offence is made by the court, then, again, the court will normally require the parent or guardian to pay (Powers of Criminal Courts (Sentencing) Act 2000, s. 137). The youth court also has power to make a *reparation order* on a young offender, the idea being that, in a straightforward and not particularly serious case, the juvenile can be required to write a letter of apology to their victim, or to perform some specified task for that person as a way of making amends (Powers of Criminal Courts (Sentencing) Act 2000, s. 73 and s. 74). The court must have a report from the responsible officer suggesting this course of action, indicating the willingness of the victim to be involved, and setting out the kind of reparation which is proposed. The order cannot require the young offender to do more than 24 hours of work. If the court does make the order, the reparation must be carried out under the supervision of the responsible officer. The law also permits a reparation order to be made for the benefit of the local community generally rather than for the victim of the offence, but it is mainly designed as a vehicle for face-to-face reparation. The youth courts have not made great use of the reparation order, and its use has declined further since the introduction of referral orders.

The principal non-custodial sentence in the youth court is the *youth rehabilitation order* (YRO), a single generic disposal which replaced a range of community sentences in 2008. The YRO can be imposed only where the offence is serious enough to justify it, and can last for up to three years. The court can insert into the order one or more requirements drawn from a list set out in the legislation (Criminal Justice and Immigration Act 2008, s. 1). These include an activity requirement for up to 90 days, a supervision requirement, an unpaid work requirement of between 40 and 240 hours (available only if the juvenile is aged 16 or 17), a programme requirement, an attendance centre requirement (of varying duration, depending on the age of the young offender), a prohibited activity requirement, a curfew requirement (for periods of between two and sixteen hours a day), an exclusion requirement, a residence requirement, a local authority residence requirement (for no more than six months, and ending as soon as the young offender turns 18), a mental health treatment requirement, a drug treatment requirement, a drug-testing requirement, an intoxicating sub-stance treatment requirement and an education requirement. The full details of each of these requirements lie outside the scope of this chapter, but it can be said that the court when selecting from this menu will be seeking to achieve a balance of punishment, public protection, prevention of re-offending, rehabili-tation and reparation. Most requirements do not need the juvenile to comply, but consent is needed for mental health, drug treatment or intoxicating sub-stance treatment requirements. A drug-testing requirement can only be required in conjunction with a drug treatment requirement. More generally, require-ments cannot be imposed which conflict with each other, or which interfere with the young offender's schooling or religious observance. Electronic moni-toring (or 'tagging') of the juvenile is also available, but as a means of securing compliance with one or more of these requirements, rather than as a 'stand-alone' requirement. Before making a YRO, the court must obtain a PSR from the responsible officer about the home and family circumstances of the juvenile. The report will suggest what combination of requirements would be suitable for the offender and at the same time reflect a level of intervention appropriate for the seriousness of the offending (Sentencing Guidelines Council, 2009: paras 10.9 to 10.22: Fox and Arnull, 2013: chapter 7).

What has been described so far can be regarded as the 'basic' YRO. Also avail-able are the *youth rehabilitation order with intensive supervision and surveillance,* and the *youth rehabilitation order with fostering.* The former can only be imposed if the court would otherwise have imposed a custodial sentence, and if so, the court must include an 'extended' activity requirement lasting between 90 and 180 hours, a supervision requirement and a curfew requirement backed by elec-tronic monitoring (see further Sentencing Guidelines Council, 2009: paras 10.23 to 10.27). The latter can only be imposed if the court would otherwise have imposed a custodial sentence, and after the court has consulted the parent or guardian of the young offender (if practicable to do so) and the local authority which is to receive the young offender. A supervision requirement must also be made. The fostering period must be specified by the court and must not exceed 12 months in total nor operate for any time after the young offender reaches the age of 18 (see further Sentencing Guidelines Council, 2009: paras 10.28 to 10.31).

If the responsible officer finds that the young offender has failed to comply with any of the requirements of the YRO, the officer must give a warning which explains the nature of the failure. A further warning may be given within a 12-month period, but if there is a third failure to comply, the officer must refer the young offender back to court. The youth court when dealing with a young offender for breach of a YRO may impose a fine, amend the requirements in the order or revoke the YRO and re-sentence. If it is re-sentencing, and the court finds that the young offender has 'wilfully and persistently failed to comply' with the order, it may replace it with a YRO with intensive supervision and surveillance. If the order which is breach was a YRO with intensive supervision and surveillance, the court may impose a custodial sentence instead. This is almost certain to be a DTO. Crown Court powers on breach are very similar. See further Staines (2015: chapter 4).

Orders against parents

Whenever the youth court makes a *financial order* (fine, order for compensation to be paid to the victim or an order for costs) against an offender under the age of 18, the court will normally order the parent or guardian to pay, and in the case of an offender under the age of 16 the court will always do so (Powers of Criminal Courts (Sentencing) Act, s. 137). There is, however, discretion not to make the parent pay if the court is satisfied that the parent cannot be found, or that it would be unreasonable to make the order. The court must give the parent an opportunity to be heard, and to make representations about their ability to pay or the fairness of requiring them to do so. It has been held that it would be wrong to make a parent pay where the parent has done all he or she reasonably can to prevent the offending (*Sheffield Crown Court, ex parte Clarkson* (1986)). In this context, where a local authority has parental responsibility for a person under the age of 18, and the young person is in care or is being provided with accommodation by them, the term 'parent or guardian' may well include the local authority. What matters is whether the services being provided by the local authority bring it within the definition of 'guardian' in section 107 Children and Young Persons Act 1933. If it does fall within that definition, the local authority, as with a parent, has the right to be heard, and in *D v DPP* (1995) it was held that no order should be made where the local authority had done all that it reasonably could to prevent the offending. In *Bedfordshire County Council v DPP* (1996) the Divisional Court went further, and said that it would be unreasonable to require the local authority to pay unless fault on the part of the council was proved, and it could also be shown that the fault had led to the offending.

The youth court has power to make a *parenting order* on the parent of a juvenile in a number of different situations, but, importantly for this chapter, where that child or young person has been convicted of an offence (Crime and Disorder Act 1988, s. 8). The power to make the order becomes a requirement to do so where the young offender is aged under 16, but the court always has discretion not to make a parenting order if it is not satisfied that it would be in the interests of preventing reoffending. If the court takes that view, it must say so in open court and explain why not (Crime and Disorder Act 1988, s. 9). A parenting order requires the parent or guardian to comply for a period not exceeding 12 months with requirements in the order and to attend within that period (but not for more than three months) counselling or parental guidance sessions as specified by the responsible officer. Such courses can be residential or non-residential, but the court must always be assured that the interference with family life is justified. In *R(M) v Inner London Crown Court* (2003) the whole legislative scheme of parenting orders survived a legal challenge that it contravened Article 8 of the ECHR which guarantees respect for private and family life. Before it makes a parenting order, the court is required to take into account the family circumstances, so this is another situation where the responsible officer is expected to advise the court as to the value or otherwise of proceeding in that way. Failure to comply with a parenting order is an offence, punishable with a fine of up to £1,000. Views as to the value of parenting orders are sharply divided (Drakeford and McCarthy, 2000). According to the Ministry of Justice, parenting courses help parents to improve their communication skills, their ability to handle conflict with their children and improve family relationships (Ministry of Justice, 2013a). Many commentators are more sceptical, taking the view that parenting orders often tend to make things worse, by placing additional burdens on families which are already struggling to cope (Burney and Gelsthorpe, 2008).

Custodial sentences

In the year ending March 2015 there were 1,834 young people who received a custodial sentence, down by 19 per cent from the year before, and down by 70 per cent over the last ten years. The average length of custodial sentence was just short of 15 months (Ministry of Justice/Youth Justice Board, 2016). The DTO is the standard custodial sentence for offenders under the age of 18 at the date of their conviction. The youth court has power to pass a DTO of up to two years in length. If a young offender is aged 17 when convicted (or when they plead guilty) but is aged 18 when sentenced, the correct custodial sentence is the DTO and not the sentence of detention in a young offender institution, which is appropriate for offenders aged 18, 19 or 20 when convicted. There are important restrictions on imposing a DTO on a juvenile under the age of 15. Under current law the DTO is unavailable if the juvenile is aged 10 or 11, and if aged 12, 13 or 14 it is only available if the juvenile is a 'persistent offender' (Powers of Criminal Courts (Sentencing) Act 2000, s. 100). That phrase is, unfortunately, not defined in the legislation, but a series of appellate decisions has established that in deciding whether a young offender is persistent or not for these purposes, the court can take into account any youth cautions (or their equivalent under earlier law) on their record (an example is *AD* (2001)). The Sentencing Guidelines Council (2009) said that a young offender should only be regarded as 'persistent' if they have been convicted or received a youth caution on at least three occasions in the last 12 months, but this proposal has been overlooked by the courts. In the leading case of *L* (2013), a 14-year-old pleaded guilty to three offences of street robbery, all committed within a few minutes of each other and in the company of slightly older youths. He had two previous cautions but this was his first court appearance. The Court of Appeal said that this was *not* 'persistent', quashed the DTO which had been imposed and substituted a YRO instead.

The DTO is a unique custodial sentence in that the youth court must impose a sentence length which is one of those approved in the legislation – orders of 4, 6, 8, 10, 12, 18 or 24 months are the only ones which are permitted. A DTO of, say, nine months, is unlawful. Clearly, since the minimum permitted period for a DTO is four months, an offence justifying less than four months must receive a YRO instead. It is worth noting that a DTO cannot be suspended, unlike a custodial sentence on offenders aged 18 or over. The Sentencing Guidelines Council says that when the court is considering the length of a DTO where the juvenile is aged 15, 16 or 17, it is appropriate to take a starting point for sentence which is from half to three-quarters of that which an adult would receive for the same offence. For someone under the age of 15, greater flexibility is required to allow for the wide range of maturity and culpability which has to be taken into account (Sentencing Guidelines Council, 2009). Ordinarily a DTO falls into two distinct parts – during the first half the young offender is detained in custody, and during the second half he or she will be under licence and supervision in the community. Supervision is carried out by a responsible officer. Exceptionally, if the young offender turns 18 by the halfway point of the DTO, on release he or she will be subject to a full 12 months of licence and supervision which will begin at that halfway point (Offender Rehabilitation Act 2014, s. 6).

If a young offender fails to comply with the supervision requirement of the DTO, the court may impose a fine, order further supervision or commit the young offender to youth detention for up to three months (Powers of Criminal Courts (Sentencing) Act 2000, s. 104).

As we have seen, the maximum term for a detention and training order is two years. Sometimes a young offender has to be dealt with for a very serious offence for which the two-year limit would be too low. If so, the matter is beyond the jurisdiction of the youth court, and should be dealt with in the Crown Court. First, if a young offender is charged with an offence involving *homicide* (murder, manslaughter, causing death by dangerous driving, etc.) then the case is auto-matically transferred to the Crown Court. Second, if the young offender has been charged with an offence (sometimes referred to as a 'grave crime', but basically any offence which carries a maximum penalty of 14 years or more in the case of an adult, plus some other offences specifically provided for in stat-ute) and that offence on its facts would justify a custodial sentence clearly in excess of two years, then the DTO cannot be used and the case is too serious for the youth court to deal with. The case must instead be sent up to the Crown Court to be sentenced under *section 91 Powers of Criminal Courts (Sentencing) Act 2000*. That court has the same sentencing powers in relation to a young offender as it has for an adult, so that in principle the Crown Court could impose a life sentence on a young offender for a robbery and up to 14 years for a domestic burglary. The High Court, in the leading case of *Southampton Youth Court* (2005), emphasised that the general policy was to deal with as many young offenders as possible in the youth court, and that there was a 'strong presumption' against sending juveniles to the Crown Court. In that case the defendant was aged 14 and he and a 15-year-old boy were jointly charged with robbing a 13-year-old boy of his bicycle. It was alleged (though denied) that the defendant had produced a broken bottle and threatened the victim with it. The defendant had not been in trouble before, which meant that the DTO was (as explained above) unavailable, and the most likely outcome was a YRO. Lord Woolf CJ said that the youth court should have dealt with the case. On the other hand, in the case of *Q* (2012) the young offender was aged 14 and, together with another 14-year-old, a 15-year-old and a 16-year-old, took part in a rob-bery of a corner shop, in which an air pistol was used to threaten the shop owner, who was seriously affected psychologically by the incident. This case was sent to Crown Court, and the judge considered a YRO for Q but decided that the offence was too serious for that. The DTO was unavailable because Q was not a persistent offender. The judge passed a sentence of 18 months detention under section 91, and that sentence was upheld on appeal despite that term being shorter than the normal two-year threshold necessary for a section 91 sentence. The case illustrates the point that while the DTO cannot be used where an offender under the age of 15 is not a persistent offender, the same limitation does not apply where a 'grave crime' has been committed.

It is worth referring briefly to two other cases where sentence was imposed under section 91, to illustrate the difficult decisions which have to be made when very young people commit serious crimes. In *P* (2006) a 12-year-old boy admitted kidnapping a boy aged eight and subjecting him to serious violence and abuse. P was said to be of very low intelligence, and having special needs. The Court of Appeal, after 'anxious consideration', upheld a sentence of three years detention. In *SP* (2010) six years detention was the sentence in a tragic case of manslaughter where a 13-year-old boy, in company with his 17-year-old brother, set fire to a derelict building in which two people sleeping in the building were killed. SP was described as being of low intelligence, and as someone who had been allowed to run wild by his parents, who had little interest in him. The Crown Court also has power, when passing a custodial sentence of this kind for a violent or sexual offence, to pass an 'extended sentence' which means that the young offender's release date depends on a decision being made by the parole board about any continuing risk posed by the young offender, and upon release there is an additional period of supervision (Criminal Justice Act 2003, s. 226B). If the offence, like manslaughter, carries a life sentence as its maximum, then in the worst kind of case, detention for life can be ordered under section 91. That sentence, although indeterminate, requires the judge to set a minimum period in custody which must be served in full before consideration can be given to releasing the young offender back into the community. An example is *JM* (2003), where life with a minimum term of three and a half years was imposed on a 14-year-old boy who had struck a man on the head with a wooden stake, fracturing his skull and causing long-term injuries. JM had a history of violent and disturbed behaviour.

Finally, in the rare situation of a young offender being convicted of murder, the mandatory sentence (called detention during Her Majesty's pleasure) is detention for life but, again, the judge will set a minimum period which must be served before release can be considered by the parole board. The 'starting point' for setting the minimum period for an offender aged under 18 convicted of murder is 12 years, but that figure always has to be adjusted for age, and relevant aggravating and mitigating circumstances (Criminal Justice Act 2003, schedule 21, para. 7).

Young offenders in custody

Juveniles who are sentenced by the court to custody serve their sentences either in a young offender institution (which also cater for offenders aged 18, 19 and 20), in a secure training centre or a secure children's home. There are just seven young offender institutions which also cater for those under 18. Six are operated by the National Offender Management Service (NOMS), and one by a private provider. The four secure training centres are all run by private companies, and the 21 secure children's homes are all operated by local authorities. Collectively these institutions are referred to as the 'youth secure estate'. The custodial population of young offenders has fallen by 56 per cent since 2004. The government has expressed serious concern (Ministry of Justice, 2013b) over the annual cost of places in these institutions, the limited number of hours of education available to the juveniles detained there and the high rate of reoffending (70 per cent reoffend within 12 months of leaving, compared with 47 per cent of adult offenders). In 2015 the government legislated for the building of the first privately run 'secure college' (Criminal Justice and Court Services Act 2015, s. 39), but following a change in policy those plans have now been abandoned.

The average population of young people in custody in the year ending March 2015 was 1,037, a reduction of 15 per cent in the last year and down 65 per cent from a peak in the year ending March 2008. This figure compares with just over 5,000 offenders aged 18–21 and 80,463 offenders aged 21 and over held in custody in the same year. It should not be forgotten that one-quarter of those held in custody have not been convicted but have been remanded by a court awaiting trial or sentence. About 8 per cent of young offenders are remanded in custody rather than being bailed, and in the year ending March 2015 on average there were 240 juveniles held in the youth secure estate at any one time (Ministry of Justice/Youth Justice Board, 2016). The average number of days young people spent in the secure estate is 52 days for those on remand, 108 days for those serving a DTO and 323 days for those on long-term sentences including section 91 disposals. There is an over-representation among young people in custody of children who are, or have been, 'looked after' children with experience of local authority care (Children Act 1989, s. 20), and some over-representation of black and minority ethnic groups (Ministry of Justice, 2016, para. 40).

The problems which these juveniles have are clear – 88 per cent of boys aged 15–17 have been excluded from school, and some 18 per cent have special educational needs (compared to 3 per cent of the general population). In the year ending March 2015 there were 7.7 incidents of self-harming per 100 young offenders, an increase from 6.6 in the previous year and 5.3 in 2010 (Ministry of Justice/Youth Justice Board, 2016). There were no deaths in custody in the secure estate in the year to March 2015, but there have been eight deaths since 2005. In the year to March 2015 there were 28 'restrictive physical interventions' recorded per 100 young people in custody (Ministry of Justice/Youth Justice Board, 2016). A *Panorama* programme broadcast in 2016 exposed serious wrongdoing, including assaults by staff on juveniles, at the Medway secure training centre. This led to dismissal of several members of staff at the centre. The private company running the centre, G4S, has since decided to end its contractual involvement in the youth secure estate (BBC News, 2016). This scandal occurred against the background of a major review of the youth justice system chaired by educationalist Charlie Taylor, which is due to present a final report in summer 2016. An interim report of emerging findings, published in February 2016 (Ministry of Justice, 2016), proposes a renewed emphasis upon education of children held in youth custody. It proposes that custodial institutions for juveniles should be 'reconceived as schools', overseen and inspected under the education framework: 'Rather than seeking to import education into youth prisons, we should create schools for young offenders in which we overlay the necessary security arrangements' (at para. 18). This is clearly an important initiative, but we must wait for the final report to see whether funding would be made available to the Education Department to set up and manage such institutions, based upon the existing alternative provision free schools.

Conclusion

As we have seen, the youth justice system is currently in a period of significant contraction, in terms of the numbers of juveniles entering the system, the numbers being sentenced by the youth court and the numbers in custody. All this is very positive, although the criminological reasons for the year-on-year fall over the last ten years are unclear. There may simply be a fall in lawbreaking by the young. Or the reduction may reflect to some extent government policy to reduce the numbers entering the system (especially for lesser offences) and the creation of more imaginative court disposals short of custody. It is possible that sentencing guidelines in the magistrates' courts and, in particular, the Sentencing Guidelines Council guideline on *Sentencing Youths* (Sentencing Guidelines Council, 2009) may have helped magistrates to resist punitive outcomes in a larger number of cases. One immediate effect in the reduction of youth court work has been to accelerate the closure of magistrates' courts, a trend already under way due to the greater use of out-of-court disposals for adult offenders. Nearly 100 magistrates' courts have closed in recent years, and a further round of cuts is currently proposed. As we have seen, youth courts are sitting at fewer venues, and less frequently. Yet, the message from youth justice practitioners, recognised by the Ministry of Justice and YJB, is that the complexity of needs of the young offenders who are still entering the system is becoming more challenging and acute. It is worrying, then, that expertise in the youth courts is a diminishing asset. As Wigzell and Stanley (2015) argue, the issue of training must be looked at again – both in the youth court (where expertise is reducing over time) and in the Crown Court, where judges receive no specialist training at all in dealing with juveniles. In the higher courts, judges encounter juveniles infrequently, but when they do, the cases are likely to be challenging and the sentencing conventions are very different from those applicable to adults. The current ongoing *Review of the Youth Justice System* (Ministry of Justice, 2016) is mainly focused on custodial provision for juveniles, but is expected to report more widely on juvenile justice measures in the community, including proposals to further devolve youth justice services (including budgetary responsibility) to local areas and to strengthen multidisciplinary partnerships within YOTs, especially with health and education.

References

AD [2001] 1 Cr App R (S) 202
Baker, K. (2004) 'Is Asset really an asset? Assessment of young offenders in practice', in R. Burnett and C. Roberts (eds), *What Works in Probation and Youth Justice: Developing Evidence-Based Practice*, Cullompton: Willan, 70–87.

Bateman, T. (2014) *Children in Conflict with the Law: An Overview of Trends and Developments*. Online, available at: http://thenayj.org.uk/wp-content/files_mf/childreninconflict withthelaw2013.pdf.

BBC News (2016) 'Four sacked after Panorama investigation into G4S unit'. Online, available at: www.bbc.co.uk/news/uk-england-kent-35290582.

Bedfordshire County Council v DPP [1996] 1 Cr App R (S) 322

Burney, E. and Gelsthorpe, J. (2008) 'Do we need a naughty step? Rethinking the parenting order after ten years', *Howard Journal of Criminal Justice*, 47(5): 470–785.

Carlile, A. (2014) *Independent Parliamentarians' Inquiry into the Operation and Effectiveness of the Youth Court*. Online, available at: www.ncb.org.uk/media/1148432/independent_ parliamentarians_inquiry_into_the_youth_court.pdf.

Crawford, A. and Newburn, T. (2003) *Youth Offending and Restorative Justice: Implementing Reform in Youth Justice*, Cullompton: Willan.

Drakeford, M. and McCarthy, K. (2000) 'Parents, responsibility and the new youth justice', in B. Goldson (ed.), (*The New Youth Justice*, Lyme Regis: Russell House, 96–114.

D v DPP (1995) 16 Cr App R (S) 1040

Field, S. (2015) 'Developing local cultures in criminal justice policy-making: The case of youth justice in Wales', in M. Wasik and S. Santatzoglou (eds), *The Management of Change in Criminal Justice: Who Knows Best?*, Basingstoke: Palgrave, 170–85.

Fox, D. and Arnull, E. (2013) *Social Work in the Youth Justice System: A Multidisciplinary Perspective*, Maidenhead: Open University Press.

Haines, K. (2000) 'Referral orders and youth offender panels', in B. Goldson (ed.), *The New Youth Justice*, Lyme Regis: Russell House, 58–80.

JM [2003] 1 Cr App R (S) 245

L [2013] 1 Cr App R (S) 317 (56)

Ministry of Justice (2013a) *Parenting Interventions: Addressing Youth Crime*. Online, available at: www.justice.gov.uk/youth-justice/prevention/parenting.

Ministry of Justice (2013b) *Transforming Youth Custody* (CP4 /2013), London: MOJ. Online, available at: www.gov.uk/government/uploads/system/uploads/attachment_ data/file/181588/transforming-youth-custody.pdf.

Ministry of Justice (2016) *Review of the Youth Justice System: An Interim Report of Emerging Findings*. Online, available at: www.gov.uk/government/publications/review-of-the-youth-justice-system.

Ministry of Justice/Youth Justice Board (2016) *Youth Justice Statistics 2014/15*. Online, available at: www.gov.uk/government/statistics/youth-justice-annual-statistics-2014-to-2015.

P [2006] 1 Cr App R (S)659

Pickford, J. and Dugmore, P. (2012) *Youth Justice and Social Work,* 2nd edn, London: Sage.

Q [2012] EWCA Crim 296

R(M) v Inner London Crown Court (2003) *The Times* 27 February

Rutherford, A. (1986) *Growing Out of Crime: Society and Young People in Trouble*, London: Penguin Books.

Sentencing Guidelines Council (2007) *Reduction in Sentence for a Guilty Plea*. Online, available at: http://sentencingcouncil.judiciary.gov.uk/docs/web_reduction_in_sentence_for_a_ guilty_plea.pdf.

Sentencing Guidelines Council (2009) *Overarching Principles: Sentencing Youths*. Online, available at: http://sentencingcouncil.judiciary.gov.uk/docs/web_overarching_principles_ sentencing_youths.pdf.

Sheffield Crown Court, ex parte Clarkson (1986) 8 Cr App R (S) 454

Souhami, A. (2008) 'Multi-agency practice: Experiences in the youth justice system', in S. Green, E. Lancaster and S. Feasey (eds), *Addressing Offending Behaviour: Context, Practice and Values*, Cullompton: Willan, 208–25.

Souhami, A. (2013) 'Youth justice', in A. Hucklesby and A. Wahadin (eds), *Criminal Justice*, 2nd edn, Oxford: OUP, 222–46.

Southampton Youth Court [2005] 2 Cr App R (S) 171

SP [2010] 1 Cr App R (S) 186

Staines, J. (2015) *Youth Justice*, London: Palgrave.

von Hirsch, A. and Ashworth A. (2004) 'Proportionate sentences for juvenile offenders', chapter 3 in *Proportionate Sentencing: Exploring the Principles*, Oxford: OUP, 35–49.

Wigzell, A. and Stanley, C. (2015) 'The Youth Court: Time for reform?', in M. Wasik and S. Santatzoglou (eds), *The Management of Change in Criminal Justice: Who Knows Best?*, Basingstoke: Palgrave, 241–58.

8

VULNERABLE AND INTIMIDATED WITNESSES: SPECIAL MEASURES, COMPETENCE, CONSENT AND CROSS-EXAMINATION

Penny Cooper

Introduction

It is a sad fact that some members of society, including the very young and those who are mentally or physically incapacitated, are particularly susceptible to abuse: an autistic man duped out of his disability benefits by his so-called friends; a deaf woman physically abused and kept locked up as a domestic slave; a very young boy stamped on by his 'carer'; a learning-disabled resident of a care home sexually abused by a member of staff. Unfortunately these are real examples from cases in the criminal justice system where the evidence of the victim has been crucial for a prosecution.

If the criminal justice system is working correctly, the police will investigate and gather the evidence, the right suspect will be charged and there will be a guilty plea or a finding of guilt after a trial. When a matter proceeds to a criminal trial, in the usual course of events, prosecution witnesses will be required to give their evidence orally and to be available for oral cross-examination. Where a witness is 'vulnerable' on account of their age, physical or mental disability or disorder or 'intimidated' through fear of distress, it raises the issue of what adjustments should be made to standard court procedures to enable the witness to give their best evidence.

This chapter examines and critically analyses the law and practice in relation to adjustments for 'vulnerable witnesses' and how 'competence' and 'consent' to cross-examination should be approached in criminal cases. It goes on to make recommendations regarding the social work approach to supporting a 'service user' who falls within the definition of 'vulnerable' or 'intimidated' witness. The focus is vulnerable witnesses as opposed to vulnerable defendants, which, although an equally important and challenging area, is outside the scope of this chapter.

Witnesses who are 'vulnerable' or 'intimidated'

In general there is no single agreed definition of who is 'vulnerable'.

> Any one single definition of vulnerability based on age, incapacity, impairment or medical condition may not reflect the nature of vulnerability that a particular individual may face at different times and in different environments.
>
> (Cooper et al., 2014)

The Department of Health *No Secrets* report in 2000 defined the vulnerable adult as a person:

> who is or may be in need of community care services by reason of mental or other disability, age or illness; and who is or may be unable to take care of him or herself, or unable to protect him or herself against significant harm or exploitation.
>
> (Department of Health, 2000: para. 2.4)

It can be argued that the term 'vulnerable' should be replaced with something else, though there is no obvious suitable alternative word or phrase:

> The paradox of employing the frame of 'vulnerability' is that it makes people more vulnerable. It does so by contributing to prejudices about disabled people though there is there is no obvious term to replace it.
>
> (Crowther, 2015)

However, within the criminal justice system, the term vulnerable witness has a specific meaning defined in legislation. 'Vulnerable' witnesses are defined in the legislation separately from, but alongside, 'intimidated' witnesses, though in reality the latter is really just another aspect of vulnerability.

Legislation sets out a range of 'special measures' for witnesses who are 'vulnerable' on the 'grounds of age or incapacity' (Youth Justice and Criminal Evidence Act 1999, s. 16) or 'intimated' on the 'grounds of fear or distress about testifying' (Youth Justice and Criminal Evidence Act 1999, s. 17).

Vulnerable witnesses eligible for special measures are those under 18 (Youth Justice and Criminal Evidence Act 1999, s. 16(1)(a)) or those for whom the 'quality' of their evidence is 'likely to be diminished' on account of their 'mental disorder' or 'significant impairment of intelligence and social functioning', or 'physical disability' or 'physical disorder' (Youth Justice and Criminal Evidence Act 1999, s. 16(1)(b)). Intimidated witnesses are eligible for special measures 'if the court is satisfied that the quality of evidence given by the witness is likely to be diminished by reason of fear or distress on the part of the witness in connection with testifying in the proceedings' (Youth Justice and Criminal Evidence Act 1999, s. 17(1)).

If a witness falls within the definition of vulnerable or intimidated, the court must determine if a special measure or a combination of special measures will 'be likely to improve the quality of evidence given by the witness' (Youth Justice and Criminal Evidence Act 1999, s. 19(2)). Only the court can put in place special measures by making a direction to that effect in relation to the witness's testimony.

'Special measures' are set out in legislation (Youth Justice and Criminal Evidence Act 1999, s. 23–30). The range of special measures is:

- A screen placed around the witness so that they cannot see the defendant

- A live-link so that witness gives evidence through a televised link to the courtroom (including with a supporter if the court directs)

- Evidence given in private when the judge excludes from the court members of the public and the press (except for one named person to represent the press)

- Removal of wigs and gowns by judges and barristers

- A video-recorded interview admitted as the witness's evidence in chief

- Pre-recorded cross-examination (though currently only a pilot scheme and not widely available)

- Examination of a witness through an intermediary

- Giving evidence using aids to communication (such as an electronic device or picture boards) or technique (such as signing).

All these special measures are potentially available to any 'vulnerable' witness (Youth Justice and Criminal Evidence Act 1999, s. 18(1)). However, only the first six (above) are potentially available to the 'intimidated'; intermediaries and aids to communication are not available to intimidated witness (Youth Justice and Criminal Evidence Act 1999, s. 18(2)).

Special measures can be applied for by the prosecution or defence for their witness or can be directed by the court of its own motion. The legislation also contains further provisions, for instance, to protect a witness from cross-examination by the accused in person, restrictions on evidence and questions about complainant's sexual behaviour, and restrictions on the reporting by the media. Further detailed guidance is available from the Crown Prosecution website (CPS, 2015).

In addition, the judge has a responsibility to ensure that a trial is fair and can utilise inherent powers to adapt the trial process. The Criminal Procedure Rules state that the court must take 'every reasonable step' to facilitate the participation of any person (Criminal Procedure Rules 2015, rule 3.8(4) (a)–(b)).

Adjustments other than the 'special measures', sometimes informally referred to as 'extra special measures', may also be directed by the judge when necessary, as these two examples from actual cases demonstrate (see Cooper et al., 2014):

Case Example One

The witness was taking a significant amount of medication to control psychiatric symptoms. Her ability to give evidence was much improved in the afternoon when her medication had the chance to start working and her mental state was most stable. It was scheduled so that she gave her testimony only in the afternoons.

Case Example Two

The judge allowed a young witness to take a very small tent into the live-link room which was not visible on the TV link screen in the courtroom. The witness was allowed to have short 'time-out' breaks (usually of just thirty seconds) in the tent when her anxiety peaked, but was not at the point where she needed a full break from giving her evidence. While the witness took this short break the live-link was temporarily turned off and the court waited until she was ready to continue.

Jacobson et al. conducted 20-month qualitative study of the Crown Court, including extensive interviews with witnesses and other court users and observations of crown court hearings:

Victims and witnesses at court take centre stage only for the (usually relatively short) period of time when they give evidence in a trial. Even at this point, they are seldom granted the freedom to tell their story in full, in the manner they wish ... The clearest divide in the courtroom, therefore, is not victim and defendant, or prosecution and defence, as might be expected; but between the legal professionals and the lay court users.

(Jacobson et al., 2014: 83)

Arguably *all* those who enter the criminal justice system as witnesses are vulnerable in the sense that they may be daunted by unfamiliar environment and language. This witness vulnerability (in the general sense) is likely to be more acute for one who is very young or physically or mentally incapacitated, or for an intimidated witness.

Professional duties to the witnesses

Every witness must be treated as an individual, and when they are eligible for special measures and wish to have them, the party calling the witness should apply for them. However solicitors' and barristers' respective codes of conduct, the basis of their regulatory framework for professional conduct, provide general guidance on the outcomes they must achieve only in respect of their 'clients', not 'witnesses'.

Solicitors must make sure that *clients* are treated 'fairly' and 'make reasonable adjustments to ensure that disabled *clients* ... are not placed at a substantial disadvantage compared to those who are not disabled' (Solicitors Regulation Authority, 2011). The code of conduct for solicitors also mandates they must be responsive to clients' needs, 'especially those who are vulnerable' (Solicitors Regulation Authority, 2011). Barristers, regulated by the Bar Standards Board, must make sure '[c]are is given to ensure that the interests of vulnerable clients are taken into account and their needs are met' (The Bar Standards Board, 2015).

The solicitors' representative body has produced guidance in the form of a 'practice note' which says they should 'adapt their practices to identify and meet the needs of vulnerable clients' (Law Society Practice Note, 2015). Their representative body for barristers said in 2013 that it 'encourages the creation and implementation of a "required training programme"', though none is in place at the time of writing (Press Release 2013). The Advocacy Training Council has produced best-practice guidance for all advocates dealing with vulnerable witnesses' (The Advocates Gateway, 2015).

The regulatory codes for barristers and solicitors place duties on them to treat *clients* fairly and ensure that their needs are met; however, there is no duty in respect of witnesses. This represents a serious lacuna since in the criminal justice system a witness is not usually the client of the barrister or the solicitor. However, the General Social Care Council places duties on social workers which include protecting the rights and promoting the interests of service users (The General Social Care Council, 2010). When their service user is a witness, the social worker needs to protect their rights as a witness and help to promote them.

Victim and witness rights

If the witness is the 'victim' of the crime, he or she is entitled to a minimum level of service from the criminal justice agencies including the police, the Crown Prosecution Service and the Witness Care Units. These entitlements are set out in the Code of Practice for Victims of Crime (Ministry of Justice, 2013a). A victim (more precisely, in law, the 'alleged victim' of a crime unless and until the facts of the crime are proved) has a number of entitlements including the right to 'arrange a court familiarisation visit and enter the court through a different entrance from the suspect and sit in a separate waiting area where possible' and to '[m]eet the CPS Prosecutor and ask him or her questions about the court process' (Ministry of Justice, 2013a).

A service user may not be the 'victim' but instead may be a bystander witness to a crime. For them there is 'The Witness Charter' which sets out 'standards of care for witnesses in the criminal justice system' (The Ministry of Justice, 2013b). It includes this:

> The police, Witness Care Unit and the prosecution/defence lawyers are responsible for identifying, at an early stage and throughout the process, whether you are a vulnerable or intimidated witness. They are also responsible for discussing with you whether you might benefit from any special measures.

Unlike the Code of Practice for Victims of Crime, lawyers and the criminal justice agencies are not legally required to meet these standards for witness care. According to Victim Support, 'in practice most of the people and organisations you deal with as a witness will meet and abide by the standards set out in the Charter' (Victim Support, 2015). It follows that social workers should recognise when their service user is a 'victim' or a 'witness' and refer to the support to which they are either entitled (in the case of a victim) or can expect (in the case of a witness).

Identifying a 'vulnerable' or 'intimidated' witness

In March 2014, Surrey County Council completed the Serious Case Review (SCR) into the death of Mrs Andrade (Brown, 2014). Mrs Andrade gave evidence in 2013 at Manchester Crown Court in the trial of her former music teacher, Michael Brewer. A few days after giving evidence and being cross-examined about her allegations of sexual abuse by the defendant, Mrs Andrade took her own life. The SCR noted that no one shared with the Witness Service the existing concerns about the witness's serious mental health condition, and therefore the Witness Service was unable to carry out a detailed needs assessment or to monitor the risk the witness presented to herself.

The court must take account of the views expressed by the witness in determining whether a witness falls into the category of being eligible for special measures (Youth Justice and Criminal Evidence Act 1999, s. 16(4) and s. 17(3)), notwithstanding that the SCR recommended judges should be 'proactive' in putting in place special measures for vulnerable witnesses even where that witness, as Mrs Andrade had, refuses them.

Ultimately it is the judge's role to decide on special measures, but the judge can only do that if the witness or someone on their behalf has alerted the relevant professionals in the case. The relevant professional/s might be, depending on the stage that the case has reached, the police officer, or if they are not available, the Crown Prosecution Service (CPS), Witness Care Unit staff, Witness Service or even the judge's clerk.

'Competence' to give evidence

Irrespective of vulnerability, fear or distress, the law says that in order to give evidence in court, a witness must be 'competent' to do so. Witness 'competence' is determined by the judge (Youth Justice and Criminal Evidence Act 1999, s. 54(1)). Parliament has clearly and helpfully set out the test for witness competence in criminal cases; it begins with the presumption that 'all persons are (whatever their age) competent to give evidence' (Youth Justice and Criminal Evidence Act 1999, s. 53(1)). However:

> A person is not competent to give evidence in criminal proceedings if it appears to the court that he is not a person who is able to –
>
> (a) understand questions put to him as a witness, and
>
> (b) give answers to them which can be understood. (Youth Justice and Criminal Evidence Act 99, s. 53(3))

This test was considered in 2010 by the then Lord Chief Justice in the watershed case of *R v B*. The Court of Appeal judgement makes clear that neither age nor vulnerability render a witness incompetent to testify:

> There are no presumptions or preconceptions. The witness need not understand the special importance that the truth should be told in court, and the witness need not understand every single question or give a readily understood answer to every question. Many competent adult witnesses would fail such a competency test. Dealing with it broadly and fairly, provided the witness can understand the questions put to him and can also provide understandable answers, he or she is competent.
>
> (*R v B*: 38)

Competence goes to the ability of the witness to understand the questions asked and answer them. It is not the same as credibility: 'At the stage when the competency question is determined the judge is not deciding whether a witness is or will be telling the truth and giving accurate evidence. Provided the witness is competent, the weight to be attached to the evidence is for the jury [or Magistrates if the case is being decided by them]' (*R v B*: 41). The witness might understand questions and give understandable answers (a competent witness), but whether they are going to be believed (a credible witness) is quite a separate matter and must be left to the judge in the magistrates' court or the jury in the Crown Court.

The witness's competence must be judged in light of any special measures that are to be put in place to support them to give their best evidence. Therefore it would be wrong, for instance, to assume that a witness who is fearful of seeing the defendant and profoundly deaf could not be a competent witness.

So long as they are able to give evidence with such adjustments as are necessary such as a screen so that they cannot see the defendant, and with a sign language interpreter so that they can understand the questions and give answers that can be understood, they are a competent witness. It would also be wrong to assume that deploying special measures for a witness mean the witness is less likely to be believed; there is no evidence that that is the case.

In *R v Watts* (2010) a vulnerable witness was assisted by an intermediary (see Cooper et al., 2015: 417–432) and aids to communication (Youth Justice and Criminal Evidence Act 1999, s. 30). To communicate her evidence to the police and in court, she gave evidence supported by an intermediary through 'the medium of her electronic communication device' which took the form of a tablet computer mounted on her wheelchair, onto which had been programmed a number of pages relating to different topics. Each page took the form of a grid on which were drawings, picture or symbols and a square for Yes or No. The defendant, a former care worker, was convicted of a number of allegations of sexual assault on four profoundly disabled women who were residents in the residential care home at which he worked.

Intermediaries have been available in all police and CPS areas since 2007 (Cooper and Wurtzel, 2014: 39–61). Their remit is now far wider than was originally envisaged. They do not act as interpreters. They are not witness supporters, and they are not expert witnesses. They assess the witness's communication needs; they advise the police how to interview the witness and help the plan the interview; they provide a comprehensive report for court regarding the type, style and length of questioning; they advise on the most appropriate special measures for that witness; they play an active part at the witness familiarisation visit prior to trial; they advise the court at the Ground Rules Hearing when the judge determines what adjustments need to be made to traditional questioning; they stand or sit next to the witness as they give testimony to intervene if needed to facilitate questioning and answering. (See P. Cooper, P. Backen and R. Marchant (2015) 'Getting to grips with Ground Rules Hearings – a checklist for judges, advocates and intermediaries', *Criminal Law Review*, 6: 417–32.)

In 2014 the Ministry of Justice recorded over 200 requests a month, on average, for an intermediary. Inevitably, over the years the intermediary special measure has become more widely known and appreciated, and the procedure for using their services (Cooper, 2015) has become more established. More recently, the demand has outstripped the supply and over 100 more were recruited and trained in 2015.

Consent to being interviewed by the police

Guidance exists for the police with the aim of ensuring witnesses are treated fairly at interview stage, including checking that they consent to being interviewed. 'Achieving Best Evidence in Criminal Proceedings Guidance on interviewing victims and witnesses, and guidance on using special measures'(Ministry of Justice, 2011) (ABE) states that it is 'a general principle that all witnesses should freely consent to be interviewed and to have the interview recorded on video'. If the police's aim is to pursue the case through to conviction of the offender, it is axiomatic that they need the witness's consent not only to recording their ABE interview but also to what might follow in the event of a not guilty plea, giving evidence at court. Giving evidence includes giving evidence in chief (the witness tells their version of events unless the court directs that a video recording of the witness's interview is played instead) and being cross-examined (when the witness is challenged on their version of events).

If the suspect is charged, the DVD recording of a witness's ABE interview, or their written witness statement if it is not recorded, will be disclosed to the defendant's solicitors. In the case of a DVD recording of an interview, if this special measure is granted, the recording may be used by the prosecution in place of the witness's 'live' evidence in chief (Youth Justice and Criminal Evidence Act 1999, s. 27).

When a witness's evidence is contested by the other party, they are usually required to attend court to be cross-examined live either in the witness box or over the court TV link. Hunter et al. (2013) also raise doubts about the extent to which witnesses are informed about the case and how it will proceed. Anecdotal reports from Registered Intermediaries suggest that police officers do not always explain to the vulnerable witnesses they assist that their interview will be disclosed and that they may be required to go to court to be cross-examined.

Concerns about witnesses not being properly consulted for consent are not new. A CPS inspection report on 'Disclosure of medical records and counselling notes' in 2013 showed lack of consultation with witnesses about disclosure of their medical records to the defence. The research was on case files in general, not simply those with vulnerable witnesses:

> It was difficult to tell whether the complainant's consent to disclosure [of medical records and counselling notes] to the defence had been obtained because in the majority of cases we could not see anything in the file to show this. With some exceptions, prosecutors are not asking the police to approach the complainant for consent, even where the original consent is limited. This means that in some cases it is possible that consent to disclosure is never obtained.
>
> (HM CPS Inspectorate, 2013)

It is possible that witnesses' participation is assumed. Consent may be glossed over by police officers who fear that if the process is explained, the witness will withdraw. This may mean that in some cases, witness consent, which it is suggested should always be explicit, is at best implied and at worst non-existent.

There are online resources with which a social worker ought to be familiar and should signpost to their service user if they need information about being a witness and going to court. This would complement, not replace, the obligations on the police to explain the process and seek consent from a witness.

Capacity to consent to being interviewed as a witness

A person can only consent if they have the capacity to do so. Capacity is a separate issue to competence (discussed above). The law on adult capacity to make decisions is contained in the Mental Capacity Act 2005 (MCA '05). Capacity means being regarded as having the mental ability to make a decision. The MCA '05 creates a statutory presumption that a person has capacity to make decision with regard to the relevant issue (one of the principles of the MCA '05 set out in section 1).

Imagine a social work service user, let's call him 'Lennie', is vulnerable on account of autism and he has been the victim of a vicious criminal attack. The police want to speak to Lennie though he is still in hospital receiving medical treatment. Lennie's social worker does not think it would be in Lennie's best interests to be interviewed by the police. She fears he may become more anxious and distressed having to recount what happened to him. If the police officer is keen to conduct the interview and pursue their investigation, whose view should prevail?

It is necessary to start with the principle that Lennie is 'assumed to have capacity unless it is established that he lacks capacity' (Mental Capacity Act 2005, s. 1(2)). Lennie would be considered to lack capacity to make a particular decision only if he is unable to make a decision for himself because of an impairment of or disturbance in the functioning of the mind or brain. Lennie has autism which could, depending on how he is affected by the condition at that particular time, be considered such an impairment. However, this impairment would have to be the reason why he is unable to make a decision for himself. This is shown if he is unable to:

(a)   understand the information relevant to the decision,

(b)   retain that information,

(c)   use or weigh that information as part of the process of making the decision, or

(d)   communicate his decision (whether by talking, using sign language or any other means). (Mental Capacity Act 2005, s. 3(1))

Among medical practitioners there is notable lack of awareness and understanding of the MCA '05 (House of Lords Select Committee, 2014) and this may be true, probably to an even greater extent, among police officers. There is also evidence that a lack of capacity is sometimes assumed 'in order to justify a decision made by the local authority, which was often resource-led' (House of Lords Select Committee, 2014: 36).

Lennie must be given the information about being interviewed as a witness 'in a way that is appropriate to his circumstances (using simple language, visual aids or any other means)' (Mental Capacity Act 2005, s. 3(2)). The MCA '05 also tells us that we cannot treat Lenny as being 'unable to make a decision unless all practicable steps to help him to do so have been taken without success' (Mental Capacity Act 2005, s. 1(3)). Lennie may for instance need visual aids (see Mattison, 2015) to help him make a choice about whether to be interviewed.

If Lennie says he wants to go ahead and be interviewed, his social worker has no legal right to stop this purely because they think he is being unwise. The presumption of his capacity would have to be rebutted on medical or other evidence. Lennie 'is not to be treated as unable to make a decision merely because he makes an unwise decision' (Mental Capacity Act 2005, s. 1(4)). 'Just because a decision is unwise does not mean that a person has lost mental capacity' (Cobb J in *Wandsworth Clinical Commissioning Group v IA (By the Official Solicitor As His Litigation Friend)* [2014] EWHC 990 (COP) at para. 34.)

The law says if a person lacks capacity, their best interests must be determined (Mental Capacity Act 2004, s. 1(5)). If Lennie does not have capacity to make the decision about being interviewed as a witness by the police, ABE guidance to the interviewing police officer states that they must 'take account of the principles set out in the Mental Capacity Act 2005 and the Code of Practice that accompanies it' and 'only proceed if it is considered to be in the witness's best interests' (Ministry of Justice, 2011: para. 2.99). It continues, the 'matters to be taken into account (as specified in Section 1(6) of the Mental Capacity Act 2005) include: The person's past and present wishes and feelings; The beliefs and values that would be likely to influence the person's decision if they had capacity; and [T]he other factors that the person would be likely to consider if they were able to do so'.

This decision about whether or not it is in Lennie's best interests to be ABE interviewed potentially creates a tension between the police officer, who has a legitimate aim of detecting crime and protecting the public, and family, medical and social care professionals who have an equally legitimate aim of protecting and promoting Lennie's health and well-being.

Resources available to support and assist Lennie in the ABE interview, such as a witness supporter (perhaps a member of his care team or family) and an intermediary, would be relevant to the decision about his best interests. However, the decision must not be resource-led.

Under the Code of Practice 2008 which accompanies the MCA '05, an 'advocate might be useful in providing support for the person who lacks capacity to make a decision in the process of working out their best interests, if: the person who lacks capacity has no close family or friends to take an interest in their welfare, and they do not qualify for an [Independent Mental Capacity Advocate]; family members disagree about the person's best interest; family members and professionals disagree' etc. (Gov.uk, 2016).

In the event of a dispute about Lennie's capacity to consent to a police ABE interview or where his best interests lie, an application would need to be made seeking a capacity and a best-interests decision from the Court of Protection.

Consent to cross-examination

An historic case from the House of Lords called *Browne v Dunn* decided that 'if it is to be suggested that the evidence in chief of any witness is false then the witness must be challenged in cross-examination' (as described by counsel in *Wade & Anor v British Sky Broadcasting Ltd*). Cross-examination is the opposing party's opportunity to challenge the witness's account, which can include testing the witness's accuracy (for example, asking questions about their eyesight or memory), testing their certainty (for example, putting their client's version of events to the witness) or challenging their motives (for example, suggesting to them reasons why they would lie).

Even robust adult witnesses, let alone the vulnerable and intimidated, can experience difficulty understanding questions in cross-examination. Recently at The Old Bailey (the Central Criminal Court, London) the author observed an advocate ask an adult male witness who had seen his mother arguing with a neighbour outside their home, 'What was it that passed between them?' The witness hesitated for a moment and then said, 'A fence'. The advocate realised what had happened and rephrased his question: 'What were they saying to each other?'

Research published in 2013, based on interviews with witnesses, concluded:

> Cross-examination was cited by witnesses as a particularly challenging aspect of the court experience; and the formal or legal language of the courtroom also posed difficulties for some. Witnesses were appreciative of judges' interventions to ensure they understood a barrister's questioning or to prevent overly hostile or aggressive questioning.
>
> (Hunter et al., 2013).

In cross-examination, special care must be taken with those who are vulnerable: 'the trial process must cater for the needs of witnesses' (*R v F* [2013]: para. 25). To that end, the Attorney General launched The Advocate's Gateway (co-founded by the author and supported by the Advocacy Training Council) in April 2013, and the 'toolkits' (primarily aimed at advocates but of wide practical assistance) are now recognised as best-practice advice on questioning vulnerable people in court. (3D.7 *Criminal Practice Directions*, [2015] EWCA Crim 1567.)

The former Director of Public Prosecutions (Head of the CPS) Sir Keir Starmer QC has spoken of poor victim experiences in the criminal justice system such that some witnesses would not be willing to give evidence a second time (Starmer, 2014). Although, see also Hunter et al.: 'almost all of our interviewees stated that they would be willing to give evidence again in a criminal case' (Hunter et al., 2013: 5). Less pessimistically, Hunter et al. found that witnesses' 'overall feelings about the court process were shaped both by their treatment within it and by the outcome of the case' (Hunter et al., 2013) and recommended that witnesses have 'access to clear and consistent information about the court process'.

Let us suppose that Lennie is interviewed by the police and some time later he is asked to be a witness at court. We can draw upon a principle established in the Court of Protection about capacity to make a decision about future residence: 'it is not necessary for a person to demonstrate a capacity to understand and weigh up every detail of the respective options, but merely the salient factors'. Lennie should be able to weigh up the 'salient factors' about going to court or not going to court as a witness. Thus he should have access to information about what is likely to happen at court, including the possibility of special measures, though not 'every detail' (*KK v STCC* [2012]: 69, Baker J) of what will happen at court.

If Lennie does not have the capacity to make a decision, whether or not he gives evidence depends on what is deemed to be in his best interests – note, not what is in the prosecution's, the criminal justice system's or even society's best interest, but in Lennie's.

Summary

What should be considered by a social worker if their service user is a prospective witness in a criminal case and is 'vulnerable' by virtue for age or incapacity or 'intimidated' by reason of fear or distress about giving evidence?

At the police interview stage:

1 Has the service user's consent been sought to being interviewed as a witness?

2 Has the salient information about being interviewed as a witness been communicated in a way that meets the witness's communication needs?

3 If the witness does not have capacity to consent to being interviewed, is it in their best interests?

4 What support would they need to communicate their evidence in a police interview?

In anticipation of a trial, very similar questions should be asked:

5 Has the service user's consent been sought to being a witness at court?

6 Has the salient information about going to court as a witness been communicated in a way that meets the witness's communication needs?

7 If the witness does not have capacity to consent to going to court as a witness, is it in their best interests?

8 What support would they need to communicate their evidence at court?

Conclusion

Being a witness is not solely or even primarily about giving evidence in court in the witness box, though that is often the impression given by film and TV programmes. Being a witness as a victim or bystander always involves a police interview and a wait, possibly for months, before going to court to give evidence if the defendant pleads not guilty.

A social worker should be there to support their service user through the police investigation, in the run up to, during the trial and in the aftermath. The social worker's responsibilities include making make sure that:

- What the service user is being asked to do is properly explained and their consent is sought

- The service user had capacity to consent to the interview/ being called a witness or if they lack capacity that it only proceeds if it is in their best interests

- And in the case of vulnerable and intimidated witnesses, the interviewing officer and lawyers take into account the services user's needs and apply for 'special measures' as necessary.

The criminal justice system has made great strides in the last decade thanks to legislation providing a presumption of witness competence and a range of special measures for those classed as vulnerable or intimidated. There is also guidance for solicitors and barristers to help them acquire the skills and knowledge to work with vulnerable witnesses in the criminal justice system.

However, other areas of the legal system, such as the civil courts, family court and the Court of Protection, which have a significant proportion of vulnerable and intimidated witnesses, have no such legislation. They lag woefully behind. Special measures and other arrangements are, at best, ad hoc. Social workers are likely to find that their vulnerable and intimated service users face even greater obstacles as witnesses trying to give their best evidence in those courts.

References

Brown, H. (2014) *The Death of Mrs A – A Serious Case Review*, Kingston Upon Thames: Surrey County Council Safeguarding Adults Board.

Browne v Dunn (1894) 6R67 HL

Cooper, P. et al. (2014) *Toolkit 10 Identifying Vulnerability in Witnesses and Defendants*, London: ATC. Online, available at: www.theadvocatesgateway.org/images/toolkits/10identifyingvulnerabilityinwitnessesanddefendants100714.pdf.

Cooper, P. and Wurtzel, D. (2014) 'Better the second time around? Department of Justice Registered Intermediaries schemes and lessons from England and Wales', *Northern Ireland Legal Quarterly*, 65(1): 39–61.

Cooper, P. (2015) *Intermediaries: Step by Step*. Online, available at: www. theadvocatesgateway.org/images/toolkits/16intermediariesstepbystep060315.pdf.

Cooper, P., Backen, P. and Marchant, R. (2015) 'Getting to grips with Ground Rules Hearings – a checklist for judges, advocates and intermediaries', *Criminal Law Review*, 6: 417–32.

CPS (2015) *Special Measures*. Online, available at: www.cps.gov.uk/legal/s_to_u/special_measures/.

Crowther, N. (2015) *It's High Time We Abandoned the Language of Vulnerability*. Online, available at: https://makingrightsmakesense.wordpress.com/2015/08/05/its-high-time-we-abandoned-the-language-of-vulnerability-2/.

Department of Health (2000) *No Secrets: Guidance on Developing and Implementing Multi-agency Policies and Procedures to Protect Vulnerable Adults from Abuse*, London: DoH, para. 2.4.

Gov.uk (2016) *Mental Capacity Act Code of Conduct*. Online, available at: www.gov.uk/government/publications/mental-capacity-act-code-of-practice.

HM CPS Inspectorate (2013) *Disclosure of Medical Records and Counselling Notes*, London: HM CPS Inspectorate. Online, available at: www.justiceinspectorates.gov.uk/crown-prosecution-service/wp-content/uploads/sites/3/2014/04/DOMRACN_thm_Jul13_rpt.pdf.

House of Lords Select Committee on the Mental Capacity Act 2005 (2014) 'Mental Capacity Act 2005: post-legislative scrutiny'. Online, available at: www.publications. parliament.uk/pa/ld201314/ldselect/ldmentalcap/139/139.pdf.

Hunter, G., Jacobson, J. and Kirby, A. (2013). *Out of the Shadows*. Online, available at: www.victimsupport.org.uk/sites/default/files/Out%20of%20the%20shaddows.pdf Date accessed 10 April 2014.

Jacobson, J., Hunter, G. and Kirby, A. (2014) *Inside Crown Court*, Bristol: Policy Press.

KK v STCC [2012] EWHC 2136 (COP) at para. 69 (Baker J)

Law Society Practice Note (2015) *Meeting the Needs of Vulnerable Clients*. Online, available at: http://lawsociety.org.uk/support-services/advice/practice-notes/meeting-the-needs-of-vulnerable-clients-july-2015/ Date accessed 27 September 2015.

Mattison, M. et al. (2015) *Toolkit 14 Using Communication Aids in the Criminal Justice System*, London: ATC.

Ministry of Justice (2011) *Achieving Best Evidence in Criminal Proceedings: Guidance on Interviewing Victims and Witnesses, and Guidance on Using Special Measures*, London: MOJ.

Ministry of Justice (2013a) *Code of Practice for Victims of Crime*, London: MOJ.

Ministry of Justice (2013b) *The Witness Charter: Standards of Care for Witnesses in the Criminal Justice System*, London: MOJ.

Press Release (2013) *Bar Council Encourages the Creation and Implementation of a 'Required Training Programme' for Cross Examination of Vulnerable*. Online, available at: www. barcouncil.org.uk/media-centre/news-and-press-releases/2013/july/bar-council-encourages-creation-of-a-'required-training-programme'-for-cross-examination-of-vulnerable-witnesses/ Date accessed 27 September 2015.

R v B [2010] EWCA Crim 4

R v F [2013] EWCA Crim 424, para. 25 citing R v B [2010] EWCA Crim 4

R v Watts (Rev 3) [2010] EWCA Crim 1824

Solicitors Regulation Authority (2011) *SRA Code of Conduct*, London: SRA.

Starmer, K. (2014) 'Britain's criminal justice system fails the vulnerable. We need a Victims' Law', *The Guardian*, 03 February. Online, available at: www.theguardian.com/commentisfree/2014/feb/03/britain-criminal-justice-system-victims-law-public-prosecutions.

The Bar Standards Board (2015) *The Bar Standards Handbook*, 9th edn, London: BSB.

The General Social Care Council (2010) *Codes of Practice for Social Care Workers*, London: GSCC.

The Advocates Gateway (2015) *Responding to Communication Needs in the Justice System*. Online, available at: www.theadvocatesgateway.org/.

Victim Support (2015) *Your Rights as a Witness*. Online, available at: www.victimsupport.org.uk/help-witnesses/your-journey/your-rights-witness.

Wade & Anor v British Sky Broadcasting Ltd [2014] EWHC 634

Wandsworth Clinical Commissioning Group v IA (By the Official Solicitor As His Litigation Friend) [2014] EWHC 990 (COP) at para. 34 (Cobb J)

9

HUMAN TRAFFICKING AND SOCIAL WORK LAW

Tom Obokata

Introduction

Trafficking of human beings is a global problem. It has been estimated that approximately 140,000 people are trafficked into or within Europe each year (United Nations Office of Drug and Crimes, 2010: 7). Of these, only 10,374 have been identified by the relevant authorities in 2013 alone (US Department of State 2014: 45, 61), suggesting that the vast majority of victims are not properly identified in practice. Within the United Kingdom, a total of 2,340 victims from 96 countries were identified in 2014 (National Crime Agency, 2014: 1). The clandestine and sophisticated nature of human trafficking means that the actual number of victims is likely to be higher than these statistics. Upon arrival at their destinations, these victims are exploited in a number of ways. While female victims are predominantly exploited sexually, male victims are trafficked for the purpose of labour exploitation (Eurostat, 2015) in sectors including agriculture, construction, catering and food processing. The annual profits generated from sexual and labour exploitation amounts to $150 billion (International Labour Organization, 2014: 13), highlighting that human trafficking and exploitation are lucrative businesses for criminals.

Human trafficking is not merely a criminal justice issue. It is also a human rights issue, as its victims experience gross violations of their fundamental rights and freedoms before, during and after their journey. This means that their protection must constitute an integral part of an overall anti-trafficking strategy, in addition to promoting a more effective criminal justice response (e.g. prohibition, prosecution and punishment). The role played by local authorities, including social workers, becomes extremely important in this regard, as the primary obligation to protect trafficked victims rests upon the public authorities. The main purpose of this chapter is to provide a critical assessment of the current legislative and other measures to identify and protect victims of human trafficking in the United Kingdom. It begins by exploring the definitions of human trafficking in national, regional and international legislation in order to clarify what this crime entails. The chapter then identifies key obligations relating to victim protection established by these legislation. Finally, it provides an analysis of state practice in the United Kingdom, with particular reference to the role of local authorities, including social workers. The main conclusion reached is that, although the United Kingdom has made some progress in identifying and protecting victims of human trafficking, there is much scope for improvement.

What is human trafficking?

Terms such as human trafficking, migrant smuggling and irregular migration have been used interchangeably in the past, creating some confusion on the part of policymakers, the media and the general public. However, there is now clearer understanding of what human trafficking entails at national, regional and international levels. A starting point is the legal definition provided by an international treaty known as the Protocol to Prevent, Suppress and Punish Trafficking in Persons, Especially Women and Children (2237 UNTS 319) (Trafficking Protocol) which is attached to the United Nations Convention against Transnational Organised Crime 2000 (2225 UNTS 209). According to Article 3 of this Protocol:

> Trafficking in persons shall mean the recruitment, transportation, transfer, harbouring or receipt of persons, by means of the threat or use of force or other forms of coercion, of abduction, of fraud, of deception, of the abuse of power or of a position of vulnerability or of the giving or receiving of payments or benefits to achieve the consent of a person having control over another person, for the purpose of exploitation.

There are three key elements in this definition: i) act, ii) means and iii) purpose. The first element refers to the main conduct of trafficking, that is, recruitment, transportation, transfer, harbouring and/or receipt of trafficked people. The second element explains how these victims are transported. Traffickers use coercion and/or deception to traffic people from one place to another. Forcible abduction is a fairly common practice for vulnerable victims such as women and children, and many victims are also deceived as to what they are supposed to do after they reach their destinations. Because of these, it is generally accepted that there is no genuine consent on the part of victims in the trafficking process. The second element is closely interlinked with the first, as they both constitute the *actus reus* of human trafficking. Finally, the third 'purpose' element refers to the reasons why people are trafficked. In this regard, the Trafficking Protocol further stipulates that 'exploitation shall include, at a minimum, the exploitation of the prostitution of others or other forms of sexual exploitation, forced labour or services, slavery or practices similar to slavery, servitude or the removal of organs'. A crucial point to highlight here is that, contrary to the popular perception which links trafficking with sexual slavery of women and girls, men (and boys) are also targeted by traffickers for exploitation in non-sex sectors.

Technically speaking, actual exploitation is not part of the *actus reus* of human trafficking. This is so because the purpose element relates to the *mens rea*, ulterior intention in particular. A good analogy is the offence of burglary in England and Wales. This offence is complete as soon as one enters into premises as a trespasser with intention to steal, even when they do not actually steal anything (Theft Act 1968, s. 9(1)(a)). An important consideration here is what one is thinking at the time of entry. By analogy, the above definition suggests that trafficking is established when a trafficker moves people from one place to another with intention to exploit them later or with full knowledge that they will be exploited by others at their destinations. When trafficked victims are actually exploited, that would be regarded as a separate offence of slavery or forced labour (sexual or otherwise), or alternatively as an aggravating factor which would increase the level of punishment. In any event, the United Kingdom ratified the Trafficking Protocol (9 February 2006) and therefore is legally obliged to fulfil obligations established by this instrument.

Regionally, there are two main legal instruments on human trafficking applicable to the United Kingdom. The first is the Council of Europe Convention on Action against Trafficking in Human Beings 2005 (ETS No. 197) (Council of Europe Convention). Article 4 provides the following definition of human trafficking:

> 'Trafficking in human beings' shall mean the recruitment, transportation, transfer, harbouring or receipt of persons, by means of the threat or use of force or other forms of coercion, of abduction, of fraud, of deception, of the abuse of power or of a position of vulnerability or of the giving or receiving of payments or benefits to achieve the consent of a person having control over another person, for the purpose of exploitation. Exploitation shall include, at a minimum, the exploitation of the prostitution of others or other forms of sexual exploitation, forced labour or services, slavery or practices similar to slavery, servitude or the removal of organs.

It becomes immediately apparent that this definition is in line with the aforementioned Trafficking Protocol. In addition, the United Kingdom is also bound by the EU Directive on Preventing and Combating Trafficking in Human Beings and Protecting Its Victims ([2011] OJ L 101/1) (EU Human Trafficking Directive), adopted under the Treaty on the Functioning of the European Union ([2012] OJ C 326/1). According to Article 1, trafficking means:

> The recruitment, transportation, transfer, harbouring or reception of persons, including the exchange or transfer of control over those persons, by means of the threat or use of force or other forms of coercion, of abduction, of fraud, of deception, of the abuse of power or of a position of vulnerability or of the giving or receiving of payments or benefits to achieve the consent of a person having control over another person, for the purpose of exploitation.

Exploitation shall include, as a minimum, the exploitation of the prostitution of others or other forms of sexual exploitation, forced labour or services, including begging, slavery or practices similar to slavery, servitude, or the exploitation of criminal activities, or the removal of organs.

Once again, the EU definition is almost identical to the one provided by the Trafficking Protocol.

At this stage, it is useful to analyse whether the United Kingdom has adopted a definition of human trafficking in line with these international and European instruments. The most recent legislation on this crime is the Modern Slavery Act 2015. It consolidated the previous statutes applicable to human trafficking and exploitation, namely the Sexual Offences Act 2003 (trafficking for sexual exploitation), the Asylum and Immigration (Treatment of Claimants, etc.) Act 2004 (trafficking for labour exploitation), and the Coroners and Justice Act 2009 (slavery and forced labour). According to section 2 of the Modern Slavery Act 2015:

(1)   A person commits an offence if the person arranges or facilitates the travel of another person ('V') with a view to V being exploited.

(2)   It is irrelevant whether V consents to the travel (whether V is an adult or a child).

(3)   A person may in particular arrange or facilitate V's travel by recruiting V, transporting or transferring V, harbouring or receiving V, or transferring or exchanging control over V.

(4)   A person arranges or facilitates V's travel with a view to V being exploited only if—
      (a)   the person intends to exploit V (in any part of the world) during or after the travel, or
      (b)   the person knows or ought to know that another person is likely to exploit V (in any part of the world) during or after the travel.

Section 3 further stipulates that 'exploitation' will include slavery, servitude, forced labour, sexual exploitation, removal of organs, and securing services by force/threat or from children and vulnerable persons. Taken together, the trafficking definition under the Modern Slavery Act 2015 is similar to the ones provided in international and European instruments. One noticeable difference, however, is the lack of the element of coercion and/or deception for the *actus reus* of this crime. This makes the definition somewhat wider, in that those who consent to be trafficked are also covered provided that traffickers intend to exploit them or know that they would be exploited by others.

It is important to highlight here that the Modern Slavery Act 2015 does not extend to Northern Ireland and Scotland due to the devolution of policing and criminal justice. In relation to Northern Ireland, the Legislative Assembly recently passed legislation, the Human Trafficking and Exploitation (Criminal Justice and Support for Victims) Act (Northern Ireland) 2015, which contains the same definition as the Modern Slavery Act 2015. Scotland is currently scrutinising the Human Trafficking and Exploitation (Scotland) Bill, and the definition of human trafficking is also akin to England, Wales and Northern Ireland. Having the same definition or shared understanding of human trafficking naturally makes it easy for law enforcement authorities in all parts of the United Kingdom to cooperate with each other, and the central/devolved governments have taken an important first step in this regard. In summary, the key elements of the international/regional definitions of human trafficking are broadly captured by the UK definition.

Human trafficking and social work law: Identification and protection of victims

Legal obligations imposed upon the United Kingdom

While the law enforcement authorities should take a leading role in promoting a criminal justice response to human trafficking by effectively prosecuting and punishing this crime, other public authorities have an important role to play in protecting the victims of human trafficking. Indeed, the aforementioned international and regional instruments contain a number of obligations in this regard. The first important obligation is to establish a mechanism capable of identifying victims of human trafficking (Council of Europe Convention, art. 10; EU Human Trafficking Directive, art. 11(4)). It goes without saying that sufficient protection cannot be provided if the national authorities are not able to identify these victims properly. A related obligation is to train public and law enforcement officials so that they have sufficient understanding of the complex nature of this crime (Council of Europe Convention, art. 10; EU Human Trafficking Directive, art. 18(3)). If there are reasonable grounds to believe that identified individuals may be the victims of human trafficking, the next obligation is to grant a so-called reflection period which allows them to recover from their ordeals and consider what they wish to do (e.g. cooperation with the relevant authorities in criminal investigations and proceedings and/or voluntary repatriation to their countries) (Council of Europe Convention, art. 13). While the Council of Europe Convention provides for the minimum of 30 days (Council of Europe Convention, art. 13), it is unrealistic to expect victims to recover and think about their future within this short period of time. Therefore, it is desirable to grant a longer period in order to promote a more victim-centred approach.

Once the relevant authorities decide that identified individuals are victims of human trafficking, they should provide more substantive protection. These include, but are not limited to, safe accommodation, subsistence, medical/psychological assistance, translation/interpretation services and assistance during criminal investigation and proceedings (Trafficking Protocol, art. 6; Council of Europe Convention, art. 12). Due to their vulnerability, additional assistance should be provided to children, such as appointment of a legal guardian or someone who can represent their interests (Council of Europe Convention, art. 10(4); EU Human Trafficking Directive arts 14(2) and 16(3)) and access to education (Council of Europe Convention, art. 10(4); EU Human Trafficking Directive, arts 14(2) and 16(3)). In addition, national governments should issue renewable temporary residence permit not only when victims are willing to cooperate with the law enforcement authorities in facilitating criminal investigation and prosecution, but also when it is necessary due to their personal situations (e.g. not being able to return to their countries due to the risk of re-trafficking) (Trafficking Protocol, art. 7; Council of Europe Convention, art. 14). Finally, a crucial point to emphasise is that protection should be provided on the basis of individual needs and not on the condition that victims assist the law enforcement authorities in investigation, prosecution and punishment of human trafficking (Council of Europe Convention, art. 12(6); EU Human Trafficking Directive, art. 11(3)).

State practice in the United Kingdom

Victim identification

Having examined these basic obligations in relation to identification and protection of victims of human trafficking, it is now useful to analyse the extent to which the United Kingdom complies with them. In relation to identification, the government established the 'National Referral Mechanism' (NRM) in 2009 in order to fulfil its obligations under the Council of Europe Convention (Group of Experts on Action against Trafficking in Human Beings (GRETA), 2012: 14). To begin with, potential victims of human trafficking have to be referred by the so-called First Responders to the 'Competent Authorities', which make decisions as to whether referred individuals are indeed victims of this crime. These First Responders consist of governmental and non-governmental entities including the police, the UK Border Agency, local authorities, Barnardos, NSPCC and Salvation Army (National Crime Agency, 2015). In relation to local authorities, Social and Children's Services, including Safeguarding Adults and Children Boards, are important First Responders.

There are two designated Competent Authorities: the UK Human Trafficking Centre and the Home Office Immigration and Visas. While the former deals with referrals relating to UK or EEA nationals, the latter examines referrals made on behalf of non-EEA nationals (GRETA, 2012: 14). When potential victims are referred, these entities will determine, normally within five working days, whether there are 'reasonable grounds' to believe that individuals concerned are victims of human trafficking (GRETA, 2012: 14). If a positive decision is given, they are given a reflection period of 45 days and can receive necessary support such as safe accommodation and access to local GPs (Home Office, 2014: 23). While the reflection period is longer than the 30 days stipulated under the Council of Europe Convention, the government should reconsider whether this is a sufficient period for victims to recover from their experiences. In this regard, it has been argued that completion of relevant assistance such as psychological counselling often requires more than 45 days (Anti-Trafficking Monitoring Group, 2013a: 39). The UK practice may be contrasted with the Netherlands and Norway, which provide for reflection periods of three and six months, respectively (GRETA, 2014: 40). These undoubtedly represent better models in victim protection, thereby enhancing a victim-centred approach. In any event, during this reflection period, the Competent Authorities make a conclusive decision as to whether, on a balance of probabilities, referred individuals are victims of human trafficking (GRETA, 2014: 40). When a positive decision is made, these victims will be provided with further support, such as temporary residence permit (discretionary leave to remain) of 12 months initially (Anti-Trafficking Monitoring Group, 2013a: 39). Many of these supports in practice are arranged and/or provided by NGOs such as the Salvation Army (England and Wales) and the Migration Helpline (Scotland and Northern Ireland) (Home Office, 2014: 23).

Compared to the past, the United Kingdom has been making some efforts in identifying victims of human trafficking. In 2014, a total of 2,340 referrals were made to the Competent Authorities (Home Office, 2014: 23), compared to 535 referrals in 2009 (Home Office, 2014: 23). It is therefore evident that the government has been utilising the NRM more proactively. Inclusion of NGOs as First Responders is also to be commended, as this demonstrates a clear recognition of their experience and expertise in relation to human trafficking and enhances a multi-agency approach. There are also examples of good practice in identifying victims. For instance, a child safeguarding team known as *Paladin* was established at Heathrow Airport. This multi-agency team, including social workers, is said to have been instrumental in detecting suspected cases of child trafficking and making necessary arrangements for proper identification, and a similar arrangement also exists in Gatwick Airport (Anti-Trafficking Monitoring Group, 2013b: 111). At the local level, a number of local authorities have developed guidance, toolkits and other training materials in order to enhance their capability to identify victims of human trafficking.

While these examples of good practice should be recognised, various issues have been raised simultaneously. To begin with, the increasing number of referrals does not necessarily suggest that the UK government has been successful in identifying most victims. Given the large number of people who are trafficked worldwide and into the UK, many people are still not properly identified (Home Office, 2014: 23). It was acknowledged by the Home Office in this regard that many frontline First Responders, including social workers, still do not possess enough knowledge to be able to identify and refer actual/potential victims of human trafficking (Home Office, 2014: 23). This in turn suggests that sufficient training has not been conducted at the local level (International Organization for Migration, 2014: 2). In addition, while the government recognises the important contributions made by NGOs as First Responders, it has emerged that their views are not always taken into consideration when it comes to determining the victims' status (GRETA, 2012: 40). Moreover, a question has rightly been raised as to whether it is desirable to have a single Competent Authority which deals with all referrals. Two designated entities have different priorities and institutional mandates, and it seems that inconsistent decisions have been made, resulting in a loss of confidence particularly among the civil society sector (Law Society (Northern Ireland, 2014: 13). Finally, of over 2,000 victims identified in 2014, only 172 referrals were made by local authorities (National Crime Agency, 2015). Therefore, their role in identifying victims is still limited. In summary, there is much scope for improvement in relation to identification of victims of human trafficking in the United Kingdom.

Protection of trafficked victims

In terms of protection of trafficked victims, the first point to note is the discrepancies in legislative frameworks in different parts of the United Kingdom. In England and Wales, Part 5 of the Modern Slavery Act 2015 touches upon protection. Section 45, for instance, provides that trafficked victims who are forced to commit crimes as part of their exploitation would not be prosecuted and convicted. There are instances of victims being forced to commit offences such as cultivation of cannabis (Anti-Slavery International, 2014; Kelly and McNamara, 2015) and subsequently prosecuted and imprisoned (*R v N* and *R v LE*). It is not appropriate to treat them as criminals given the level of their victimisation, and this statutory provision is a step in the right direction. In addition, special measures for witness protection, civil legal aid and appointment of an independent child trafficking advocate are also provided for (Modern Slavery Act 2015, s. 46–48). However, these support mainly relate to the legal proceedings/processes, and the Modern Slavery Act 2015 does not go far to stipulate more substantive protection such as accommodation, medical assistance and so on. Although the Secretary of State 'may' issue regulations relating to protection, the language is rather weak, and their decision inevitably will be influenced by political considerations. Consequently, protection continues to be provided on a discretionary basis, and the authorities cannot be held accountable if they choose not to do so. These certainly go against the spirit of a victim-centred approach to human trafficking.

Indeed, a number of problems have been identified in relation protection of victims in England and Wales. For instance, many of them have been held in immigration detention centres or police cells (GRETA, 2012: 40). This is problematic, as this setting is not conductive in providing sufficient and appropriate protection and also enhances a perception that these victims are criminals. It has also been reported that victims are forced to wait for services such as psychological counselling because they are not readily available, and it is often not possible to receive them within the period of 45 days (Anti-Trafficking Monitoring Group, 2013b: 111). This once again strengthens the argument for extending the reflection period in the United Kingdom. In addition, the grant of temporary residence permit seems to be inconsistent due to the lack of understanding on the part of the relevant public authorities, and a degree of reluctance to grant longer-term permits has been recognised (Anti-Trafficking Monitoring Group, 2013b: 111). Moreover, while the appointment of the Independent Anti-Slavery Commissioner under the Modern Slavery Act 2015 (Part 4) is a welcome development, their role in victim protection is limited to 'encouraging good practice in relation to identification of victims' (s. 41(1)(b)), despite the fact that many stakeholders and experts recommended a more expansive role, such as monitoring and oversight, during the drafting stage (Public Bill Committee, 2014).

This situation in England and Wales may be contrasted with the devolved governments. In Northern Ireland, the aforementioned Human Trafficking and Exploitation (Criminal Justice and Support for Victims) Act (Northern Ireland) 2015 contains much better provisions for protection of victims. Section 18(4), for instance, specifies a period of 45 days during which the Competent Authorities make a decision as to the status of the victims, and makes it clear that assistance and support must not be conditional upon victims participating in criminal investigation or proceedings (s. 18(5)). In addition, those in a position to provide assistance must pay particular attention to vulnerabilities of victims, such as their gender, age or physical/mental illness, including disabilities (s. 18(5)). Further, the Act stipulates non-exhaustive list of assistance measures, which include, but are not limited to, safe accommodation, financial/material assistance, medical and psychological assistance and legal representation. In Scotland, the Human Trafficking and Exploitation Bill is currently being debated. Clause 8 stipulates a duty to secure assistance and support and a non-exhaustive list of measures which is similar to the Northern Irish legislation. It is evident therefore that the legislative frameworks in the devolved governments represent better models in terms not only of victim protection, but also of legality and accountability of public bodies. These discrepancies can lead to a fragmented, rather than integrated, approach to victim protection in the United Kingdom and undermine fairness as victims in Northern Ireland and Scotland are likely to receive more attention and care compared to England and Wales. It is therefore essential that the Secretary of State stipulates concrete and sufficient protection measures through regulations under the Modern Slavery Act 2015 in the future.

Having said this, there are additional legislative frameworks designed to protect vulnerable groups generally, which can be used to protect trafficked victims. In relation to protection of vulnerable children, the primary pieces of legislation are the Children Act 1989, the Social Services and Well-being (Wales) Act 2014, the Children (Scotland) Act 1995 and the Children (Northern Ireland) Order 1995. These place clear obligations on local authorities to safeguard the welfare of all children regardless of their immigration status, including foreign children trafficked into the United Kingdom (HM Government, 2011: 23). When a potential child victim of trafficking is referred to a local authority, a qualified and experienced social worker should make an assessment as to whether the child in question is in need, including section 47 investigations (HM Government, 2011: 23). This includes assessment of any evidence presented by the referrer as well as interviewing children where appropriate (HM Government, 2011: 23). When there is an immediate risk of serious harm to the child, then the local authority in question must secure their safety (HM Government, 2011: 22) in the same way as other children, including the development of an individual care plan (HM Government, 2011: 31). In addition to these procedures, the Modern Slavery Act 2015 provides for an appointment of an independent child trafficking advocate, as explained elsewhere. It is also worth highlighting that, unlike adult victims of human trafficking, the reflection period can be extended for child victims (HM Government, 2011: 38–39). Further, even when the Competent Authorities make negative decisions on children's status as victims of human trafficking, assigned social workers must continue to make their assessment on children's needs and provide support when necessary (HM Government, 2011: 38–39). In summary, child victims of human trafficking can receive protection outside of the Modern Slavery Act 2015.

However, a number of pressing issues have been raised in relation to protection of child victims of trafficking, highlighting the inadequacy of the current system. For instance, it has been reported that the age assessment for potential child victims is not conducted properly at times, as there seems to be over-reliance on the part of local authorities and social workers on physical appearance without sufficiently paying attention to cultural and ethnic variations (Anti-Trafficking Monitoring Group, 2013a: 108). A practical consequence of this is that these children may not receive protection under the child protection legislation. In addition, many trafficked children placed in care by local authorities go missing (GRETA, 2012: 57). This is so because traffickers or exploiters still retain control over them and actively contact them even after they are taken into care (ECPAT International, 2013: 2). The Centre for Social Justice estimates the proportion of these children to be as high as 60 per cent (Centre for Social Justice, 2013: 19) and almost two-thirds are never found again (Child Exploitation and Online

Protection Centre (CEOP), 2010a). This disturbing picture clearly casts doubt on the ability of local authorities to safeguard child victims of trafficking. This problem has been attributed to a lack of knowledge and expertise surrounding child trafficking on the part of stakeholders and also of financial resources to provide safe and secure accommodation and other assistance (All-Party Parliamentary Group for Runaway and Missing Children & Adults and All-Party Parliamentary Group for Looked After Children and Care Leavers, 2012: 13–14). A related concern is the arrangement for private fostering. While private foster carers are legally required to notify their local authorities of their fostering arrangements, it has been reported that this does not happen in practice (Refugee Council and the Children's Society, 2013: 30). In this regard, the British Association for Adoption and Fostering has noted with concern that only a little over 10 per cent of the fostering arrangements have been notified to local authorities (Baaf. org, 2015). This makes trafficked children extremely vulnerable to exploitation (HM Government, 2011: 28). To illustrate this with an example, the private fostering arrangement has been misused to claim a variety of benefits fraudulently or to facilitate domestic servitude (CEOP, 2010b; CEOP, 2011; ECPAT International, 2011). In view of these, the need for specialist foster care arrangements, including safe accommodations (All-Party Parliamentary Group for Runaway and Missing Children & Adults and All-Party Parliamentary Group for Looked After Children and Care Leavers, 2012: 17–18) has been highlighted by relevant stakeholders.

Similar to protection of vulnerable children, there are several key statutes for vulnerable adults. The relevant legislation in England is the Care Act 2014, which has made a number of reforms to the pre-existing legislative frameworks. It places obligations on local authorities to safeguard the well-being of vulnerable adults. For instance, when there is reasonable cause to suspect that an adult in its area has needs for care and support, or is at risk of abuse/neglect but is not able to protect themselves, then the local authority in question must make enquiries and decide on the course of actions to be taken (s. 42). The Statutory Guidance for the Care Act 2014 lists modern slavery and human trafficking as examples of abuse and neglect (Department of Health, 2014: 234) and therefore the legal duties of local authorities, including their Safeguarding Adults Boards, extend to the victims of these crimes. Other duties include conducting a needs assessment (s. 9), developing care and support plans (s. 25), and meeting adults' needs by providing appropriate protection.

Once again, there are several issues to be highlighted in relation to the Care Act 2014. For instance, local authorities can ask the vulnerable adults to pay for part of the care costs if they are determined to have financial resources (s. 14–17). Generally speaking, the profits generated from human trafficking as well as sexual/labour exploitation are retained by traffickers and/or exploiters, and therefore their victims are not likely to have sufficient financial resources. Consequently, the relevant part of the Care Act 2014 should not affect them.

However, the current wording of the legislation leaves open a possibility of trafficked victims being charged, and this is inappropriate given that they are the victims of gross violations of human rights. Another issue is the victims' immigration status. Many non-EU victims are trafficked into UK illegally without the right to enter or remain. Under the Nationality, Immigration and Asylum Act 2002 (schedule 3), local authorities are prevented from providing support/assistance to those who are unlawfully present, unless such support is necessary to avoid a breach of their rights under the European Convention on Human Rights 1950 (ECHR) or European Union law. In practical terms, those who have been exploited in the UK should receive assistance, as their right under Article 4 (prohibition on slavery/forced labour) of the ECHR has clearly been breached. However, if victims are not exploited, it can become difficult to prove the existence of a breach of their human rights, thereby preventing local authorities from providing necessary assistance. A crucial role of the public bodies, including local authorities, then, is to make an accurate assessment of whether repatriating these victims would breach the well-established principle of *non-refoulement*. Simply put, national governments are prevented from returning foreign nationals to their countries if doing so can breach their human rights (see *Soering v United Kingdom*). It is worth mentioning in this regard that, in *AM and BM (Trafficked Women) Albania CG*, it was recognised that returning the appellants to Albania could breach Article 3 of the ECHR due to, among others, the risk of re-trafficking and persecution by traffickers, as well as a lack of sufficient protection provided by the relevant authorities. This is a very important decision which should be remembered by the relevant stakeholders. In addition, it has been held in *Kimani v Lambeth London Borough Council* (49) that there was no duty to provide support where foreign nationals are in a position to return to their countries freely. This is problematic, as it allows the UK government to shift the burden of victimisation to countries of origin. In summary, a degree of uncertainty remains within the Care Act 2014 and its impact on trafficked victims, particularly non-EU nationals.

In relation to the devolved governments, similar arrangements as the Care Act 2014 exist in Wales (Social Services and Well-being (Wales) Act 2014) and Scotland (Adult Support and Protection (Scotland) Act 2007). Some of the issues raised above therefore are pertinent to these jurisdictions In Northern Ireland, however, there is no statutory basis for safeguarding vulnerable adults as yet, although it has developed a number of policies in which human trafficking and modern slavery have been mentioned. The Northern Ireland government issued a public consultation on the development of an adult safeguarding policy in November 2014 and published its report in April 2015 (Department of Health, 2015). Interestingly, there was a lack of consensus among those who responded in relation to the need for legislation like other jurisdictions, and the Northern Ireland government concluded (also bearing in mind the Northern Ireland Assembly election in 2016), that it was premature to introduce a bill.

From the point of view of legality and accountability, it is desirable that Northern Ireland seriously consider enacting legislation on safeguarding vulnerable adults. Having said this, this gap is mitigated to some extent by the specific legislation on human trafficking in this jurisdiction which is more advanced than England and Wales or Scotland.

In any event, it is to be appreciated that protection of trafficked victims puts some financial and other pressures on local authorities. However, this should not be used as an excuse not to provide assistance, as this problem can be ameliorated if they are able to use the confiscated criminal proceeds. The Proceeds of Crime Act 2002 (as amended) is an important piece of legislation as it provides a general framework for confiscation. However, there is scope to change the ways in which confiscated proceeds are allocated. The Home Office has initiated the Asset Recovery Incentivisation Scheme (ARIS) whereby 50 per cent of the proceeds are returned to the law enforcement authorities to enhance their capacity in confiscation, while the other half is retained by the Home Office (Home Office, 2014: 3). While there is no doubt that capacity building important, the other 50 per cent should be returned to local authorities or NGOs which are in a position to safeguard trafficked victims. As part of the Modern Slavery Strategy, the UK government has stated that the first priority in using ARIS is repatriation of these victims (HM Government, 2014: 39). Although facilitation of voluntary repatriation with full consent of victims is reasonable, the proceeds should be used to provide immediate assistance such as subsistence and medical assistance in the first instance. This emphasis on repatriation can also be interpreted as the reluctance or unwillingness on the part of the UK government to embrace and implement a victim-centred approach. In summary, the central and local authorities must work harder to protect the victims of human trafficking.

Conclusion

This chapter has examined the United Kingdom's approaches to identification and protection of victims of human trafficking, which are two areas relevant to social work law. Although some progress has been made compared to the past, a number of issues must be carefully considered and tackled simultaneously. Consequently, the United Kingdom is not fulfilling its obligations under the relevant international and European instruments entirely. The present analysis also underscores a disconnect between ongoing policy debates on protection of trafficked victims and the actual practice on the ground. While all stakeholders, particularly the civil society sector, acknowledge that victim protection is vital, this is not followed by concrete and effective action. This casts some doubts on the commitment of the United Kingdom to advance and implement a victim-centred approach to human trafficking.

At a micro-level, it is evident that the potential of local authorities in victim identification and protection has not been fully realised also, and there are a number of steps which should be taken. The First Responders, including social workers, need to be trained sufficiently so that they become fully aware of relevant indicators and the complex nature of human trafficking. In particular, all of those concerned should not treat trafficked victims as illegal, irregular or economic migrants who breach the UK immigration and criminal laws, but rather as victims of gross violations of human rights who are in need of protection. This switch in their perceptions will make it easier to promote a victim-centred approach. These First Responders must also be more proactive in referring potential victims to the Competent Authorities. In this regard, for those local authorities which have not done so already, they must develop and circulate clear guidelines and toolkits on victim identification. It should also be remembered that these victims are more likely to approach NGOs for assistance, due to a fear of enforcement action by public authorities. Therefore, closer communication and coordination with the civil society sector is vital so that local authorities can take appropriate action sooner rather than later. Finally, all local authorities should be able to use confiscated criminal proceeds to provide sufficient protection, and the central government should seriously facilitate this. When the capacity of the relevant stakeholders at the local level is enhanced, it increases the likelihood of promoting a more victim-centred approach to this heinous crime of the contemporary society.

References

All-Party Parliamentary Group for Runaway and Missing Children & Adults and All-Party Parliamentary Group for Looked After Children and Care Leavers (2012) *Report from the Joint Inquiry into Children Who Go Missing from Care*, 13–14.

AM and BM (Trafficked Women) Albania CG [2010] UKUT 80

Anti-Slavery International (2014) *Trafficking for Forced Criminal Activities and Begging in Europe*.

Anti-Trafficking Monitoring Group (2013a) *Hidden in Plain Sight: Three Years On: Updated Analysis of UK Measures to Protect Trafficked Persons*, 39.

Anti-Trafficking Monitoring Group (2013b) *In the Dock: Examining the UK's Criminal Justice Responses to Trafficking*, 111.

Anti-Trafficking Monitoring Group (2014) *Briefing: Anti-Slavery Commissioner*.

Baaf.org (2015) *Leading Charities Warn Over 10,000 Children at Risk Because 91% of the UK Adult Population Don't Know What Private Fostering Is*. Online, available at: www.baaf.org.uk/node/7936.

Child Exploitation and Online Protection Centre (CEOP) (2010a) *Strategic Threat Assessment: Child Trafficking in the UK*

CEOP (2010b) *The Trafficking of Children into and within the UK for Benefit Fraud Purposes*.

CEOP (2011) *Hidden Children: The Trafficking and Exploitation of Children within Home.*

Centre for Social Justice (2013) *It Happens Here: Equipping the United Kingdom to Fight Modern Slavery*, 19.

Department of Health (2014) *Care and Support Statutory Guidance Issued under the Care Act 2014*, 234.

Department of Health (2015) *Social Services and Public Safety and Department of Justice, Draft Safeguarding Adult Policy: Consultation Summary Report.*

ECPAT International (2011) *Understanding Child Trafficking and Private Fostering.*

ECPAT International (2013) *Trafficking Children and Missing*, 2.

Eurostat (2015) *Report on Trafficking in Human Beings*, 11.

Group of Experts on Action against Trafficking in Human Beings (GRETA) (2012) *Report Concerning the Implementation of the Council of Europe Convention on Action against Trafficking in Human Beings by the United Kingdom*, 17.

GRETA (2014) *Report Concerning the Implementation of the Council of Europe Convention on Action against Trafficking in Human Beings by the Netherlands*, 45.

Home Office (2014) *The Proceeds of the Crime Act 2002*, 3.

HM Government (2011) *Safeguarding Children Who May Have Been Trafficked: Practical Guidance*, 23.

HM Government (2014) *Modern Slavery Strategy*, 39.

Home Office (2014) *Review of the National Referral Mechanism for Victims of Human Trafficking*, 23.

International Labour Organization (2014) *Profits and Poverty: The Economics of Forced Labour*, 13.

International Organization for Migration (IOM) (2014) *Review of the National Referral Mechanism: Written Submission to the Review Team*, 2–3.

Kelly, A. and McNamara, M. L. (2015) '3,000 children enslaved in Britain after being trafficked from Vietnam', *The Guardian*, 23 May. Online, available at www.theguardian.com/global-development/2015/may/23/vietnam-children-trafficking-nail-bar-cannabis.

Kimani v Lambeth London Borough Council [2003] EWCA Civ. 1159

Law Society (Northern Ireland) (2014) *NRM Review – Full Response*, 13.

National Crime Agency (NCA) (2014) *National Referral Mechanism Statistics – End of the Year Summary*, 1.

National Crime Agency (2015) *National Referral Mechanism*. Online, available at: www.nationalcrimeagency.gov.uk/about-us/what-we-do/specialist-capabilities/uk-human-trafficking-centre/national-referral-mechanism.

Public Bill Committee (2014) *Modern Slavery Bill: Written Evidence*, 8.

Refugee Council and the Children's Society (2013) *Still at Risk: A Review of Support for Trafficked Children*, 30.

R v N and R v LE [2012] EWCA 182

Soering v United Kingdom (1989), Application No. 14038/88

United Nations Office of Drug and Crimes (2010) *Trafficking in Persons to Europe for Sexual Exploitation*, 7

US Department of State (2014) *Trafficking in Persons Report*, 45 and 61.

10

GOOD REVIEW? GOOD QUESTION

Margaret Flynn and Hilary Brown

Background

This chapter examines the arrangements for review in services for adults-at-risk and explores whether they achieve their aims. New provisions within the Care Act 2014 restate the primacy of achieving systemic change, as opposed to the holding of individual service providers to account, but in a fragmented market-place of health and social care provision this often proves illusory. Meanwhile, the mechanisms for review often provide a clumsy vehicle for managing the distress of relatives or for recalibrating the standards of staff.

Definitions of the noun 'review' confirm that it is a *formal assessment* of an event or process *with the intention of instituting change if necessary.* The verb 'to review' refers to a process of *going over a subject.* It is helpful to keep these definitions in mind as we consider some familiar responses to tragedies and scandals, all of which promise learning and reform. These are variously mandated as 'inquiries', serious case reviews (SCRs), post-incident reviews, statutory domestic homicide reviews (DHRs), serious incident reviews or serious incidents requiring investigation.

As this list testifies, there is no shortage of review mechanisms in health and social care services for adults, but there is a shortage of systematic learning from these exercises. When abuses have taken place in service settings, inquiries underscore inter alia the limitations of institutions where poor practice slides into abusive and anti-therapeutic practice; where restraint and over-sedation trump credible person-to-person support; and where an absence of informed 'management' undermines stated policies and values. The arrestingly familiar themes in reviews concerning individual adults in community settings, for example, bring into sharp focus the tensions between concepts of choice, risk, self-determination and mental capacity and the potential for any of these laudable principles to be used in perverse ways. So when we hear it said that reviews 'all say the same things', there is a grain of truth in this, in that these reviews do gravitate towards the same fault lines, but they also raise different kinds of concerns relating to specific conditions and unhelpful mindsets that often influence the way that legislation is used or risk managed. While there are clearly specific features unique to each tragic situation, there are also well-trodden routes to service failure that have already been mapped out but that are still routinely followed.

In this chapter we examine how, in theory, inquiries could achieve more lasting change and set out the guidance for the conduct *and implementation* of these reviews. We follow that by describing some salient issues emerging in recent reviews into abuse in service and in community settings to unpack the most common findings of these reviews and to suggest ways in which these insights could be incorporated into new ways of working in a more history-sensitive way.

An overview of the way inquiries have been used in adult services

Too many or too few?

Reviews are a form of qualitative research in that they uncover the ways in which policies operate in real world situations. They are also the focus of research in themselves, but until the advent of statutory responsibilities to instigate reviews, and the adoption of shared thresholds, they have not been seen as a credible source of data. In children's services these conditions have been met and there has been a tradition of meta-analyses of both causative factors and of recommendations for organisational change (Reder et al., 1993). So when Reith (1998) brought together 28 homicide and other high-profile inquiries about people known to mental health services published between 1998 and 1997, she noted that: 'by gaining a greater grasp of the issues and learning what can be done to achieve better services, it becomes possible to feel empowered as a professional mental health worker to improve services, rather than to feel defeated by the range of difficulties often associated with this area of our welfare system' (195–96). Reith accepted the danger of *inquiry overload* and yet saw the merit in learning from experience and understanding the factors favourable to service delivery – irrespective of the most consistent finding: the necessity of improving inter-professional communication.

Fast forward to 2015 and there are fewer high-profile inquiries about people known to mental health services per se but a proliferation of SCRs about *adults-at-risk,* as a result of age or disability, (formerly referred to as *vulnerable adults*), who should have been protected by local safeguarding systems. These reviews have not, until now, been conducted on a statutory basis and do not have the same status as a judicial review or inquiries chaired by clinicians, but despite the intense scrutiny they represent there is no obligation to publish them. It is not possible, therefore, to state the quantity, nor identify the populations whose circumstances are most likely to trigger such reviews in a definitive way. Some authors have followed in Reith's footsteps and sought to abstract learning from reviews with disparate origins (e.g. Aylett, 2008; Benbow, 2008; Bestjan, 2012; Brown, 2009; Braye et al., 2015; Manthorpe and Martineau 2011: Parry, 2013). *The National Confidential Inquiry into Suicide and Homicide by People with Mental Illness Annual Report 2015 England, Northern Ireland, Scotland and Wales* (University of Manchester, 2015) provides one quantified, bird's-eye view which counterbalances Reith's summaries of detailed case studies and listing of all recommendations.

In 2015, more change is heralded by the requirement that local safeguarding adult boards *must* undertake *safeguarding adult reviews* in all circumstances when an adult in its area dies as a result of abuse or neglect, whether known or suspected, and there is concern that partner agencies could have worked more effectively to protect the adult (Department of Health, 2014: 266). What will this open-ended responsibility entail? Will mandatory reviews in this context be used to gather and act on significant weaknesses in service provision or coordination, or will they become routine and easy to overlook? Will Safeguarding Adults Boards (SABs) clarify the reach of such reviews by addressing such requests as: 'You need to get it down to seven sides of A4 – it's too detailed … We've written the executive summary and it's on the website … because you didn't state whether or not the tragedy was predictable or preventable, we have … the family insist that the Terms of Reference should be extended to include their concerns … no we will not remove your name from the review … why no reference to the detail of the torture?'

What are they for?

As the preceding observations testify, the purpose of reviews may not always be explicit from the outset. Formulaic conformity with reviews being *a means of holding agencies to account but not individuals to blame* does not mean that vested interests, expectations and demands are spelt out to authors. The reality is that there are often multiple, and sometimes competing, objectives for such reviews. They perform human functions as well as administrative ones in working through issues of grief, blame and anger. They sit on busy roundabouts with legal routes running off in one direction, commercial ones in another, registration and inspection taking a separate direction from that of contract compliance and adult safeguarding – and professional standards and personal responsibility looking for a crossing. It is disingenuous to claim that these reviews are primarily there to hold individuals or organisations to account when they could be brought into the legal arena or used to establish liability or inform disciplinary procedures. That is, there might be an inquest, a criminal prosecution, a disciplinary hearing or regulatory action taken against a service provider and employees. The review is therefore a highly charged context in which distress, suspiciousness and accentuated defensive behaviour impinge on fact- finding and cause-seeking.

The recommendations arising from such reviews cover a great deal of ground depending on the nature of the difficulties that the review reveals.

Where, for example, policies are sound but have not been followed, this is more easily remedied than those situations in which policies have been shown to be unworkable or unreasonable. Where policies are unrealistic given the challenges of the work, capacity or the level of available time and resources available, they can open up a gap between laudable but unachievable standards and a kind of 'learned helplessness' (Seligman, 1972) that leads to cynicism and avoidance. In conducting reviews, we ask 'What should have been done?' 'Could this have worked?' 'What is it reasonable to expect staff in these circumstances to improve?' So, for example, in a locality with a clear safeguarding policy and explicit thresholds for referral, one team failed to refer a woman with enduring mental health problems into the safeguarding system despite awareness that she was in a violent relationship, choosing instead to work with her through its normal channels. Their less formal approach met many of the goals of safeguarding work, but it did not bring other agencies to the table or engage local domestic violence agencies or formal risk management mechanisms; that required different actions to a county council where the thresholds for referral into safeguarding were unclear and contested so that a man with difficulties associated with an Autistic Spectrum Disorder (ASD) died having evidently been self-neglecting and not engaging with services.

Sometimes there is an assumption that changes of policy and procedure will translate into changes in practice. However, these instances show that the knowledge and mindset of workers affects how they interpret guidance and legislation, whether they err on the side of intervention or take a more hands-off approach when faced with people who do not fit their stereotypes of 'vulnerability' or 'capacity'.

Recent SCRs involving individuals seem to constellate around these problematic ideals, and the notion that restating rules without acknowledging the extreme ambiguity at their heart means that change can be illusory. The issue is that these matters are complex, and workers must be equipped to deal with complexity, and that guidance or leadership cannot shy away from these difficulties by putting forward such aspirations in one-dimensional ways. Always there is a tension at the heart of all these processes as to how far a review focuses on the specific as opposed to the overarching – which may be less amenable to change.

Safeguarding Adults Reviews (SARs) – what the guidance requires

The Department of Health (2014) guidance states that in addition to undertaking a review when an adult dies *as a result of abuse or neglect*, Safeguarding Adult Boards:

must also arrange a SAR if an adult in its area has not died, but the SAB knows or suspects that the adult has experienced serious abuse or neglect ... where, for example the individual would have been likely to have died but for an intervention, or has suffered permanent harm or has reduced capacity or quality of life (whether because of physical or psychological effects) as a result of abuse or neglect. SABs are free to arrange for a SAR in any other situations involving an adult in its area with needs for care and support.

The SAB should be primarily concerned with weighing up what type of 'review' process will promote effective learning and improvement action to prevent future deaths or serious harm occurring again. This may be where a case can provide useful insights into the way organisations are working together to prevent and reduce abuse and neglect of adults. SARs may also be used to explore examples of good practice where this is likely to identify lessons that can be applied to future cases. (266)

Since this guidance replaces *No Secrets* (Department of Health, 2000), it is the first time that the Department of Health has set out the criteria which should determine whether or not a review is merited in the event of an adult at risk being harmed. Arguably the guidance is a response to the insistent question in such an eventuality: *What do we do?* Adult SCRs moved into this space having borrowed some of their characteristics from children's services, where SCRs have been mandatory.

Thus by naming the array of situations – which are considerable and which must nudge SABs into embarking on a review – there is a danger of local authorities being overwhelmed by the requirement. This is most particularly so when financial constraints have inevitable consequences for local services. Historically, the motivation for undertaking reviews in adult services was various. Until the Care Act 2014 there was no requirement to conduct and publish reviews of the circumstances of adults who had been harmed. This is not to suggest that adult services were incurious or even relieved that there was no expectation of scrutiny. There are executive summaries of adult SCRs on many local authority websites, but they are not easy to find and few are subject to external scrutiny or critique (Scourfield, 2010 is an exception).

The impact of Westminster's sustained austerity will reach beyond the tenure of the current legislature. There is no dedicated funding for SARs, and yet instead of SABs defining the problems and their context, or even drawing on the attempts of others to summarise the findings of similar reviews, they are mandatory. The guidance goes on to propose that:

Early discussions need to take place with the adult, family and friends to agree how they wish to be involved. The adult who is the subject of any SAR need not have been in receipt of care and support services for the SAB to arrange a review in relation to them.
(Department of Health, 2014: 267)

It is likely that the families who become *involved* in SARs are in pain from which they cannot readily escape and/or have been bereaved. They may have sought to bring attention to their concerns by talking to support staff or making a complaint, for example. In whatever way the involvement of families is negotiated, unless the anticipated *outcome* of a SAR is explored, there is a danger that it may be perceived as their only opportunity to find out what went wrong.

The guidance identifies the principles which should be applied *to all reviews*:

- There should be a culture of continuous learning and improvement across the organisations that work together to safeguard and promote the well-being and empowerment of adults, identifying opportunities to draw on what works and promote good practice

- The approach taken to reviews should be proportionate according to the scale and complexity of the issues being examined

- Reviews of serious cases should be led by individuals who are independent of the case under review and of the organisations whose actions are being reviewed

- Professionals should be involved fully in reviews and invited to contribute their perspectives without fear of being blamed for actions they took in good faith

- Families should be invited to contribute to reviews. They should understand how they are going to be involved and their expectations should be managed appropriately and sensitively. (Department of Health, 2014: 268)

Such officially espoused principles are helpful in addressing the difficult issues facing SABs. However, they appear remote from the processes which require SABs and the authors of reviews to address conflict, tension, uncertainty and risk. Sometimes there are no readily identifiable causes, and sometimes matters are so complex or profound in the consequences of their resolution that the principles may require re-examination. For example, although loyalty to organisational hierarchy is not an end in itself, it may prove unsusceptible to the principles. In contrast, there is little that a review can do to address responses to requests for information such as, 'All the senior managers have left who were dealing with the matter ... the person who was contributing to the review has only just got access to the papers ... the IT system has changed so we can't access records ... the organisation was taken over by another provider and it doesn't appear that the records were archived'.

There is welcome specificity concerning what it is that SARs *should seek to determine,* that is: 'what the relevant agencies and individuals involved in the case might have done differently that could have prevented harm or death. This is so that lessons can be learned from the case and those lessons applied to future cases to prevent similar harm occurring again ... It is vital ... that reviews are trusted and safe experiences that encourage honesty, transparency and sharing of information to obtain maximum benefit' (Department of Health, 2014: 268).

It follows that the process should not 'hold any individual or organisation to account. Other processes exist for that. Furthermore, if individuals and their organisations are fearful of SARs their response will be defensive and their participation guarded and partial' (Department of Health, 2014: 268).

Here lies a challenge. Concerns about harms are typically fragmented into a patchwork of successive problems and the kinds of problem they appear to encapsulate may not have been imagined. There are also chains of events which may have hard to pinpoint origins, and the available means of reacting are likely to have been wanting, most particularly when management functions are spread, when the after-effects persist and when a growing number of agencies become involved.

The guidance asserts that 'the process for undertaking SARs should be determined locally according to the specific circumstances of individual circumstances. No one model will be applicable for all cases' (Department of Health, 2014: 268).

While no single *model* has been deployed in undertaking adult reviews, they are the close relative of *case studies,* that is, a concentrated, pan-disciplinary inquiry offering opportunities for learning (Stake, 2000). As noted elsewhere (Flynn et al., 2011), the method used can affect the outcome, and as noted in children's safeguarding, an overly prescriptive, Ofsted-evaluated process has attracted increasing criticism (Munro, 2011). Reviews are commissioned in physical, economic, ethical, legal and political contexts, and a consideration of the interplay of systems as well as the decision-making of individuals is merited. There is a further snag, however: professional decisions in health and social care are rarely discrete events (Schon, 1996). For example, it may not be possible to specify a timeframe within which a critical decision was made unless it was clearly documented.

The guidance states that:

> The focus must be on what needs to happen to achieve understanding, remedial action and, very often, answers for families and friends of adults who have died or been seriously abused or neglected. The recommendations and action plans from a SAR need to be followed through by the SAB.

> The SAB should ensure that there is appropriate involvement in the review process of professionals and organisations who were involved with the adult. The SAR should also communicate with the adult and, or their family. In some cases it may be helpful to communicate with the person who caused the abuse or neglect.
>
> (Department of Health, 2014: 268).

It is assumed that the 'professionals and organisations who were involved with the adult' will want to learn from the adverse incident. It is from announcements such as 'there will be a serious case review ... let's wait and see what the home itself can tell us ... the police investigation has begun and this has primacy' that a less absolute starting-line is drawn. Furthermore, there is a long tradition of health services conducting parallel inquiries following adverse incidents which remain confidential to the NHS, irrespective of expectations of transparency (Department of Health, 2010).

The guidance states:

It is expected that those undertaking a SAR will have appropriate skills and experience which should include:

- Strong leadership and ability to motivate others

- Expert facilitation skills and ability to handle multiple perspectives and potentially sensitive and complex group dynamics

- Collaborative problem-solving experience and knowledge of participative approaches

- Good analytic skills and ability to manage qualitative data

- Safeguarding knowledge

- Inclined to promote an open, reflective learning culture.

(Department of Health, 2014: 268–69)

This confirms that since progress depends on working together, SAR authors should not be graduates of the command-and-control school of management but rather those who are interested in participatory and collective approaches:

The SAB should aim for completion of a SAR within a reasonable period of time and in any event within six months of initiating it, unless there are good reasons for a longer period being required; for example, because of potential prejudice to related court proceedings. Every effort should be made while the SAR is in progress to capture points from the case about improvements needed; and to take corrective action.

(Department of Health, 2014: 269)

Reviews involve receiving and gathering information, asking questions and sifting out unfounded judgements. To ascertain and describe events as accurately as possible involves identifying the key actors, their perceptions, issues, checking facts and outlining the known sequence of events. With the necessary details known, it is important to edit, contextualise and offer explanatory frameworks, champion multiple perspectives and promote inter-professional conversations.

While urgency characterises reviews at their outset, typically they not only hinge on messy incidents, they occupy territory in which values and principles pull individuals in different directions. For example, there are obligations to managers which contribute to the best interests of an organisation and there are public interest obligations to citizens. Local authorities would be hard-pressed to identify the number of reviews which have been delivered within a six-month time frame.

The guidance proposes that there will be occasions when there are separate statutory requirements in statutory guidance to undertake a child SCR and a DHR:

> Where such reviews may be relevant to SAR (e.g. because they concern the same perpetrator), consideration should be given to how SARs, DHRs and SCRs can be managed in parallel in the most effective manner possible so that organisations and professionals can learn from the case. For example, considering whether some aspects of the case can be commissioned jointly so as to reduce duplication of the work for the organisations involved.

> In setting up a SAR the SAB should also consider how the process can dovetail with any other relevant investigations that are running parallel, such as a child SCR or DHR, a criminal investigation or an inquest.

> (Department of Health, 2014: 269).

This expectation would appear to gloss over the reality. A focus on a victim-perpetrator dyad is consequential; and the primacy of a police investigation, of unknown duration, cannot be compromised by parallel fact finding:

> It may be helpful when running a SAR and DHR or child SCR in parallel to establish at the outset all the relevant areas that need to be addressed, to reduce potential for duplication for families and staff. Any SAR will need to take account of a coroner's inquiry, and, or any criminal investigation related to the case, including disclosure issues, to ensure that relevant information can be shared without incurring significant delay in the review process. It will be the responsibility of the manager of the SAR to ensure contact is made with the Chair of any parallel process in order to minimise avoidable duplication.

> (Department of Health, 2014: 269)

In terms of *findings from SARs,* the guidance states:

> The SAB should include the findings from any SAR in its Annual Report and what actions it has taken, or intends to take in relation to those findings. Where the SAB decides not to implement an action then it **must** state the reason for that decision in the Annual Report. All documentation the SAB receives from registered providers which is relevant to CQC's regulatory functions will be given to the CQC on CQC's request.

> (Department of Health, 2014: 269)

This is the only reference to the Care Quality Commission in the context of reviews.

Finally, the guidance states that SAR reports should:

- Provide a sound analysis of what happened, why and what action needs to be taken to prevent a recurrence, if possible

- Be written in plain English and

- Contain findings of practical value to organisations and professionals.

(Department of Health, 2014: 269)

How can SCRs be harnessed to achieve real change?

Even when the 'diagnosis' of the problem has been accurate and the recommendations sound, including as a basic principle that specific concerns about individual workers are translated into system-wide changes, the implementation of those recommendations requires high-level and sustained commitment to learn and change.

In the highest profile cases, national governments have sought to take recommendations forward into managed processes of policy change and local renewal. Two examples demonstrate the potential for difficulties within those programmes, especially where social care is organised across a network of privately owned, geographically dispersed and relatively fragmented provision. Both the scandal of Winterbourne View Hospital in South Gloucestershire and the concerns raised by Operation Jasmine in south-east Wales were within the sights of the Westminster government and the Welsh government, respectively.

Winterbourne View Hospital was a private facility. Its parent company was Castlebeck Care Ltd, which was 'part of a group called CB Care Ltd, which is itself owned, via Jersey, by Swiss based private equity group Lydian, backed by Irish billionaires' (Private Eye, 2012). During May 2011, BBC *Panorama* broadcast 'Undercover Care: The abuse exposed' which showed hospital staff mistreating and assaulting adults with learning disabilities and autism. The BBC asserted that this hospital represented 'a huge failure at the heart of our system of care ... the worst kind of institutional care'.

In addition to the police investigation, the SCR concerning Winterbourne View Hospital was one of six parallel reviews, that is, Castlebeck Care Ltd reviewed the company's *culture, medical protocols and communication systems* the Care Quality Commission produced a *compliance review* prior to embarking on a *responsive review* and a *learning disability inspection programme*; the NHS South of England, on behalf of NHS England and with the agreement of the Department of Health, coordinated an investigation of the NHS' role in commissioning services for 48 former Winterbourne View Hospital patients; NHS South Gloucestershire PCT (Commissioning) reviewed collaboration in the NHS in south Gloucestershire and Bristol; the Equality and Human Rights Commission investigated the commissioning function of Primary Care Trusts and the steps these bodies took to discharge their duties under the Human Rights Act 1998; and, finally, the Department of Health undertook to abstract the general themes from the sum of the reviews.

Ultimately there was a Joint Improvement Programme (involving the Department of Health, NHS England and the Local Government Association) which had three directors in a short timeframe. In terms of outcomes, and, crucially, that of reducing the numbers of patients, there were more people with learning disabilities and autism living in assessment and treatment units/mental health hospitals than there were at the time of the 2011 BBC broadcast (National Audit Office, 2015).

Norman Lamb, the Minister of State at the Department of Health, has described the work to move people with learning disabilities out of such assessment and treatment provision as an 'abject failure'. An article by Williams and Wiggins (2014) in the *Health Services Journal* reported '"institutional inertia" among NHS and local government commissioners which had undermined efforts to hit the deadline. His part in driving the transition programme had been his "most depressing and frustrating" task'. He accused NHS England, one of multiple health and local government organisations which agreed to the June [2014] target, of failing to prioritise the transition effort. 'A significant proportion' of those who remained inappropriately accommodated in hospitals were NHS England cases, he said. 'There hasn't been enough challenge within commissioners to do this.' The metaphor of a distress flare comes to mind, as well as one the lessons identified by the review of Operation Jasmine: *scandals fix nothing, permanently.*

In Search of Accountability: A Review of the Neglect of Older People Living in Care Homes Investigated as Operation Jasmine was published by the Welsh Government in July 2015. It hinged on what was described on BBC Wales as 'Britain's biggest investigation into the neglect of the elderly in nursing homes. [The trial at Cardiff Crown Court at the beginning of 2013] collapsed in dramatic fashion, leaving families ... with a host of unanswered questions' (Flynn, 2015).

This review was commissioned by the First Minister for Wales following police and Health and Safety Executive investigations which cost £15m and delivered a legal impasse. Although there were challenges, the First Minister accepted the recommendations in full – including a very different approach to responding to older people's deep pressure ulcers. Critically, the review fed into the Regulation and Inspection of Care and Support (Wales) Bill, and a government-endorsed series of workshops are to be held throughout Wales. The First Minister expressed his disbelief that although the injuries, pain and deep pressure ulcers of older people were unobserved, unreported, reported inaccurately and/or reported belatedly in homes owned by General Practition-ers, no crimes were identified by the Crown Prosecution Service.

Both reviews pointed to the disquieting dynamics which arise when all con-trol is yielded to *the market*; when profits are privatised and losses are socialised (Taleb, 2010); and when there are weaknesses in the legal position concerning private, non-listed companies. An additional lesson from Flynn (2015) is that 'private interest pursued at the expense of others has a long history, however, the public interest cannot be subordinate to the short term personal gains or even the criminality of a minority of directors of care homes' (231).

Abuse in more community settings

When considering the cruelties endured by Steven Hoskin in Cornwall or Michael Gilbert in Luton, or reviews where self-neglect, non-engagement with services or failures to intervene where services are refused, the difficulties have often arisen as a result of workers misreading the ability of a person to manage their circumstances, and a naivety about the intentions of people's networks. Vulner-able people are at risk of predatory and parasitic relationships in which they are often targeted and exploited. Without skilled leadership, professionals in the network of support around such individuals may read their compliance as 'choice' and take refusals of help at face value. Many of these situations involve a failure to engage the Mental Capacity Act 2005 in a timely manner. The review process often calls into question assumptions that have been made about a person's view that they can manage alone. It is easy to see how this happens when services are stretched, so for example, it is not surprising that the older woman who is difficult to deal with tells her carers to go away on a Friday afternoon and they do so even though she needs them to change her inconti-nence pad and to ensure that she has water within reach to drink. A man whose household had fallen apart when his primary carer died is assumed to be able to manage even though it seems with hindsight that he had an undiagnosed ASD and although he could articulate his views strongly he was unable to act on them. His extreme self-neglect resulted in the coroner suggesting that in prior-itising an assumption of autonomy in his case over the most basic elements of his well-being was 'wrong thinking.' It is as if the pendulum has swung so far away from paternalistic involvement that the most severe deprivation does not trigger intervention. This man could not maintain his home, which became a public health hazard, and he died alone in squalor and discomfort.

Non-engagement, pursuant on depression, ASD, dementia or anxiety, is not addressed sufficiently in the Mental Capacity Act's guidance, which has at its heart an exclusively cognitive model of decision-making. This fails to take into account the way that these conditions manifest, that is, as a series of knee-jerk and often avoidant actions and/or the failure to read the intentions of others accurately, or the inability to act in one's own best interests. These difficulties do not require changes in law but in perception (Brown, 2009; Brown and Marchant, 2011).

Moreover, under pressure from lack of resources, there is often a lack of continuity in the way that individuals are supported and their case work reviewed, which means that the annual reviews work on the basis of a series of unconnected snapshots rather than foregrounding knowledge of people's history, development and the trajectory of their condition. The tension between ongoing work and independent assessment seen at the heart of mental health and mental capacity legislation encourages these one-off windows to be privileged over long-term involvement and coherent decision-making. Timing is of the essence when working with people whose lives are gradually spiralling out of control, but the emphasis on single decisions taken out of context does not match with the reality of many people's lives. Conditions such as diabetes or dental health can be left until it is too late to intervene in ways that could lead to good outcomes. Practitioners responding to a review often say that 'it rests on hindsight', but they forget that they also have opportunities to work with hindsight if they approach case work with a sense of history, context and incremental change.

How can these lessons be used to create an agenda for change?

Whether or not harms occur in an institution or in a person's own home, reviews can provide insight and distinguish the individual and system factors that have led to cruelties and the breakdown of appropriate standards. Recent SCRs have highlighted glaring problems in the services that support adults whose staff are often left to manage complex conditions with little knowledge, oversight, support or scrutiny. In community settings, critical information from comprehensive history-taking is not consistently shared, and the person's ability to manage their environment, declining health or unstable mental states is not sufficiently taken into account when their decision-making and ability to act on the basis of those decisions is being assessed. The tension between informal and formal mechanisms for assessment and risk management is often resolved in favour of a 'wait and see' approach which leaves very vulnerable people in circumstances that would not be valued for the general population and should not be tolerated by professional networks. Preventative action is not taken, because there is insufficient oversight or absent coordination and distant consequences disappear from view because decision-making has been conceived as a series of one-off events rather than as milestones in the inexorable passage of time. 'Wait and see' has a tendency to lead to 'too little and too late'. Where once we would have sought valued interdependence as the bedrock of a person's life, we seem to have moved into territory where the quality of relationship in which vulnerable people are held is no longer deemed an appropriate focus of assessment or intervention until the spotlight of a review is turned onto this hinterland.

In addition, there are system factors which Operation Jasmine showed that reviews cannot address, for example, the public sector underwriting companies which have produced considerable rewards for the few at the expense of the many; companies providing services where a single director has powers of decision-making unfettered by non-executives; the use of chains of companies to disguise the financial position of a company providing services – including the money invested in service delivery, salaries, dividends and benefits in kind; and only prosecuting employees provides companies with incentives to scapegoat them, thereby shifting attention from its corporate structure, culture and goals (see Hamilton and Micklethwaite, 2006).

Meanwhile, service provision in the care sector rests on employing people on low wages often with a minimum of professional leadership. The result is that those staff either work to, or work around, the letter of the law rather than embedding its spirit in their everyday practice and decision-making.

References

Aylett, J. (2008) 'Learning the lessons in training from abuse inquiries – findings and recommendations', *The Journal of Adult Protection*, 10(4): 7–10.

Benbow, S. M. (2008) 'Failures in the system: Our inability to learn from inquiries', *The Journal of Adult Protection*, 10(3): 5–13.

Bestjan, S. (2012) *Learning from Serious Case Reviews on a Pan-London Basis*, London: Joint Improvement Partnership.

Braye, S., Orr, D. and Preston-Shoot, M. (2015) 'Learning lessons about self-neglect? An analysis of serious case reviews', *The Journal of Adult Protection*, 17(1): 3–18.

Brown, H. (2009) 'The process and function of serious case review', *The Journal of Adult Protection*, 11(1): 38–50.

Brown, H. and Marchant, L. (2013) 'Using the Mental Capacity Act in in complex cases', *Tizard Learning Disability Review*, 18(2): 60–69.

Department of Health (2000) *No Secrets: Guidance for the Development and Implementation of Multiagency Policy and Procedures to Protect Vulnerable Adults from Abuse*, London: Department of Health and Home Office.

Department of Health (2010) *Clinical Governance and Adult Safeguarding: An Integrated Process*, London: Department of Health.

Department of Health (2014) *Care and Support Statutory Guidance Issued Under the Care Act 2014* London: Department of Health.

Flynn, M., Williams, S. and Keywood, K. (2011) 'Critical decisions and questions regarding serious case reviews – ideas from North West England', *Journal of Adult Protection*, 13(4): 213–29.

Flynn, M. (2015) *In Search of Accountability: A Review of the Neglect of Older People Living in Care Homes Investigated as Operation Jasmine*, Cardiff: Welsh Government.

Hamilton, S. and Micklethwaite, A. (2006) *Greed and Corporate Failure: The Lessons from Recent Disasters,* Basingstoke, Hampshire: Palgrave Macmillan.

Manthorpe, J. and Martineau, S. (2011) 'Serious case reviews in adult safeguarding in England: An analysis of a sample of reports', *The British Journal of Social Work,* 41(2): 224–41.

Munro, E. (2011) *The Munro Review of Child Protection: A Child-Centred System,* Cm 8062, London: HMSO.

National Audit Office (2015) *Care Services for People with Learning Disabilities and Challenging Behaviour,* London: NAO.

Parry, I. (2013) 'Adult safeguarding and the role of housing', *The Journal of Adult Protection,* 15(1): 15–25.

Private Eye (2012) 'Private care: passing the "beck"', *Private Eye,* 1327: 31, 16–29 November.

Reder, P. Duncan, S. and Gray, M. (1993) *Beyond Blame: Child Abuse Tragedies Re-Visited,* London: Routledge.

Reith, M. (1998) *Community Care Tragedies: A Practice Guide to Mental Health Inquiries,* Birmingham: Venture Press.

Schon, D. A. (1996) 'From technical rationality to reflection in action', in J. Dowie and A. Elstein (eds), *Professional Judgement: A Reader in Clinical Decision-Making,* Cambridge: Cambridge University Press.

Scourfield, P. (2010) 'Reflections on the serious case review of a female adult (JK)', *The Journal of Adult Protection,* 12(4): 16–30.

Seligman, M. E. P. (1972) 'Learned helplessness', *Annual Review of Medicine,* 23(1): 407–12.

Stake, R. E. (2000) 'Case studies', in N. K. Denzin and Y. S. Lincoln (eds), *Handbook of Qualitative Research,* 2nd edn, London: Sage.

Taleb, N. N. (2010) *The Black Swan: The Impact of the Highly Improbable,* London: Penguin Books.

University of Manchester (2015) *The National Confidential Inquiry into Suicide and Homicide by People with Mental Illness Annual Report 2015: England, Northern Ireland, Scotland and Wales,* July.

Williams, D. and Wiggins, K. (2014) 'Winterbourne View scheme an "abject failure", minister admits', *Health Services Journal,* online, available at: www.hsj.co.uk/news/commissioning/winterbourne-view-scheme-an-abject-failure-minister-admits/5070443.article#.U3ivS_ldV4w.

INDEX